AF728850

Rybnik 2025–2026

Mateusz Wrazidlo

RAPTURE
A Journey to the Lost World

Foreword by Dr Jane Goodall, DBE

Dedicated to all the Creatures who accompanied me on my journeys
and who were generous enough to show me my place in the world.
Those human and nonhuman
those lurking in the shadows
and those audacious enough to venture into the daylight.

And, most importantly, to all the spectres and murky apparitions
always whispering
from behind the moonlit curtains of wet, mossy branches.
May this work be my tribute to you
until we meet again.

FOREWORD

The first time I met Mateusz Wrazidlo, we talked about our love for the natural world and for wild, relatively unexplored places. He told me about his love for botany, particularly carnivorous plants, and of his fascination with the high plateaus of the Guiana Shield. "They are often called the 'Lost Worlds'," he said, and asking me if I had ever read Arthur Conan Doyle's novel of that name, about a group of intrepid men exploring an unknown plateau in South America. Of course I had read that book – in fact, as a child, I read all the books I could find about adventuring into wild and unknown parts of the world. I longed to go to places like that – the wilder and more dangerous the better! It was Edgar Rice Burroughs' *Tarzan of the Apes* that started my fascination with Africa and my dream of going to the jungle to live with wild animals. I ended up, of course, exploring the unknown lives of wild chimpanzees in the forests of Tanzania.

Mateusz also followed his dreams. As I said, he too wanted to explore wild places, but for him it was as a self-taught botanist. This eventually led him to the Guiana Highlands, to the isolated sandstone tablelands that are known to the local Indigenous communities as tepuis. This area is one of the least explored places on Earth and is home to many species of indigenous plants that are especially fascinating to Mateusz. Not surprising, then, that he returned again and again, leading expeditions to further explore the area.

As a result of his fascination with the unique environment of the tepuis and their surroundings, as well as his skill with a camera, Mateusz has produced a book of stunning beauty that captures the very atmosphere of the Guiana Shield. I thought my exploring days were over, but although this is true physically, as I looked at the images from this book, I found I was indeed exploring the area, for the photographs are so vivid that they took me there in spirit. I travelled with Mateusz as he pushed his way through the forests, stood with him high in the mountains on sandstone tepuis, gazed with awe at one of the many great waterfalls, and shared his excitement at discovering plants found nowhere else on the planet. He was especially thrilled to find a giant pitcher plant, one of his favourite carnivorous species.

Unfortunately, Mateusz tells me, environmental disruptions will undoubtedly push some of these species to extinction, as those growing at high altitudes are unlikely to be able to adapt to a warming planet, and they cannot migrate higher. Mateusz, with his passion for botany, desperately hopes that some of these endangered endemic species can be collected, responsibly cultivated and propagated in botanical gardens and conservatories before it is too late. Of course, though they may survive, they will be living in alien conditions – like so many humans forced to leave their homes due to climate change. The cultivated plants, however, if exhibited along with photographs of their ancestors growing in their beautiful original environment, will enable future generations to understand the harm we have done to the natural world.

But there is a more immediate threat to the area: unfortunately, there are rich deposits of gold, which has led to unsustainable mining operations. Moreover, because of the mercury used in the process, this mining not only causes terrible harm to the environment, but also to the local people. I have seen the effect of gold mining in the Brazilian Amazon when I flew in a Greenpeace plane over miles and miles of rivers polluted with mercury. All life in the rivers was killed, and many of the Indigenous tribes who depend heavily on the rivers were horribly affected, losing not only their main source of food, but also their hair and teeth due to mercury poisoning.

Before I read this book, I did not know about the Guiana Highlands. Now that I have seen this work, I understand how important it is to protect as much as we can of this unique and hauntingly beautiful landscape before it is too late. There is so much more to learn, so many more species to be identified. But protecting it is not only important for scientists, it is even more so for the local Indigenous people. For it is their home, and naturally there are many sacred places that are of great spiritual importance in their lives. Unlike Westerners, but like other Indigenous people with whom I am familiar, they maintain a close relationship with nature. It is tragic that people in the West are increasingly distancing themselves from the natural world. They forget that we are a part of that world and that we actually depend on it for food, water, clothing and so much more. We still depend on healthy ecosystems, and because of our materialistic lifestyles, because the acquisition of wealth is more important than preserving the environment for the sake of future generations, we are placing unsustainable demands on the natural resources of Planet Earth. We have lost wisdom and make decisions that may benefit a person or a business or a politician in the short term, but without considering the effect on future generations or on the people who still live close to the land. And so, all around the world, ecosystems are being destroyed.

I hope with all my heart that steps can be taken to establish more protected areas within the Guiana Shield; to preserve the mystery and beauty of that haunting landscape before it is too late. And I hope that the citizens of the countries within it, particularly the children, can somehow visit 'Lost Worlds' such as these so as to realise the national treasure that is theirs. And as, for most of them, such a visit will likely be difficult or impossible, I hope that *Rapture* can be made available in their schools and libraries. For the photographs and Mateusz's words will surely enable them to explore these 'Lost Worlds' and to fall in love. Just as I have.

Jane Goodall

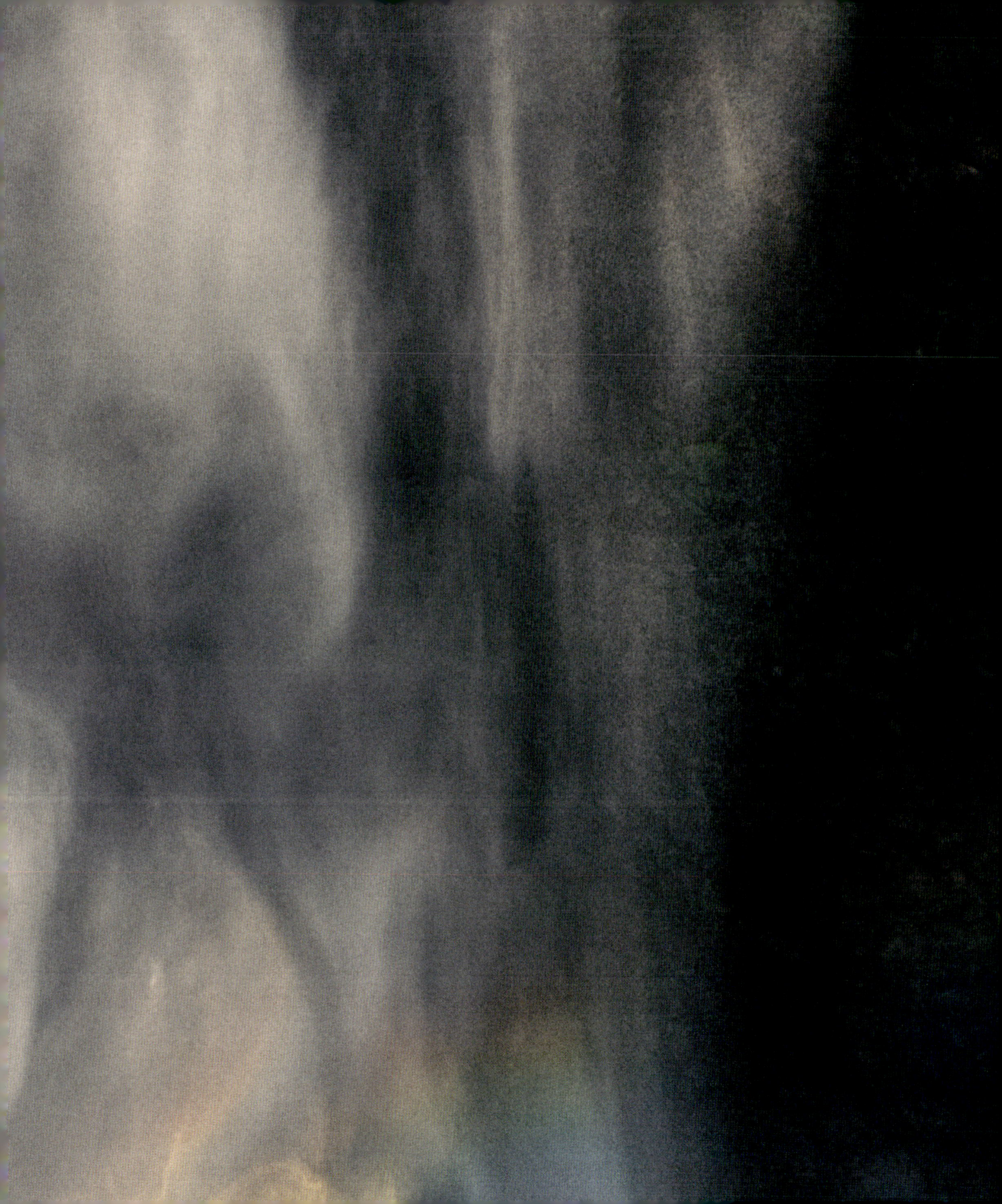

We have come to believe the age of exploration is a thing of the past. Living in a world saturated with modern technology, descendants of a space age that has left our home world monitored to its last inch by constellations of satellites constantly zooming far above our heads, it is easy to romanticise the past and think of the great mysteries of nature as something that belongs to a bygone era. Out of yearning, some of us tend to cling on to old artefacts, to photographs and books full of magical tales left by those who were inquisitive enough to challenge the boundaries of human knowledge and step into the unknown, nurturing our collective curiosity. Invoking the names of the great explorers, we think of them as the lucky ones, born just in time to have the privilege to experience the great mystery in its purest form.

But Earth is a jealous creature, keeping her deepest secrets out of sight, vaulted securely where our prying digital eyes cannot penetrate. This is a tale of one such place. Nestled within the dark heart of the lush South American interior is a place which evades all forms of human comprehension. A raw, primordial world still thriving in stubborn isolation despite centuries of humankind's daring exploits. A gateway to some of the oldest geological formations on our planet – a truly 'Lost World', 1.8 billion years in the making, filled with ancient landscapes and relic life forms straight out of a fantasy novel.

What follows is an attempt at telling a story about a place which probably means more to me than any other place in the world. A place so distant and so different from all the things I had known before that, for a long time, it remained for me in the domain of sheer childish fantasies. Yet still, that very place, through some force I cannot really grasp or comprehend, became a stage where I was able to experience a sequence of rather strange events which would eventually transpire to become some of the most formative moments of my life. At some point, probably acting against my own common sense, I allowed it to penetrate my soul so deeply that in many ways it has become closer to my heart than the place where I was born, brought up and learned to call my home. If the industrial landscape of Uppe

Silesia is somewhere that raised me, then Guiana – that mystical land lost in time, along with everyone I met and everything I experienced there – shaped and forged me as an adult.

Over the years, as I came to be obsessed more deeply with her secrets with every return, I ceased seeing Guiana as merely a place and began to treat it as a conscious being who, for reasons known only to herself, had decided to appear in my life as an unannounced companion. Gradually, with every step taken through the vast expanses of her pristine frontiers, she would come to consume my thoughts and feelings to such an extent that I became intrinsically linked to her. At some point I realised, with equal amounts of dismay and delight, that without her I would never feel complete again. What had once enriched my existence like nothing else now condemned me to a sense of constant unfulfillment and hunger that could only be satisfied in those brief, fleeting moments when, often against my own better judgement, I would get another opportunity to enter into that parallel dimension, into the embrace of a dark, damp, primordial world, as if to meet the truest love of my life after months of unbearable separation. I start and finish nearly every single day with my thoughts always hovering somewhere above that place far away, yet strangely always feeling so close. After spending years in this peculiar state of disjoint, I can no longer imagine it ever being any different.

I have spent a considerable amount of time wondering about the most suitable way or form to share this story. After all, we are talking about a region that spans six different countries, starting along the Amazon tributaries flowing down from the Andean spine of the continent, through the lowland forests and savannas around the meandering Orinoco, to the estuaries of the Essequibo, the Demerara, the Corentyne and other rivers forming the inhospitable muddy coastline of the western Atlantic. It is a tale of a place that assaults the traveller's senses, with an unimaginable diversity of environments and landscapes, ranging from the stifling humidity and heat of the Amazon selva, through sun-scorched grassy highlands, the cold montane cloud forests shrouded in a perpetual veil of mist, to the mystical, dark and eerily silent landscape of the tepui plateaus, so unlike anything we know that they seem – for lack of any better reference – probably best compared to the surface of a different planet. The tepuis, being quite literally the heart of the entire region – a teeming source of life-giving water pulsating from ancient springs and falling down gigantic sandstone cliffs – sculpt a network of river arteries that create a perfectly nourished blend of unique ecosystems covering nearly 15 per cent of the entire South American continent. It is no coincidence that Guiana means "Land of Many Waters", and that the Indigenous communities have come to call Roraima, the most famous of the tepuis, the "Mother of All Waters", worshipping it as a place of sanctity – which she definitely is.

It would have been rather easy to tell this story as yet another alarming account of just how negative humanity's impact can be on the world around us. Of how the unsustainable use of our planet's resources and relentless disruption of the environment has called into question the future of the natural world as we know it. Of how as humankind, in all our hubris and misplaced sense of self-importance, we have indulged ourselves with visions of colonising other worlds, all whilst mastering the craft of modifying the only world which allows us to thrive, tirelessly preparing it for the emergence of life forms that are ecologically incompatible with our own species in place of the ones we keep wiping out, and testing the limits of natural processes of adaptation and sustenance like thoughtless children playing with tools we do not fully understand. But I deliberately chose not to follow this path; not because I disagree with these views, but rather because I do not see myself fit to be placed on some moral or intellectual high ground to pass judgement on how to make things better. I will leave this to those with far more insight and expertise – especially to the Indigenous communities who call the lands I had the enormous privilege of experiencing their home. I believe they are the true wardens of Guiana and those who should be the first to benefit from her generosity, as well as those who should decide about their own fate in her everlasting presence, having the rights and resources to preserve their heritage and way of life for future generations to come.

With all that being said, I have instead chosen to act as a mere observer. In this sense, I am not really a creator, for what I did was simply witness the most extraordinary expressions of life capable of invoking feelings so overwhelming – and often so contradictory – I have come to consider them to be part of the spiritual world just as much as they are part of the reality we so desperately try to grasp with our scientific minds. I tried my best to document them and, with my camera in hand, carefully curate a narrative that will hopefully let you experience at least a fraction of something that I have come to love and revere so much. Choosing photography as a medium to present this story also has its roots in the influence Guiana has had on my life – it was in fact only thanks to her that I became interested in nature and landscape photography and decided to buy my first proper camera set. And it was not a decision fuelled by some need for artistic expression, but rather because I wanted to capture, preserve and share as much as I could from the unique position I found myself in, being able to interact with something so remote, so ancient, and so vulnerable. *Rapture* is in no way a work of science or a precise representation of the workings of a typical expedition, despite having some aspects of both. It is a work of a deeply personal nature. Through the images and texts in this book, I try to give the reader an opportunity to walk in the shoes of a wanderer and to invoke the ephemeral feelings one can expect when exploring the wilderness in the hinterlands of Guiana in its full spectrum.

This book was created out of scarcity – and I am well aware of how pretentious this might sound in the age of digital photography, when nearly every single one of us has the ability to capture every moment, with the most adequate take selected out of hundreds of shots using nothing more than a mobile phone. However, this is not the kind of scarcity I have in mind, but rather a scarcity of time. The photographs represent mere fleeting moments amidst long weeks I spent absorbed by tropical downpours, under the scorching sun of the savanna, and after covering hundreds of kilometres, often being gifted with the priceless opportunity to sojourn in some of the least explored places of our planet. And given how quickly these places are changing, I am aware of how painfully temporary what has been captured might be. It is my hope that through those images I was able to preserve some of those fragile manifestations and express at least a small portion of the wonder for you to behold and contemplate.

Welcome to the Guiana Shield.

Mateusz Wrazidlo

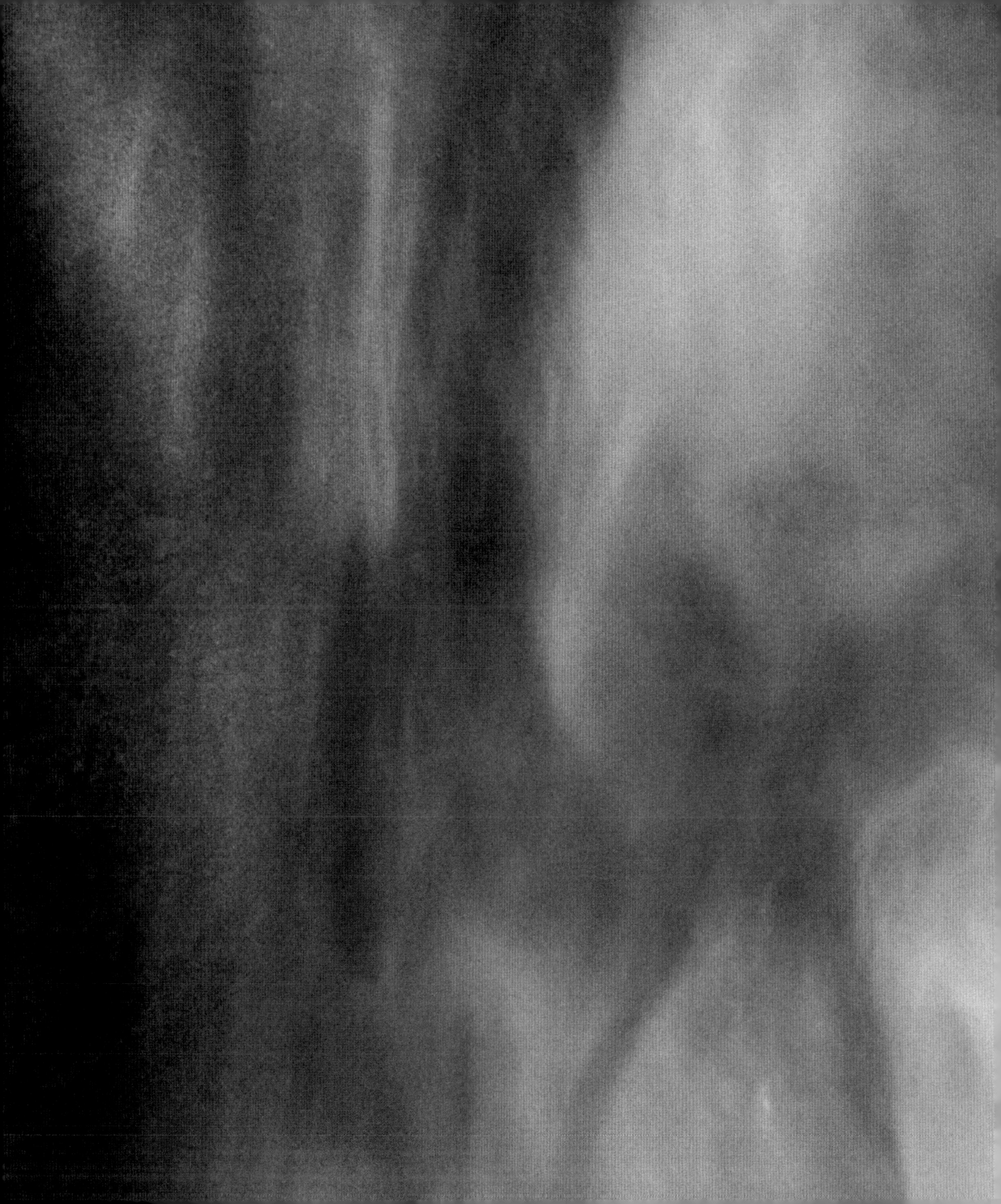

CHAPTER 1
Emerald Entanglement

"The formidable activity sunk into the apparent stillness, the evil silence, the hallucinating perspective ... The remote song of the bellbird, melancholy clapper of the immense green concavity, the crash of a tree ending its life of centuries without having been blown over by a gust of wind, of a giant tree, almost without roots, because there is hardly any space left for so many seeking nourishment in the soil ... The fallen column, the somber broken dome through which a shaft of light falls on the disquieted clearing ... The vast and profound echo resounding in the green abysses ... The pause, the grave silence after the crash. That which is impressive without sensitive shapes, the anguishing wait ... And the sad tolling of the bellbird, this time for the fallen tree.
The jungle disease, already getting hold of his spirit."

Rómulo Gallegos – *Canaima*, 1935

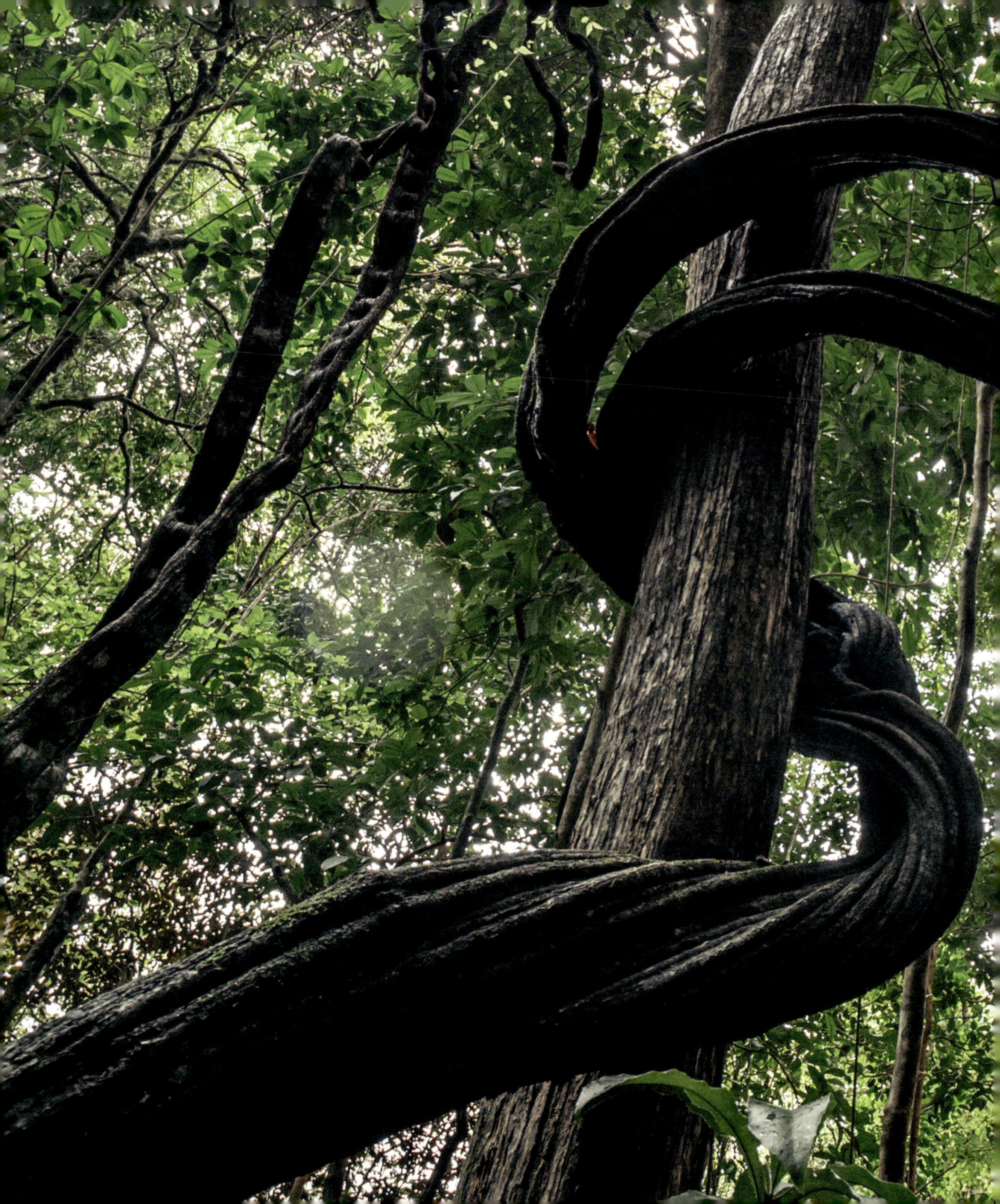

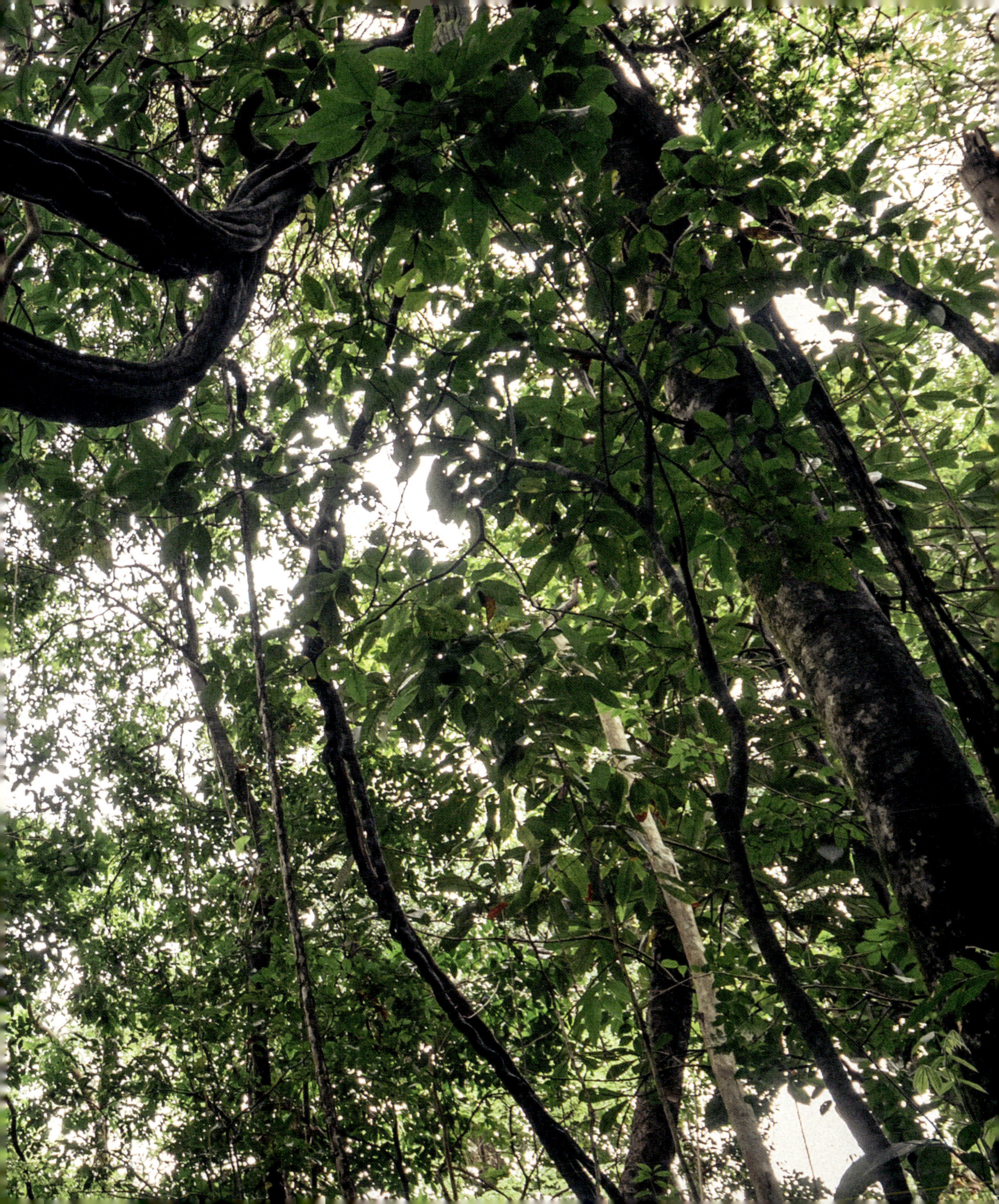

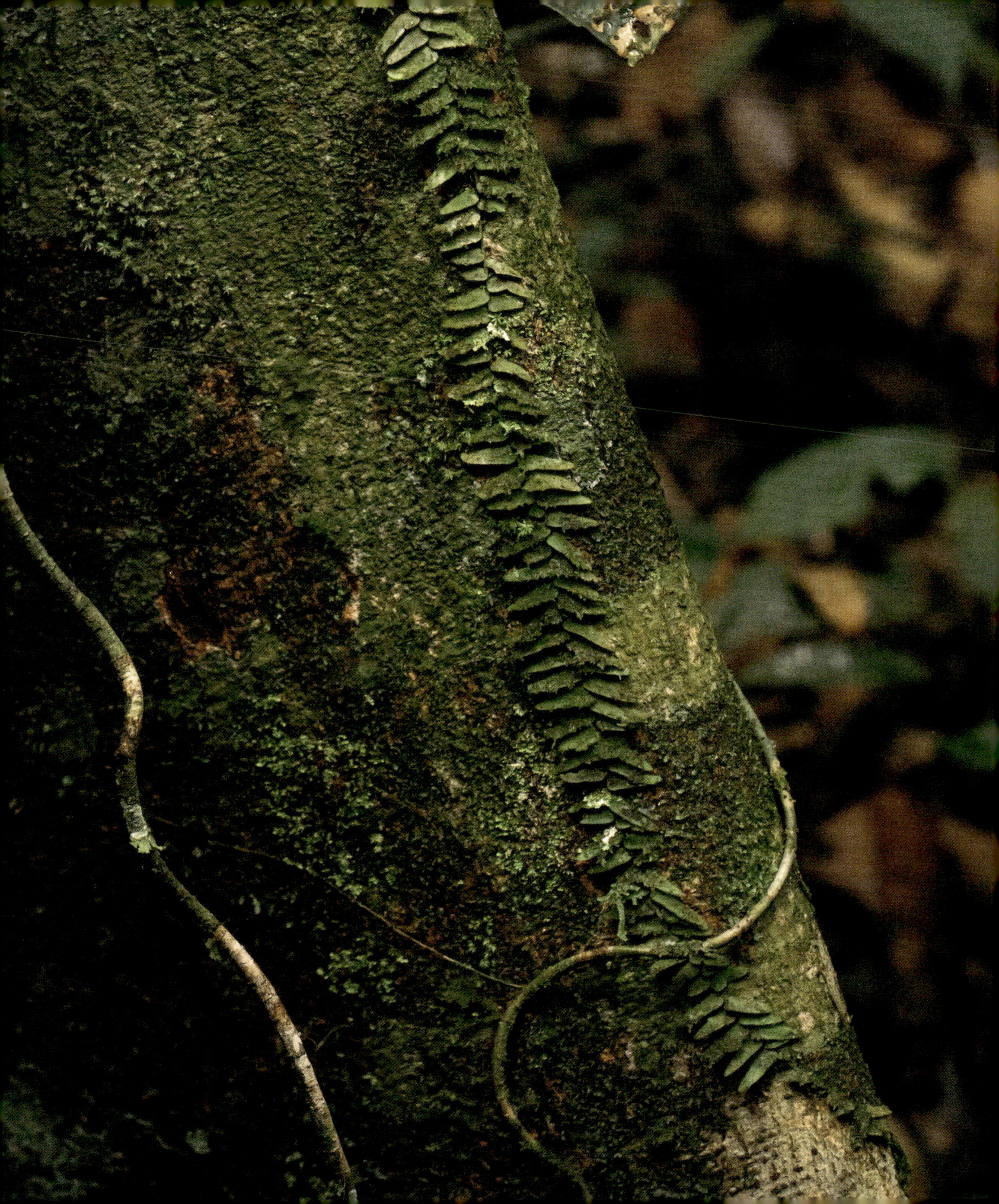

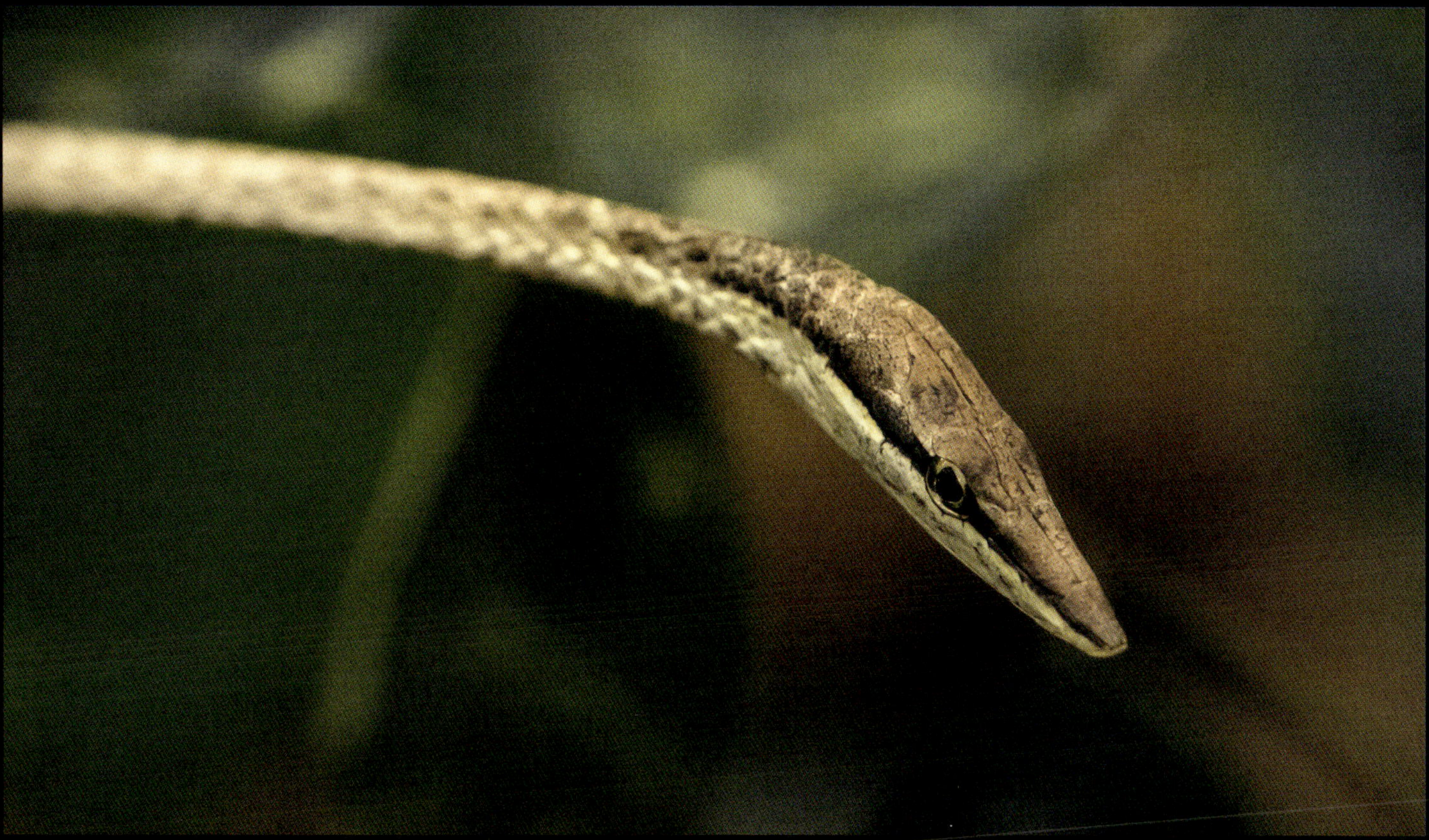

The moment I step out of that rusty truck, I feel the stifling air fill my lungs. It was bearable at first, in the hours rushing along the muddy roads, with a refreshing breeze coming through the broken windshield. But now, suddenly, there's only that overwhelming stillness and feeling of... dread? I stand here at the start of a barely visible trail leading into the shadows ahead, surrounded by imposing, living walls separating me from something I can only describe as an emerald void, luring me in with that otherworldly, chaotic cacophony I so longed to hear, now feeling nothing but intimidation at the very thought of taking a step forward. I brush aside a curtain of frail vines, only to be welcomed with a scene that makes my heart skip a beat. Before me, sunk in a shallow pool of mud, is a tree enveloped in gnarly vines, its twisted branches reaching out beyond the all-encompassing twilight like a petrified demigod stretching out its many arms in a desperate plea to grasp even the faintest rays of sunlight falling from the nurturing skies...

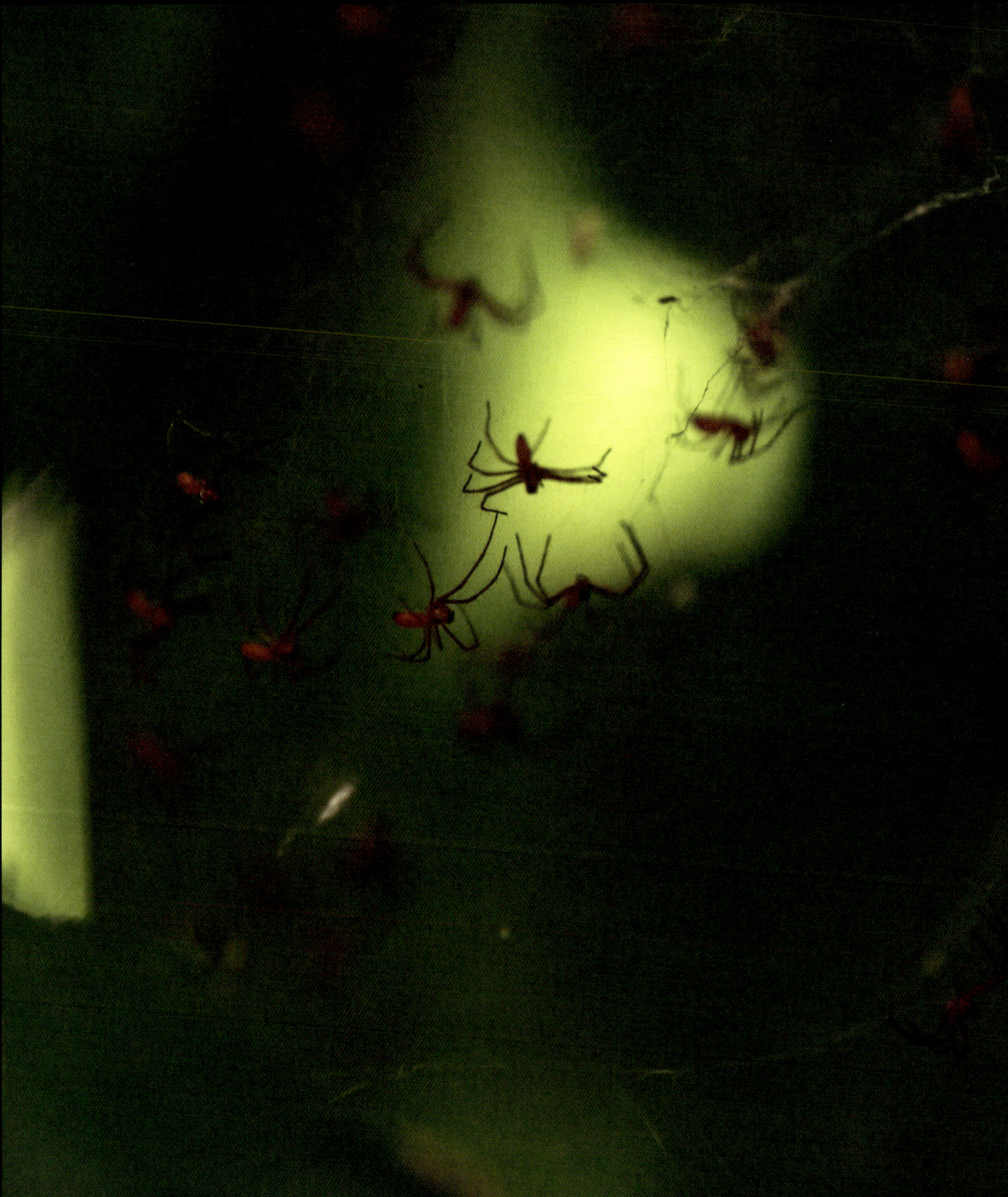

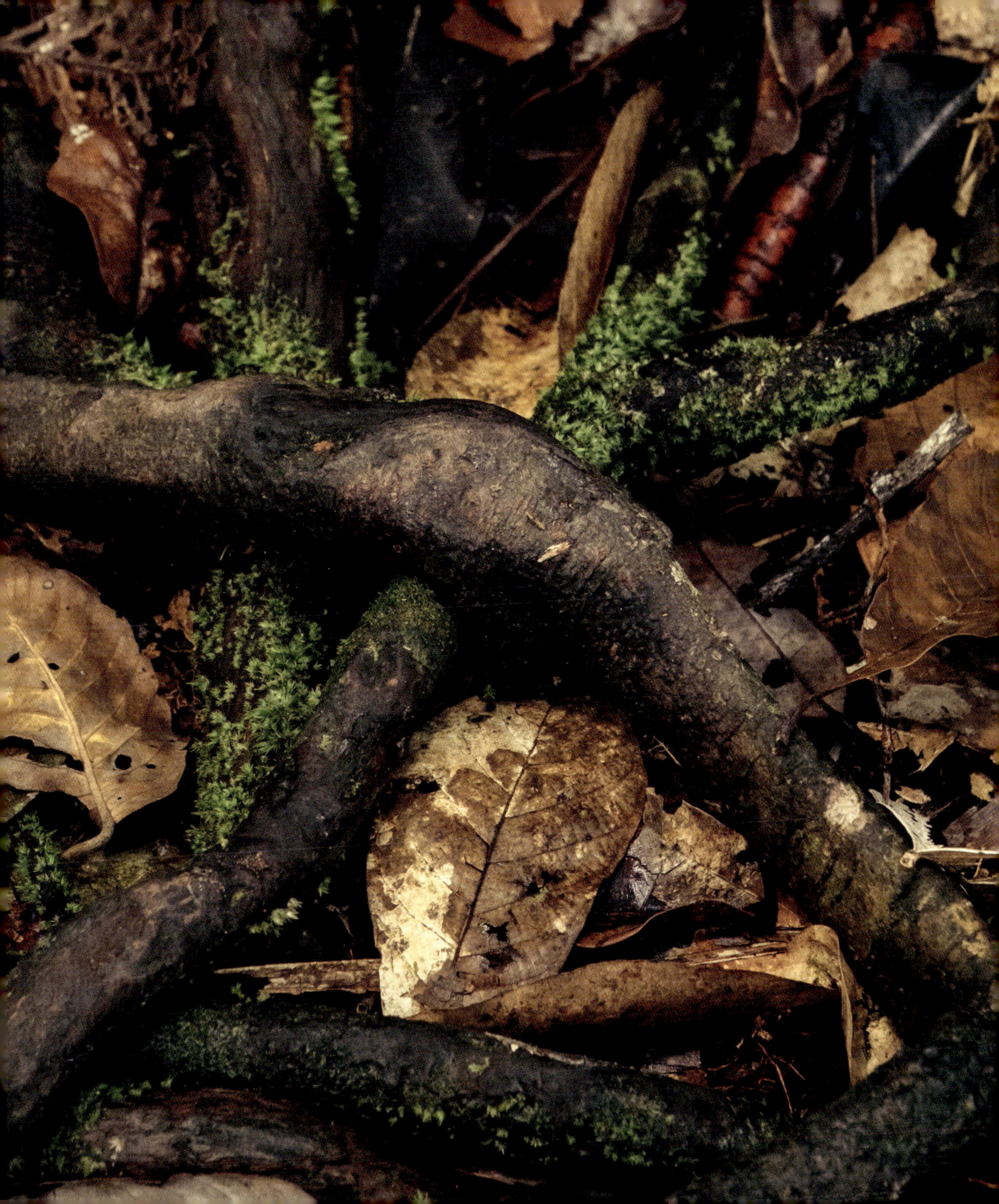

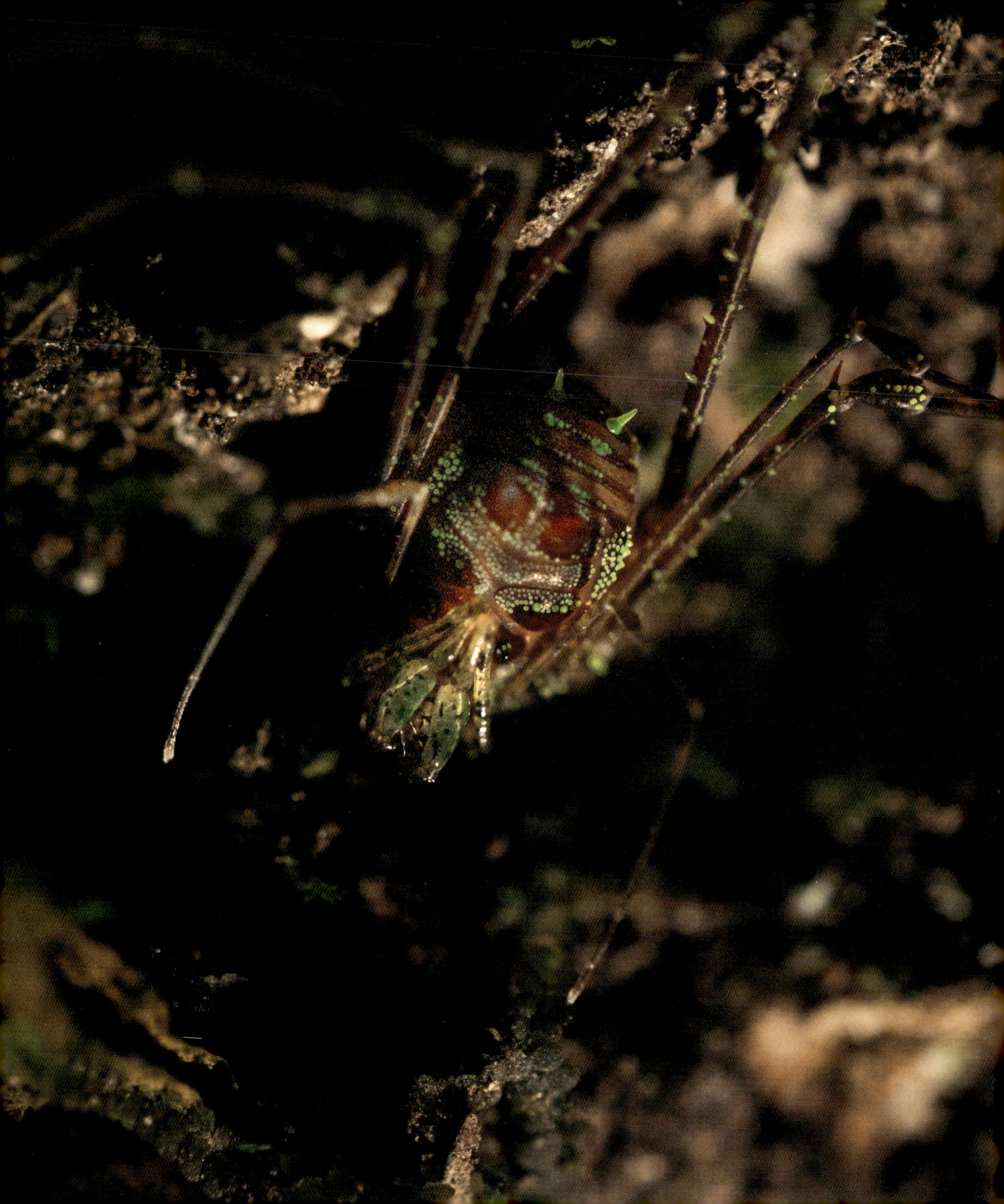

I've been marching thoughtlessly, trying to mollify the overwhelming sense of stifling heat and discomfort. I recall the stories of Humboldt and Darwin, their recollections of stunning luxuriant vegetation described so vividly in their diaries, but feel nothing but frustration growing within me. Why is it that where they were enchanted by a spectacle of life, I see only chaos and despair? I expected harmony and tranquillity here, yet what I see reminds me more of a Dantesque scene of collective asphyxiation and struggle, saturated by that overwhelmingly peculiar scent of birth and decay blended into one. The steady trickle of sweat coming from my forehead has already permeated everything – including my very thoughts.

I take my backpack off and sit down to catch my breath. As soon as I stop moving, my body becomes engulfed in a sudden, cold shiver. I hastily take off my shirt and toss it aside so that, at least for a moment, I don't have to feel that wet, dirty rag wrapped around my body. I lean my back against a tree trunk, feeling its intricate texture rub against my skin. Exhaustion makes me zone out when suddenly, through squinted eyelids, I catch sight of a flock of faint green specks glowing in the dark, drifting slowly towards my face as it presses against the bark. As I open my eyes wider, the green dots become attached to eight long, spiky legs protruding from a round carapace, in the middle of which is a set of eyes directed at me in curious anticipation. As I feel the pedipalps begin to probe my skin, I bolt upright and decide to move on.

When I bend down to grab my shirt, I notice it being invaded by a crowd of bees feasting on my sweat. My face twists into a grotesque grimace the moment my skin touches the cold wet fabric once again. I stand and gaze up at the skies, obscured by the thick canopy cursing myself for the decisions that brought me here – but not for long. My blasphemies are suddenly interrupted by a series of stings followed by a wave of painful heat across my back. I throw my shirt off once again and see a swarm of fire ants crawling furiously out of the sleeves, probably unable to believe my own foolishness for being so careless and instantly putting me back in line. I finally walk on and notice my frustration slowly giving way to humble admiration.

This place is not what I expected. But maybe it was never meant to be?

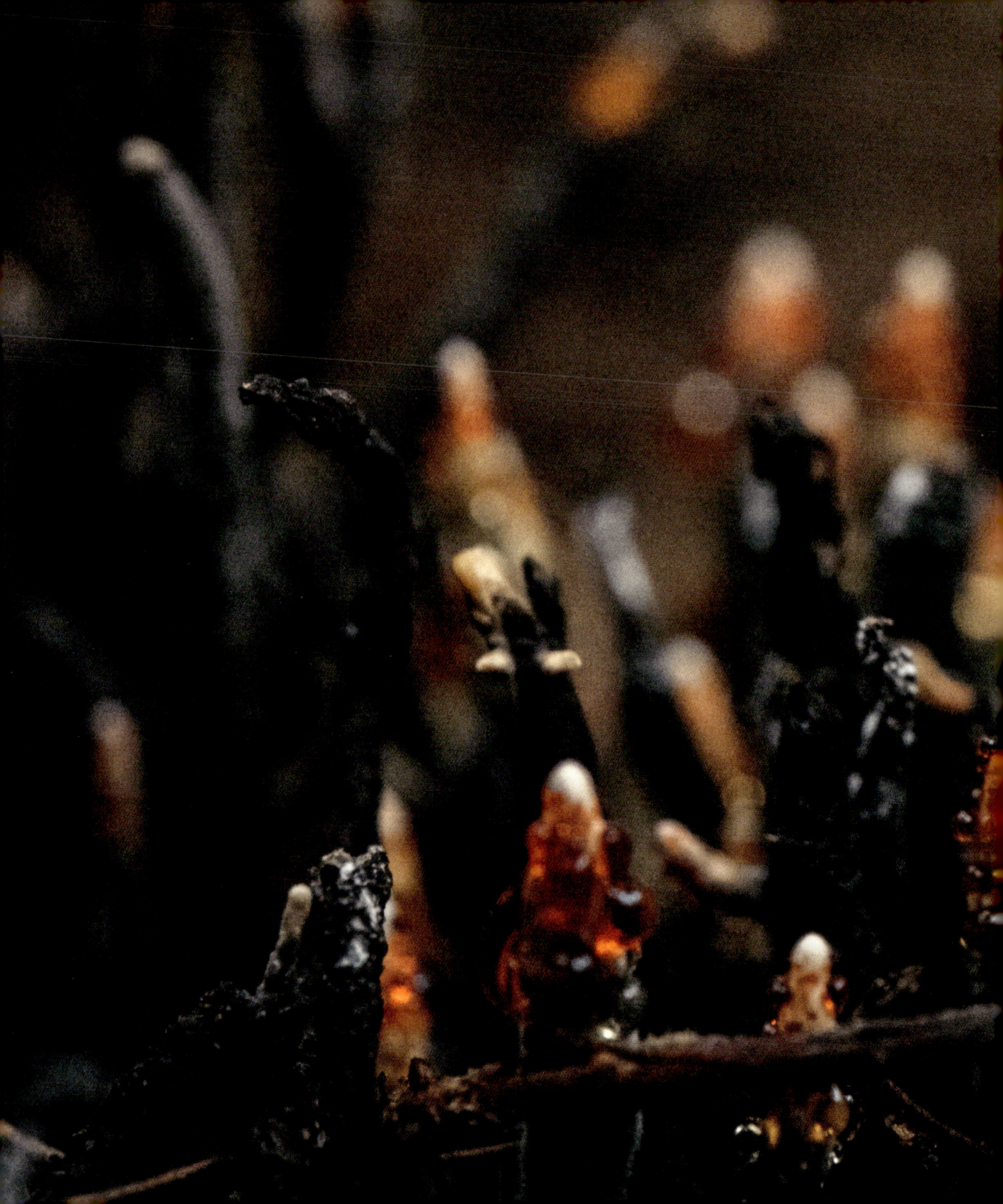

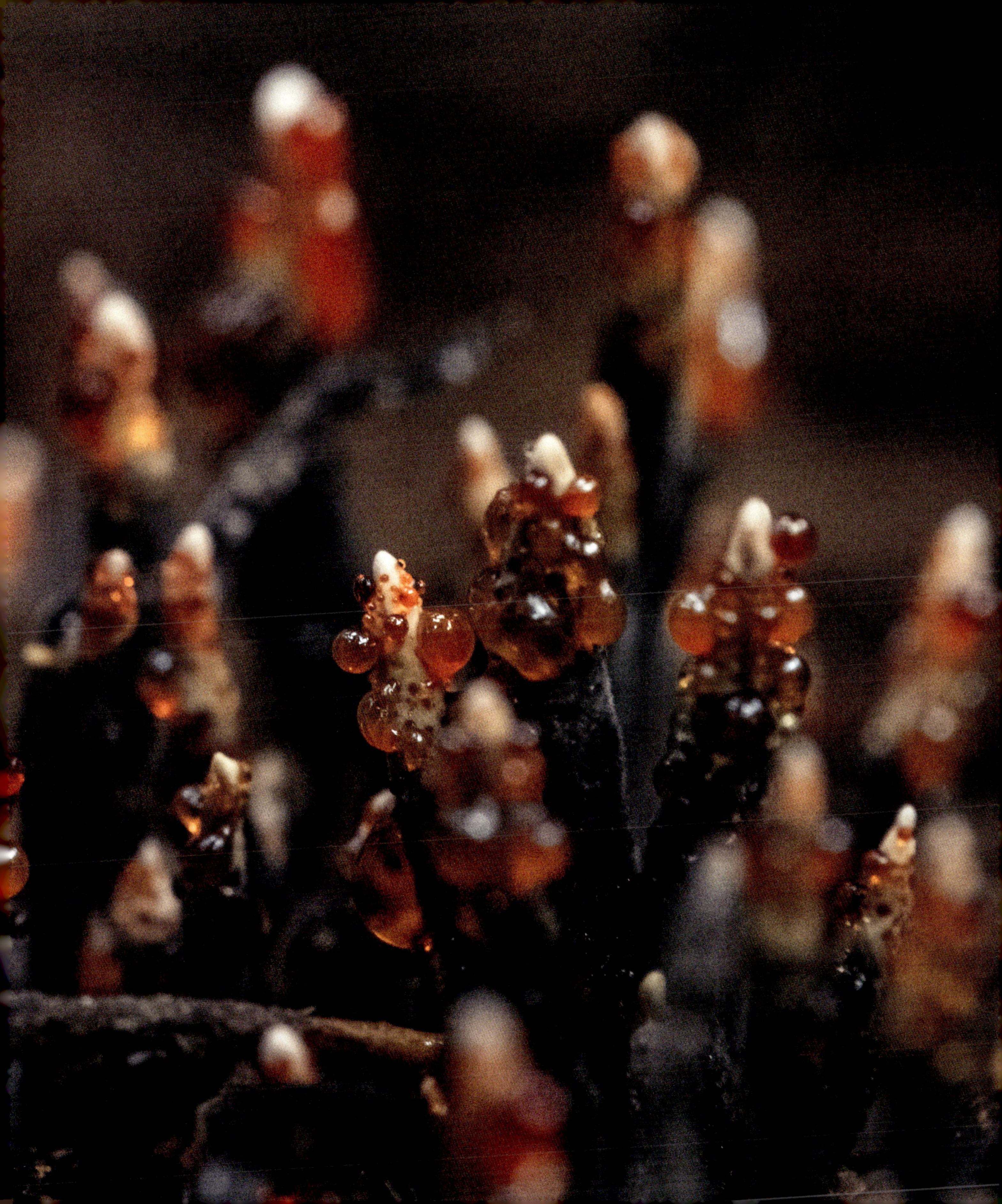

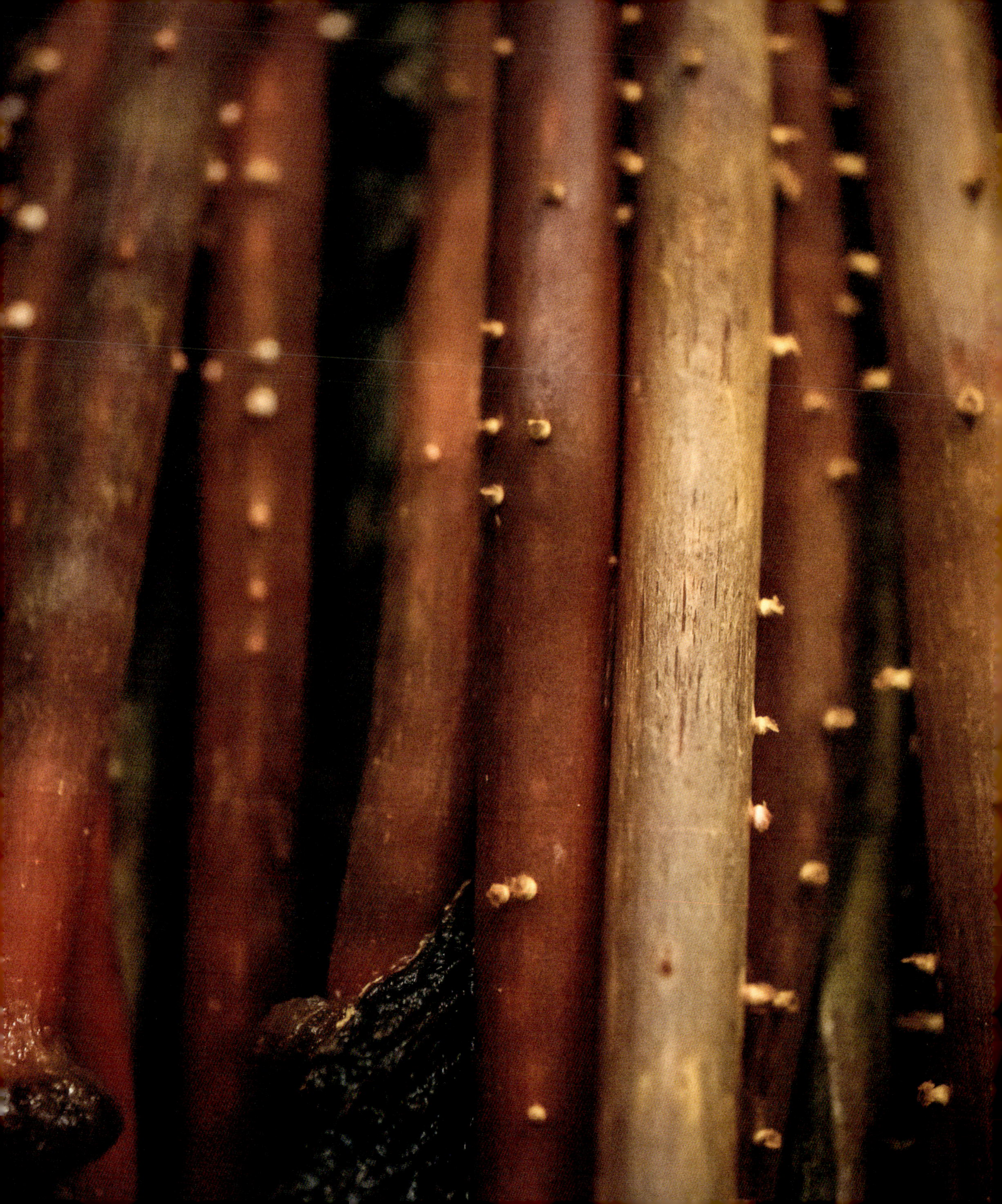

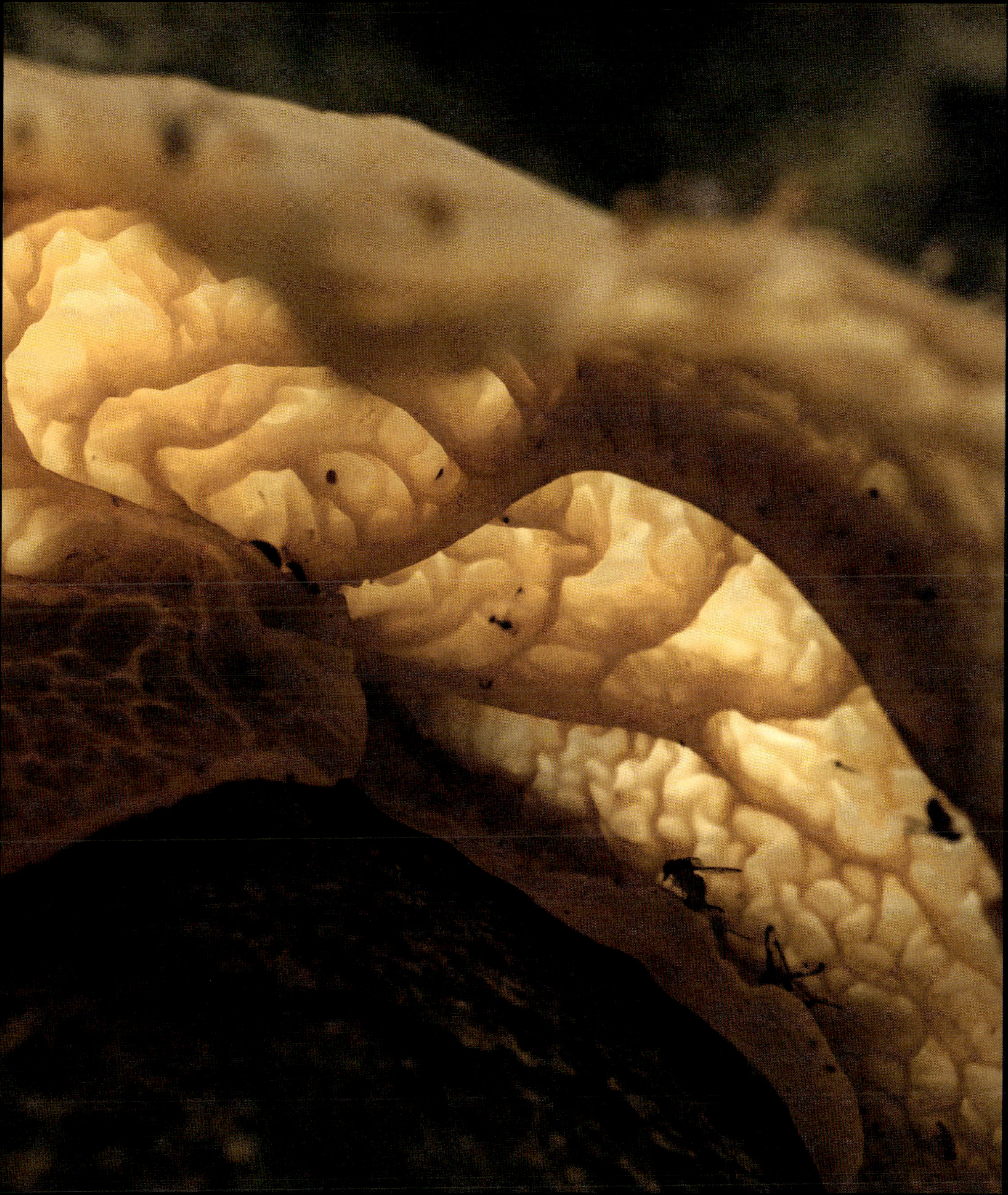

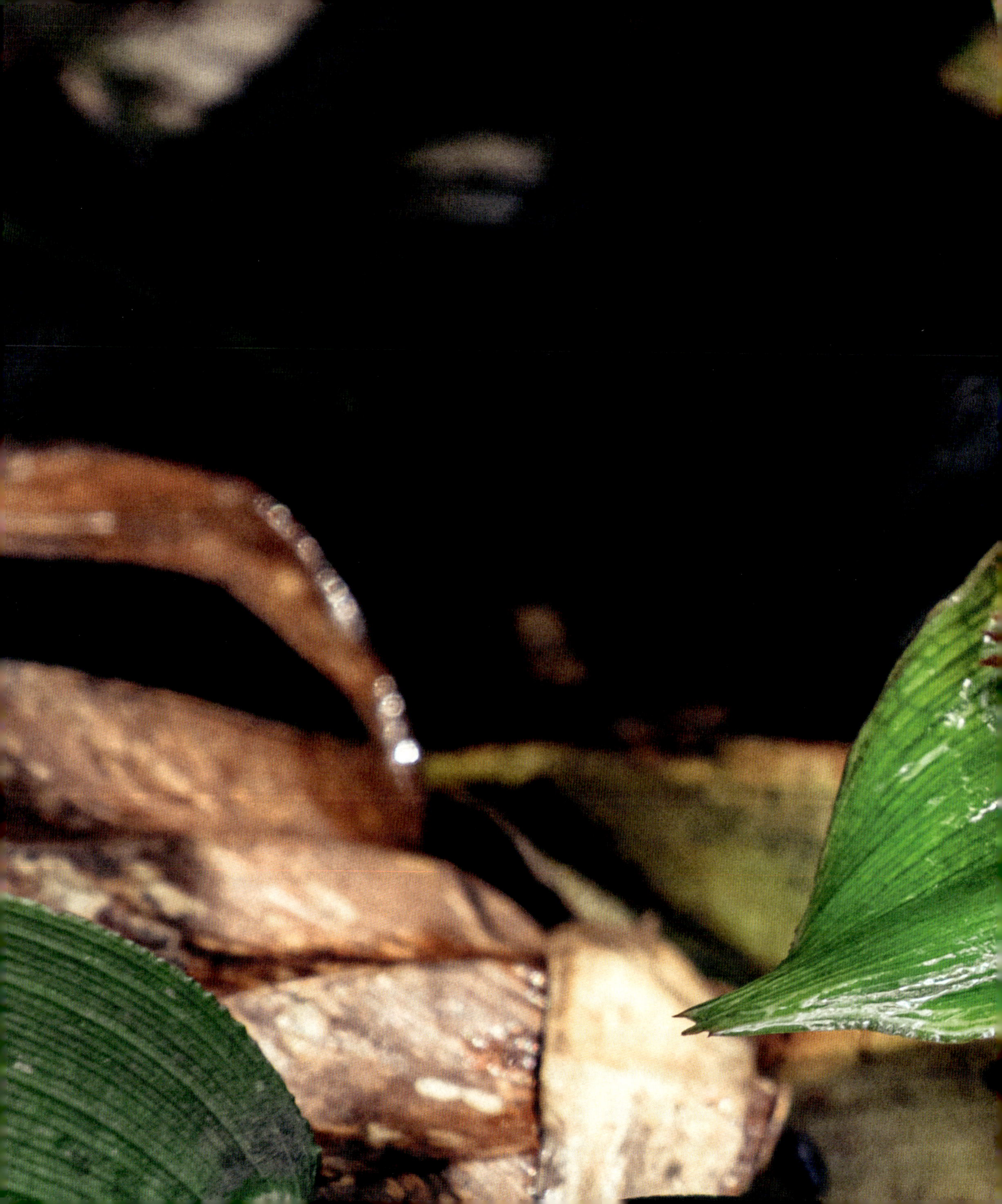

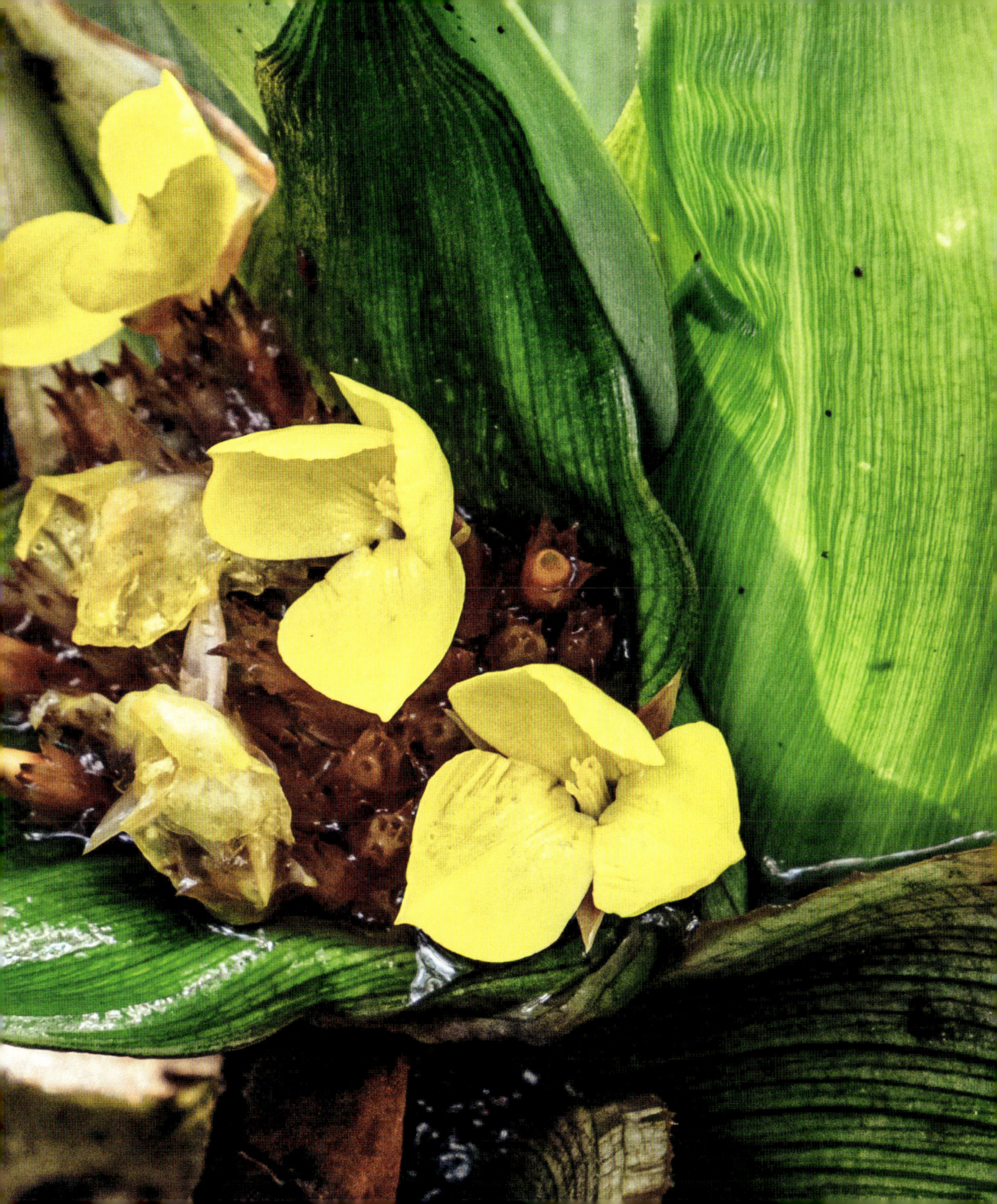

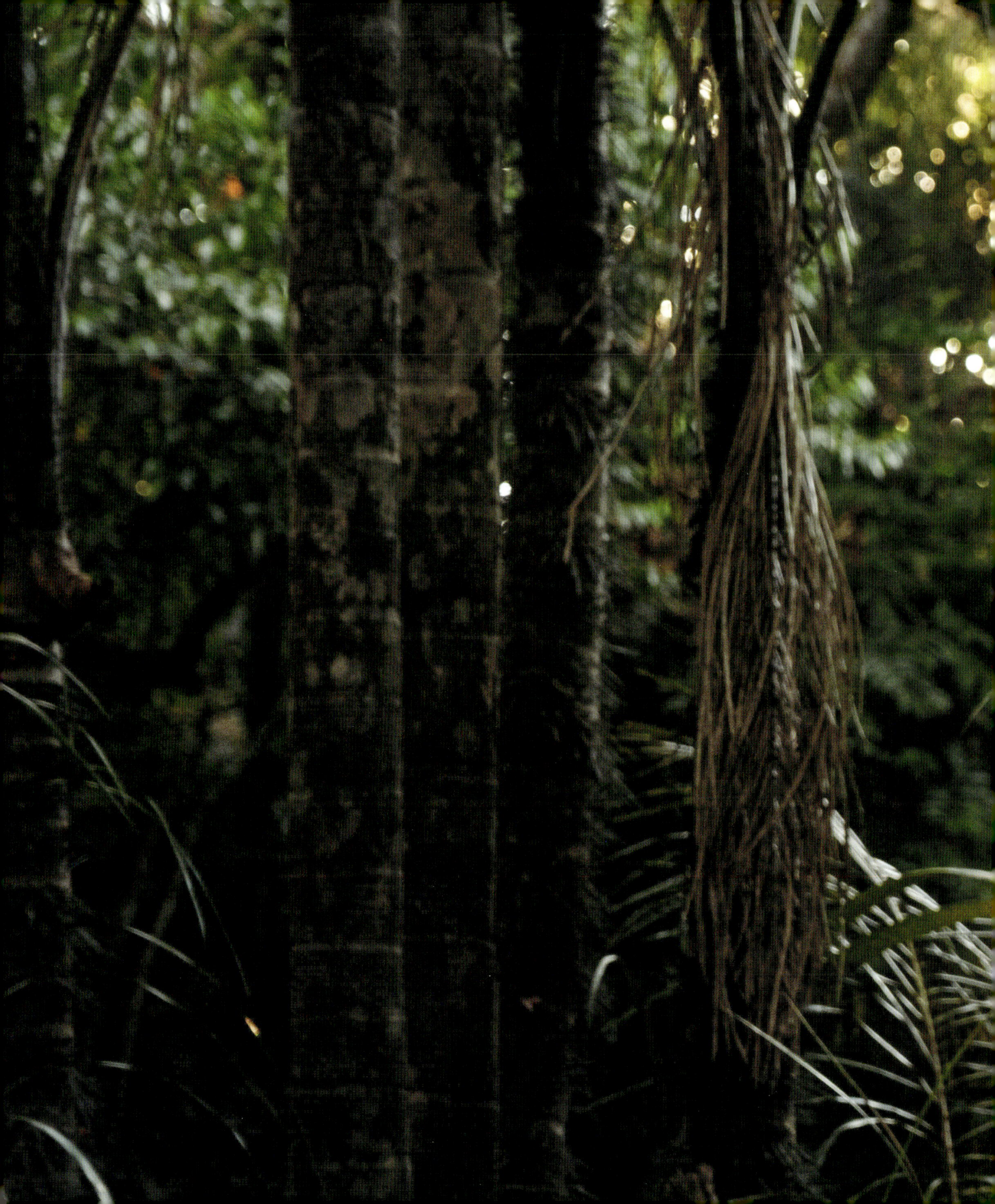

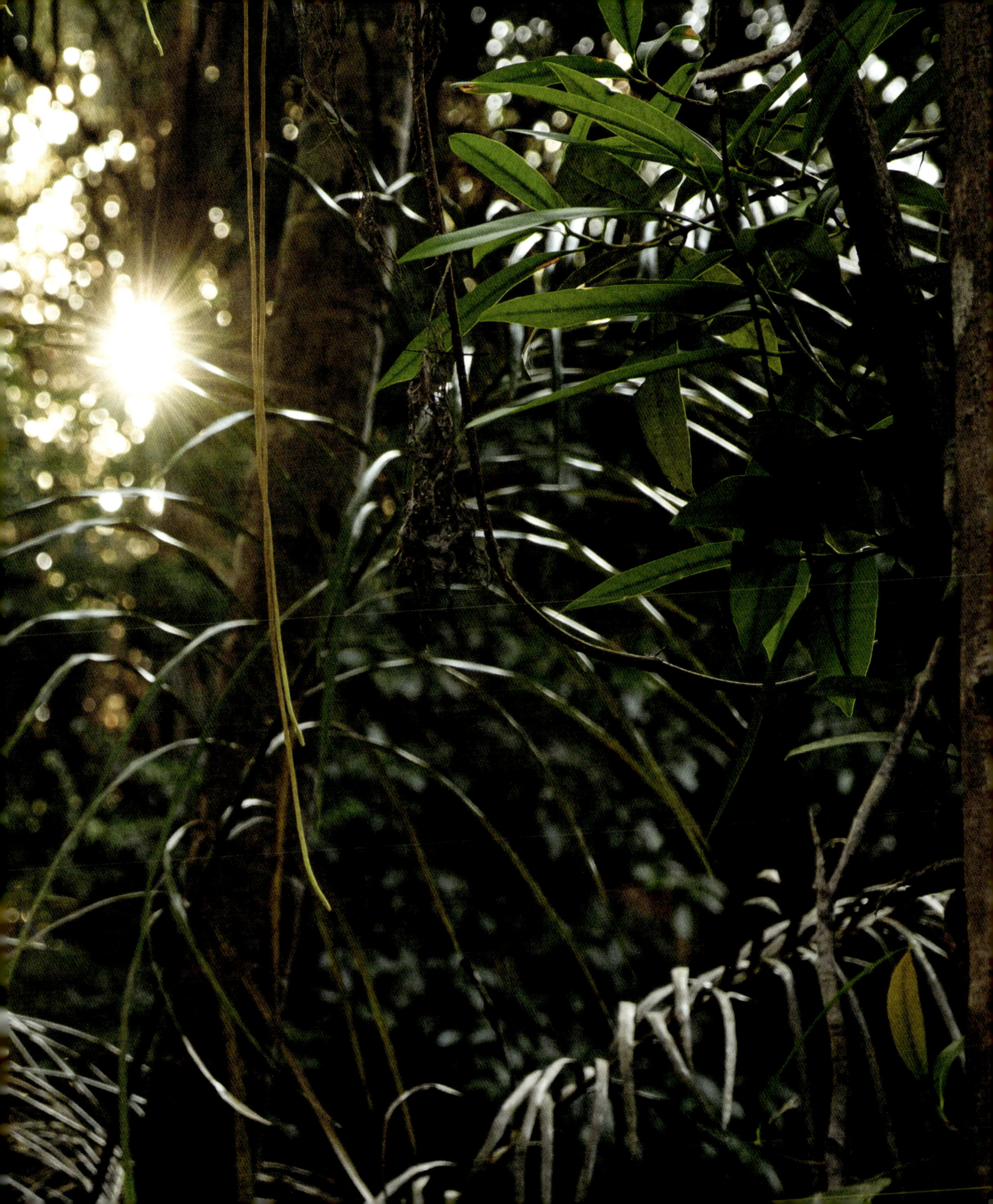

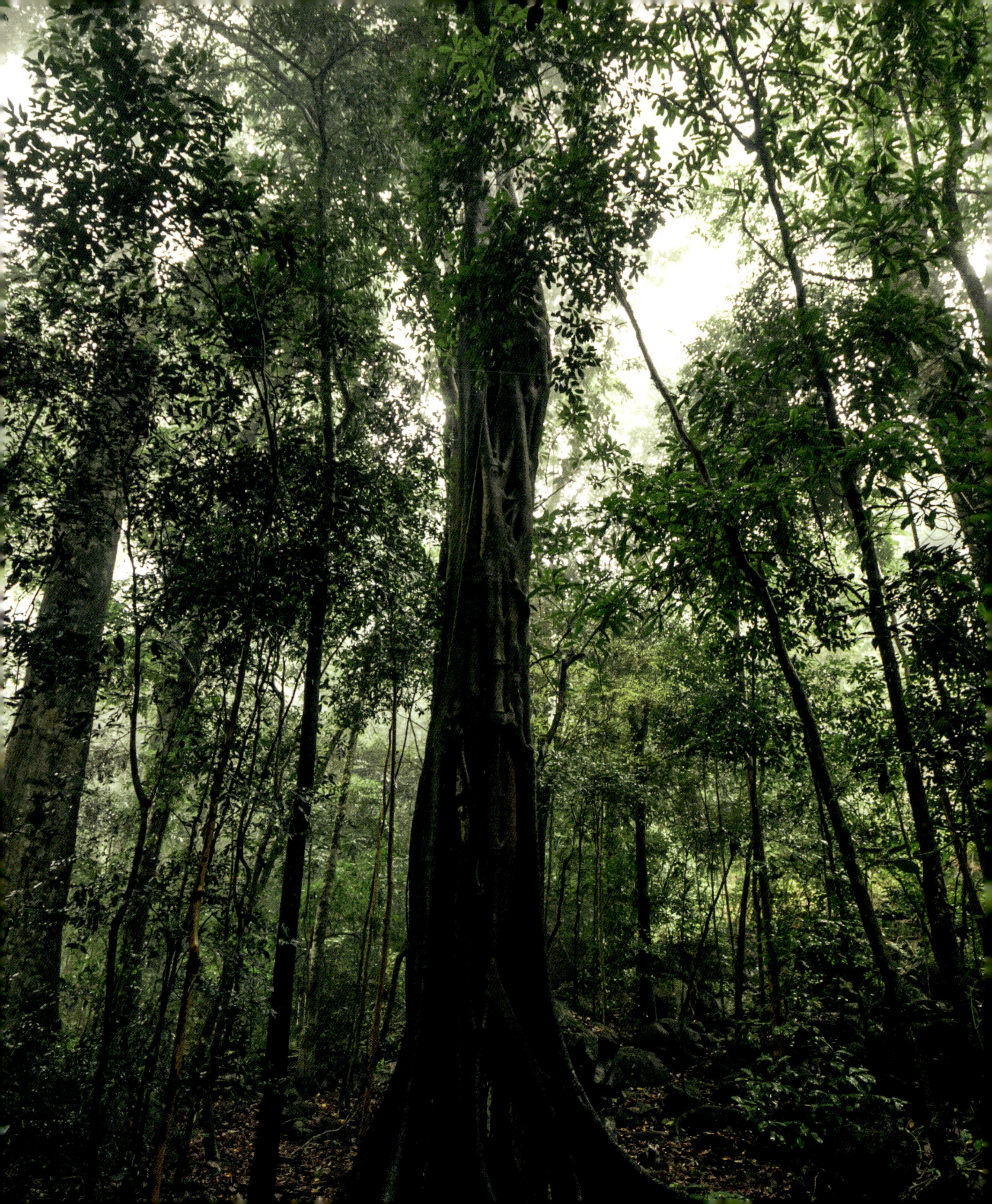

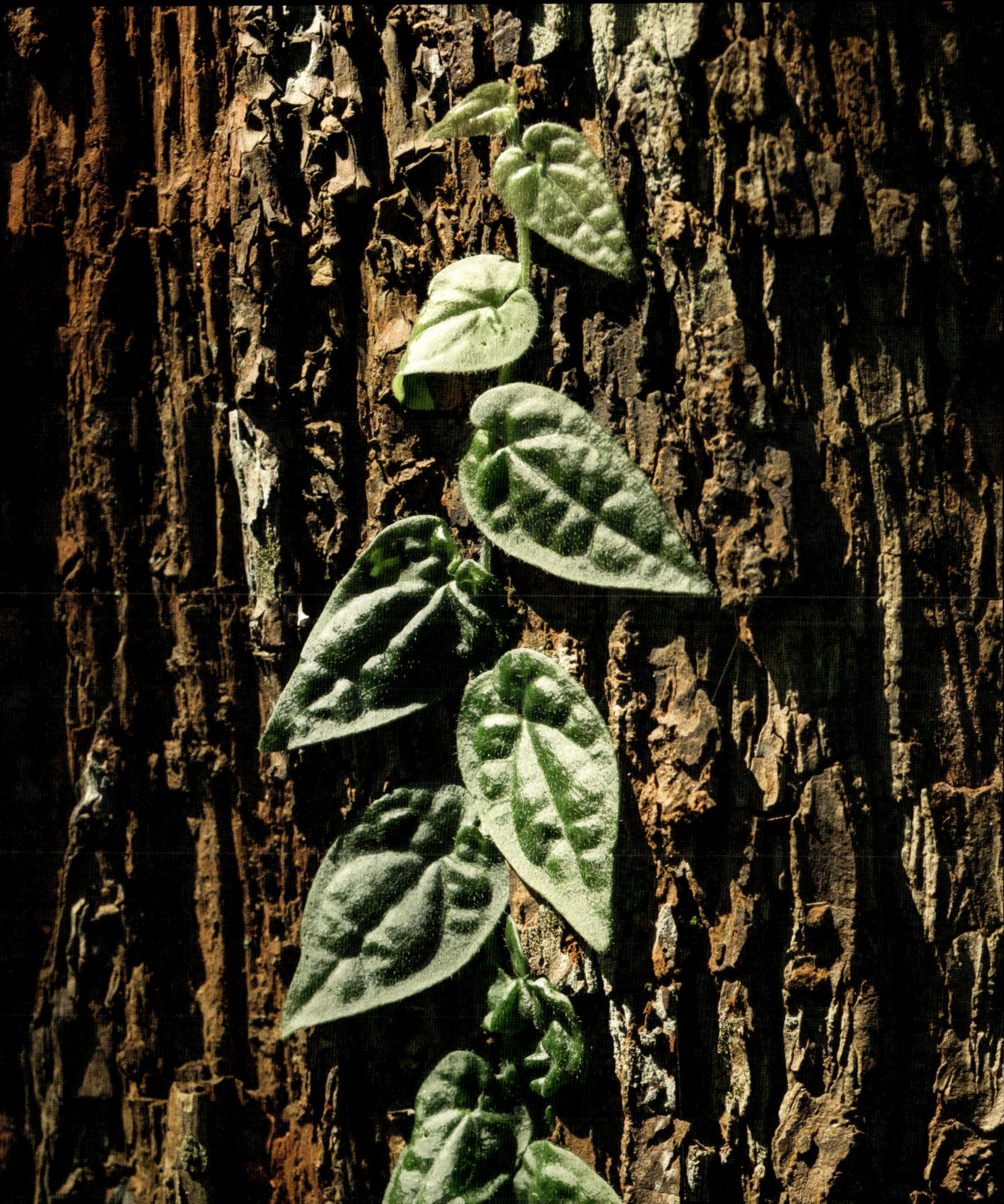

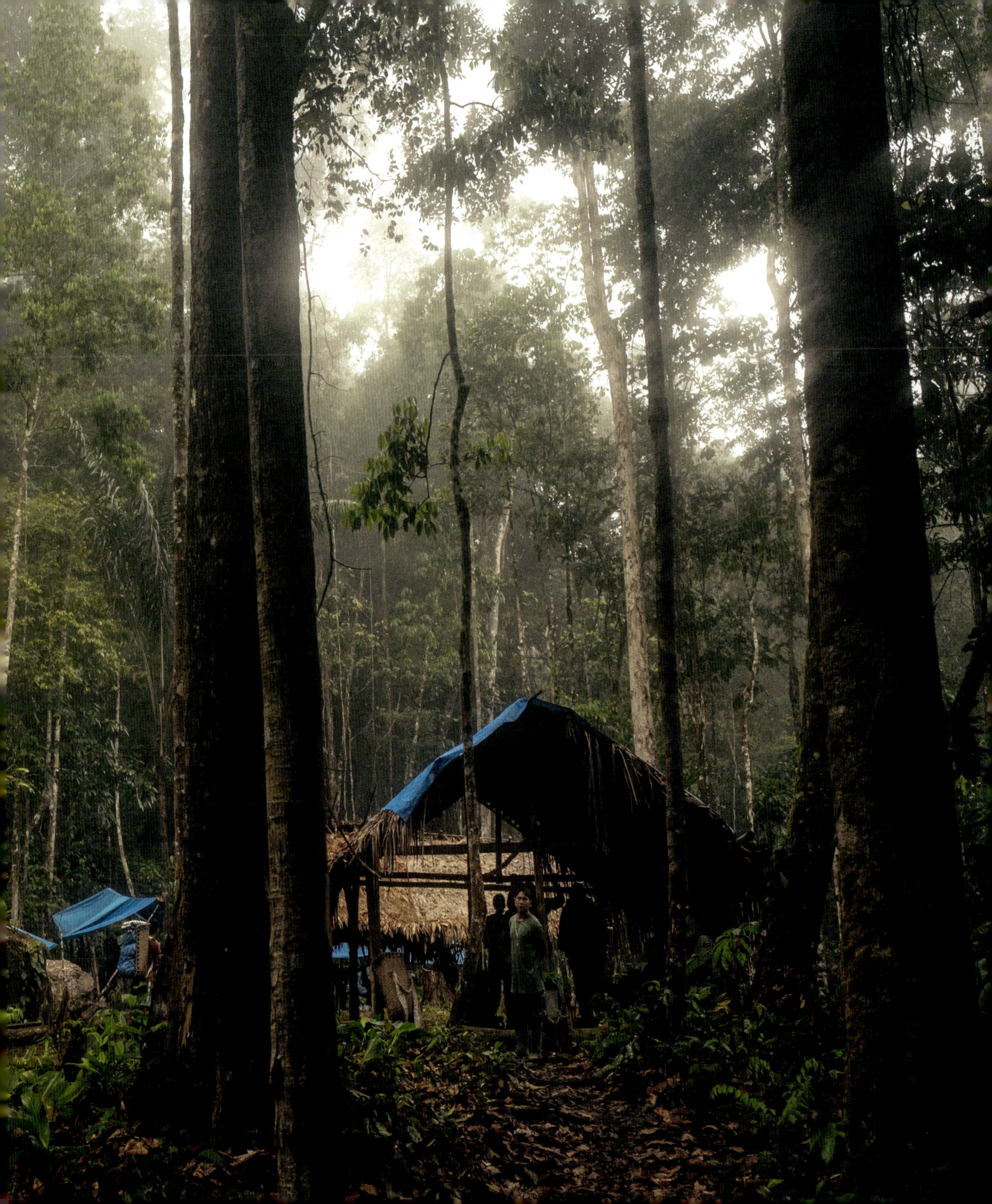

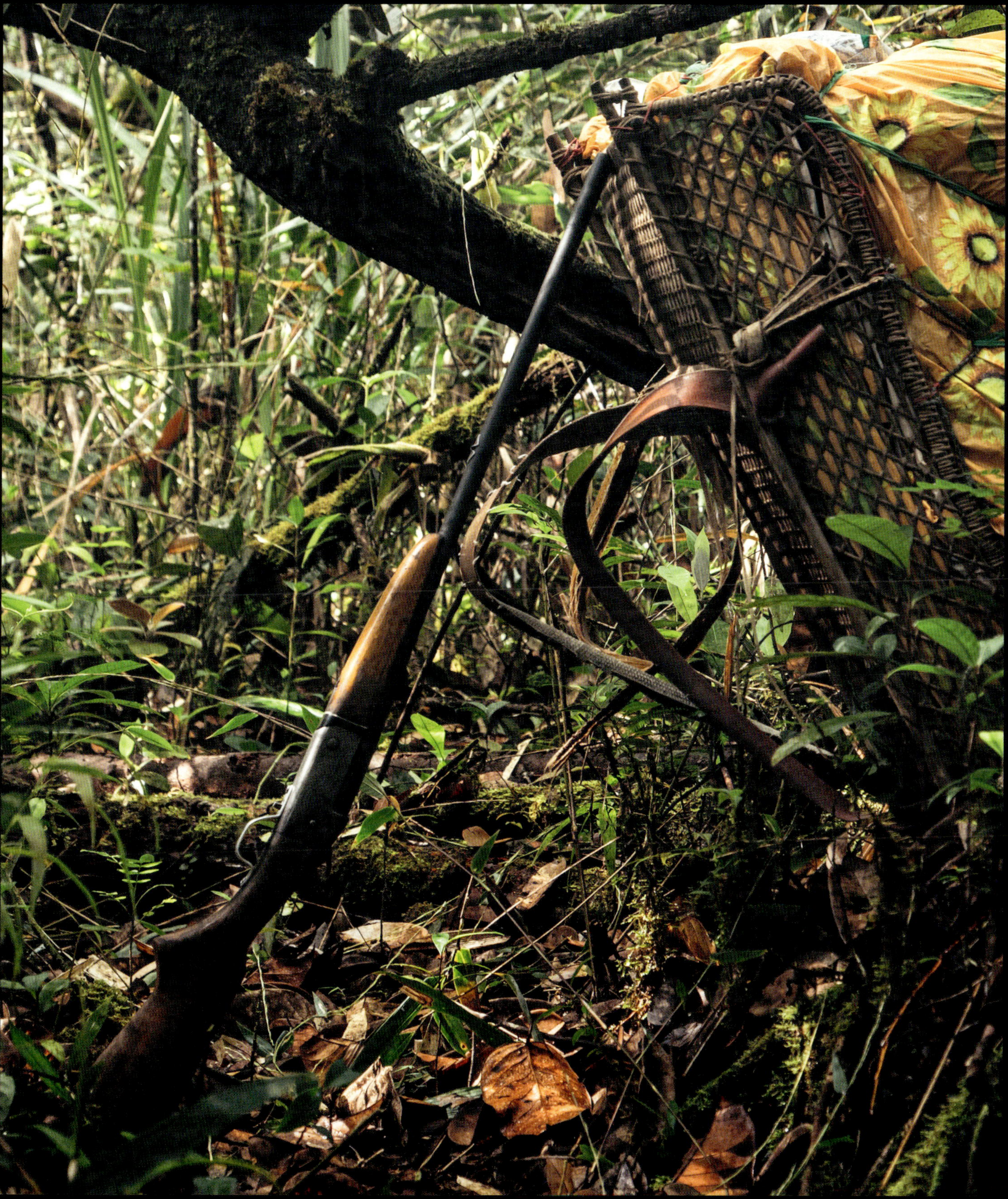

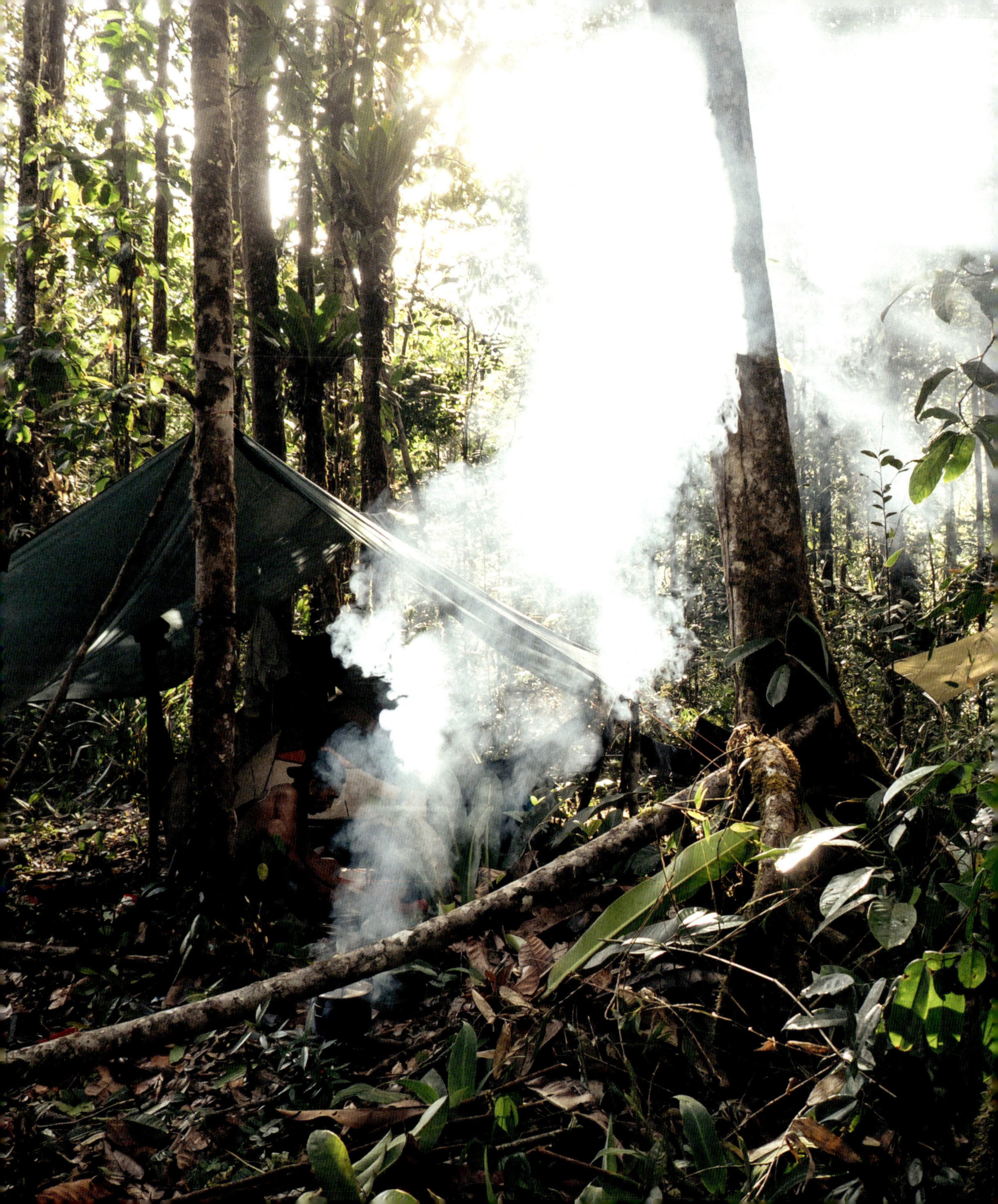

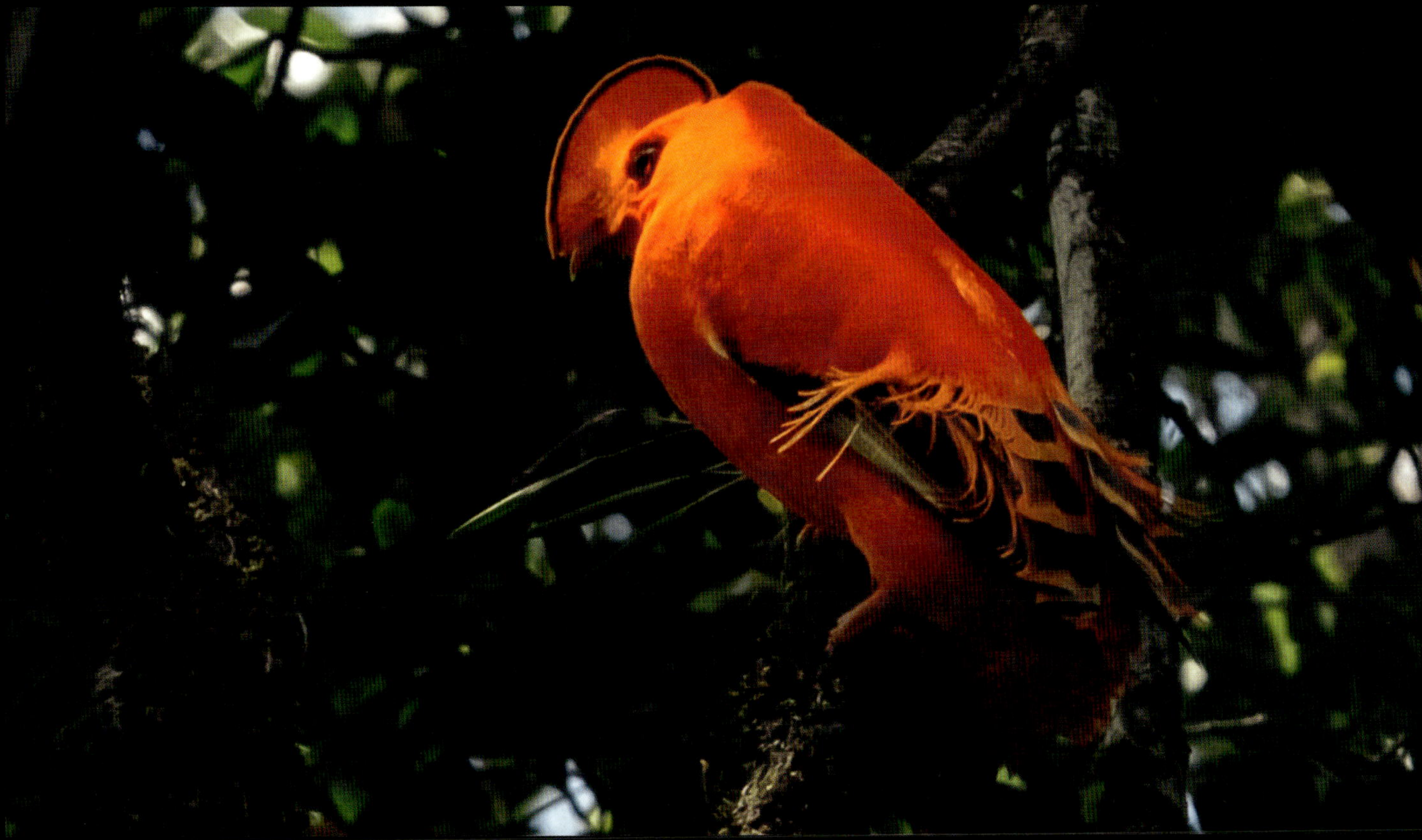

Filled with contrition after my earlier mishap, I begin to notice the forest get dimmer with each passing minute. In the soft beams of golden light, I notice a brilliant, almost electric speck of orange suddenly appear amongst the branches ahead. As I move closer, I hear it give out the most cheerful of calls – it's a bird, the magnificent Rupicola, enthusiastically greeting me upon my arrival at what appears to be a campsite. I'm thrilled for a chance to finally change into something dry for the night, leaving my wet clothes to hang next to my hammock. Suddenly, a sound of a distant thunder makes the air shudder. At first, I take it for a gunshot from a party hunting nearby – but only until I hear the first droplets of rain fall on the thatched palm roof above my head, announcing a night of wet misery.

The air is filled with a stench of damp clothes and boots as I drift off to sleep, listening to the raging downpour – along with something I can't really make out from the other noises all around me. Is that the rain hitting the gigantic aroid leaves or are they... whispers?

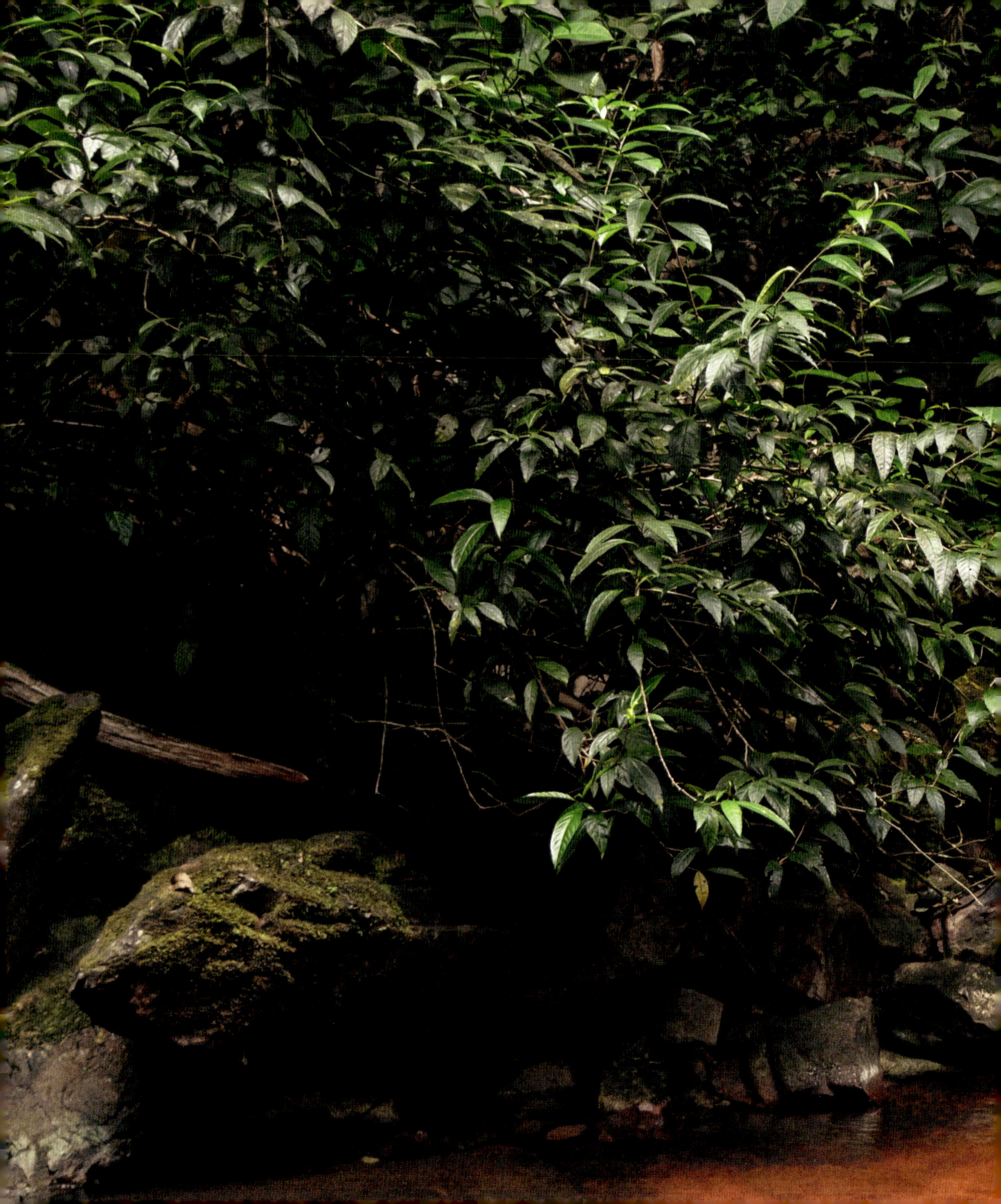

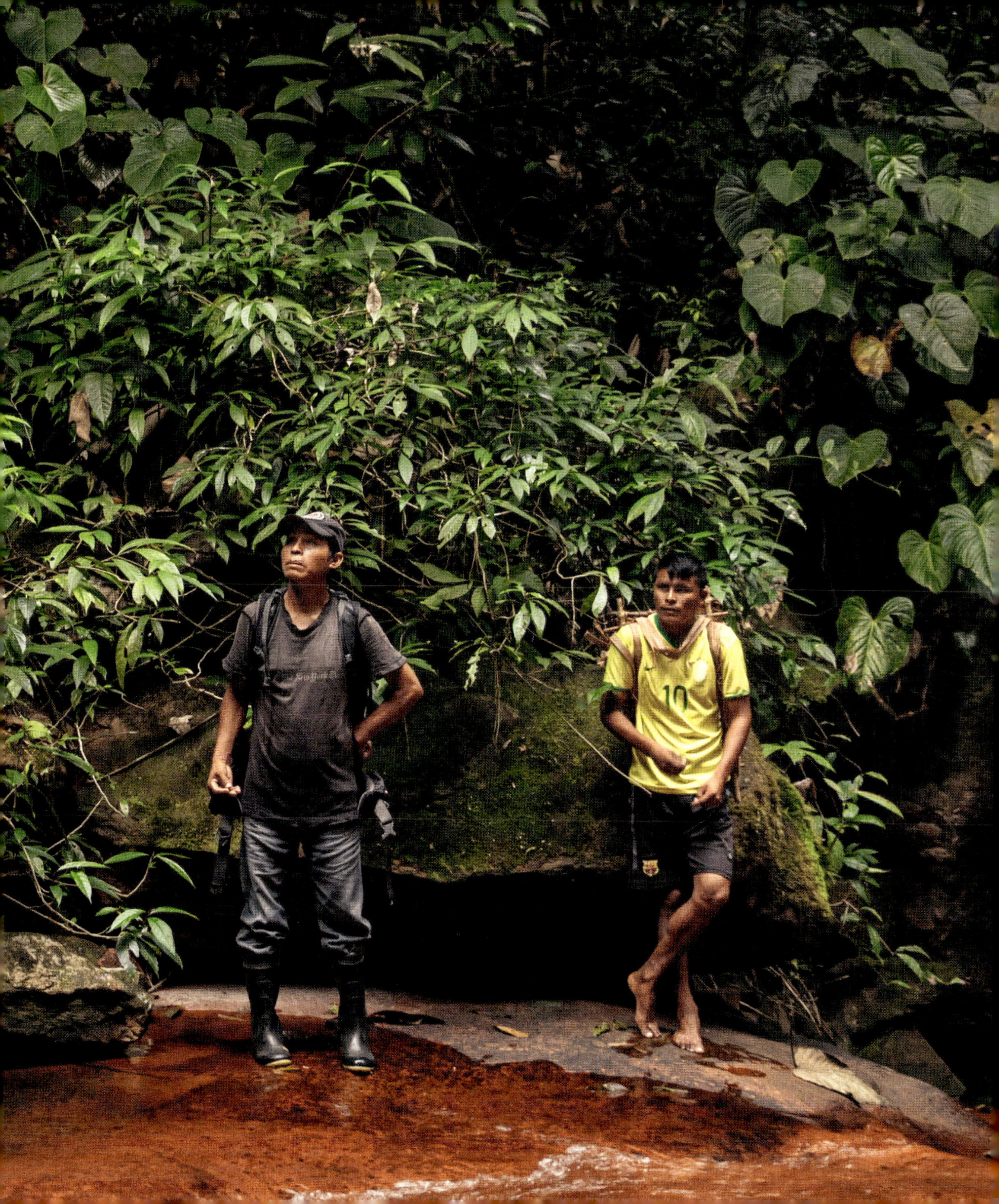

CHAPTER 2

...of All the Waters

"Against the pure blue sky the sharp outlines of the softly-coloured mountain stood out in perfect relief, and the atmosphere was so clear that we fancied we could hear the roar of the falls. What messages were those waters carrying to earth? They alone knew the secret of Roraima, but their language, like that of the birds, is understood only by themselves."

John W. Boddam-Whetham – *Roraima and British Guiana*, 1879

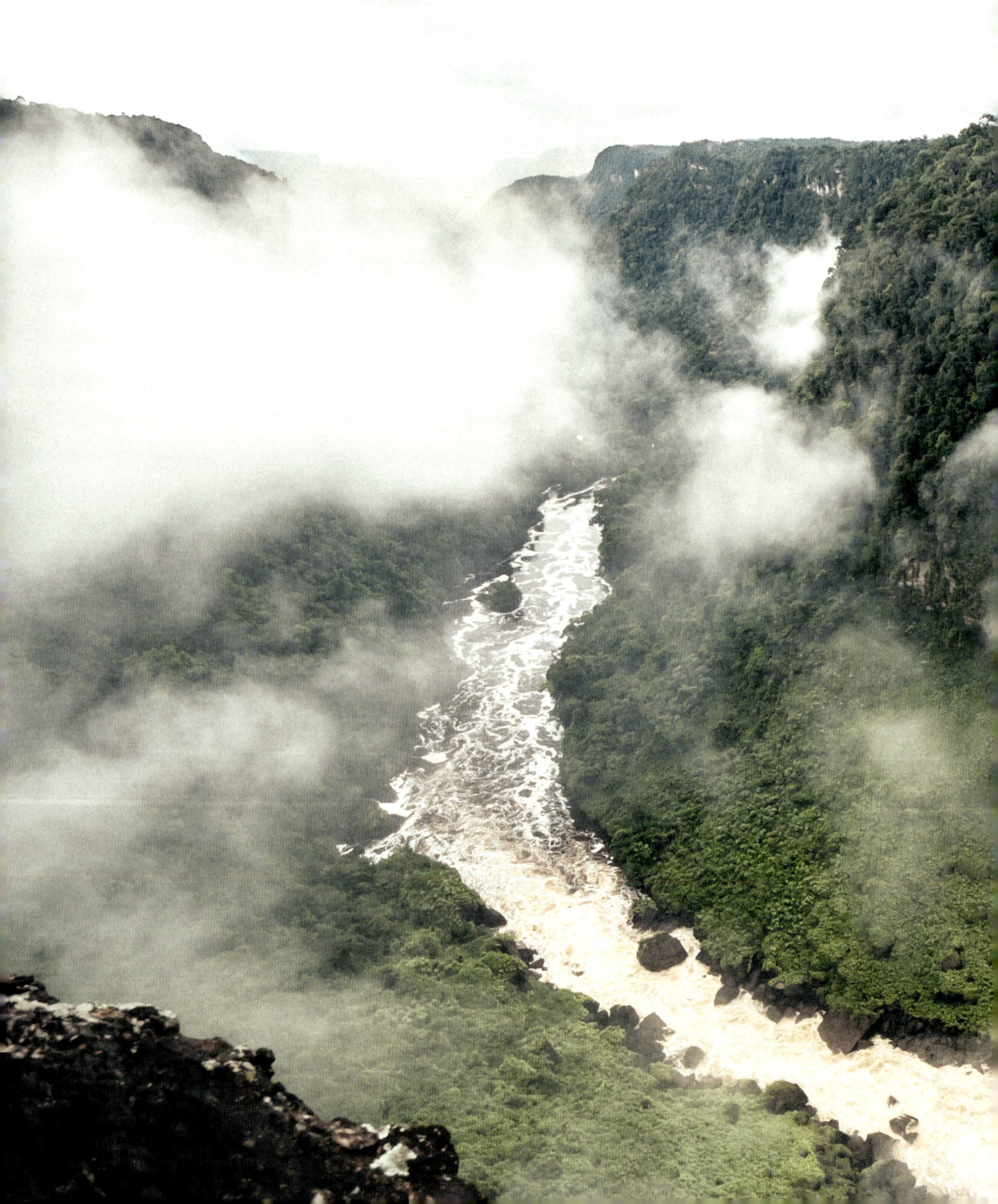

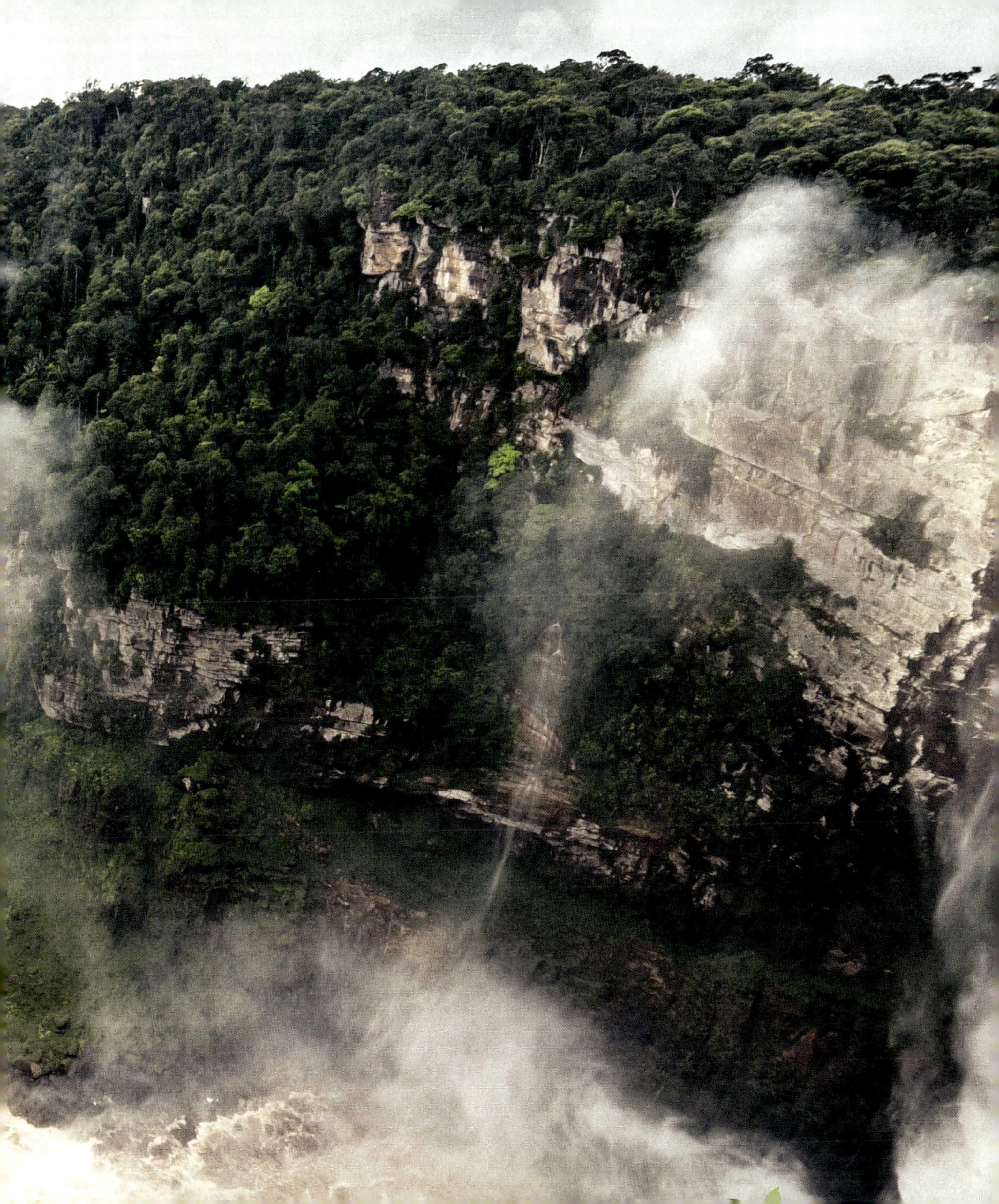

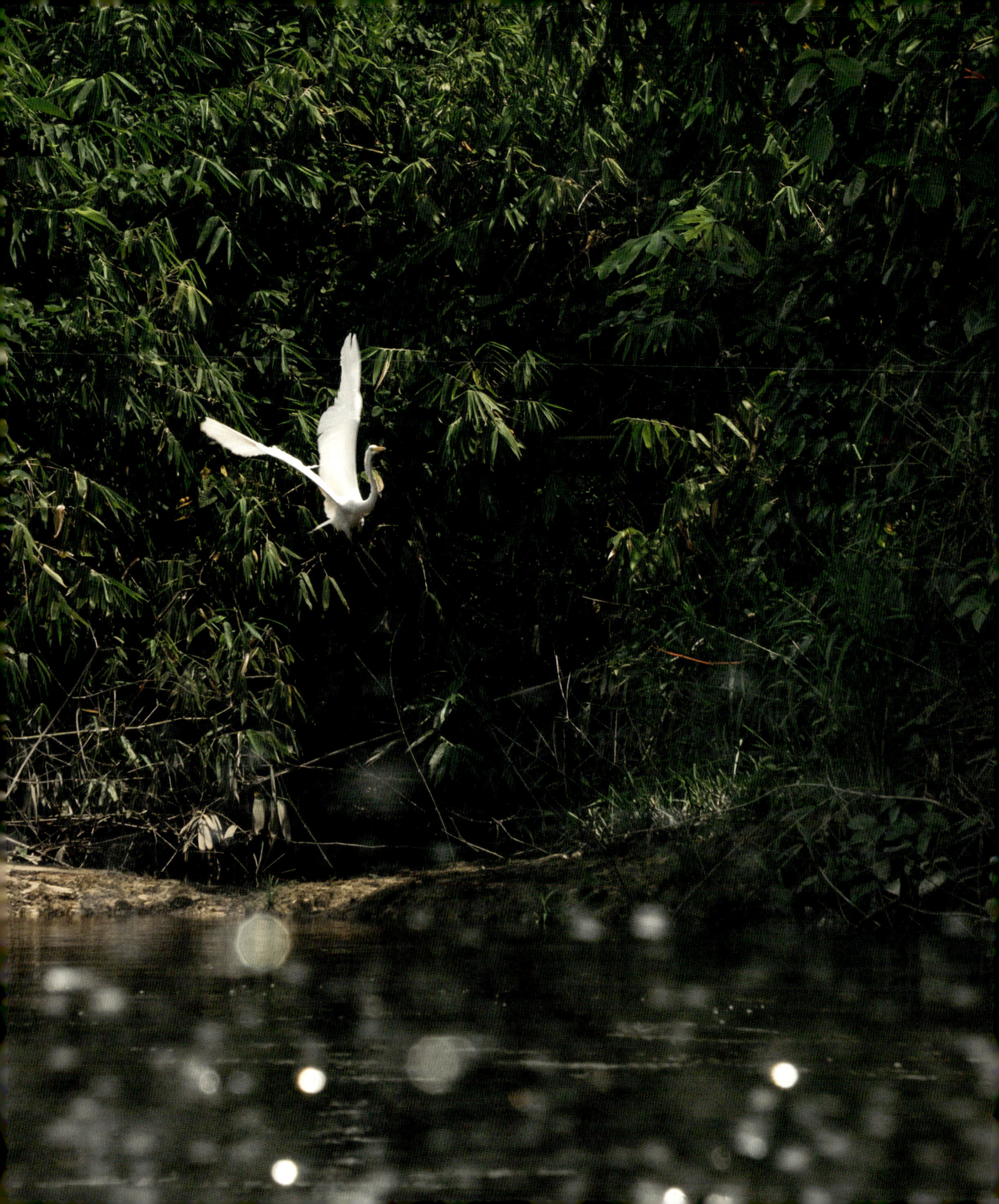

After a few days of slow progress through the lowland forest, daily frustration and discomfort give way to a tedious but manageable routine. The first glimmers of morning sun cause the forest, nurtured by the rain that comes almost every night, to fill with swathes of stifling mist as I set about the ritual of breaking camp to begin another day of my journey. Today, however, will be different – from behind the trees, I hear people talking and a roar of an outboard motor being started, accompanied by morning calls of howler monkeys hiding high among the canopies. Without even thinking, I throw on the rags that have been wet for days now; I've grown so used to them that I've stopped even trying to get them dry – I know by now that there's no point in doing so here. I throw my soaked backpack inside the boat. From here on, the river becomes both guide and pathway.

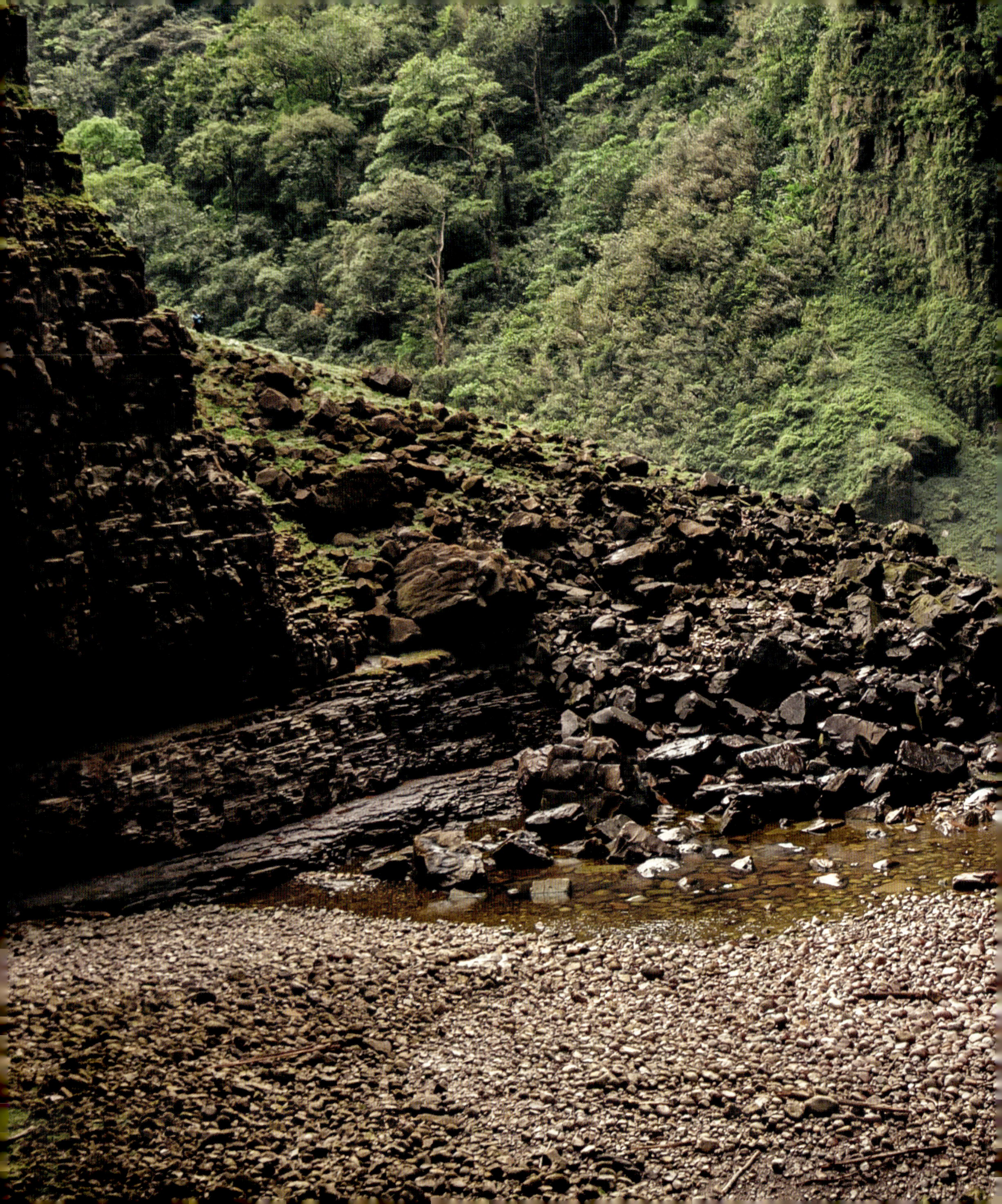

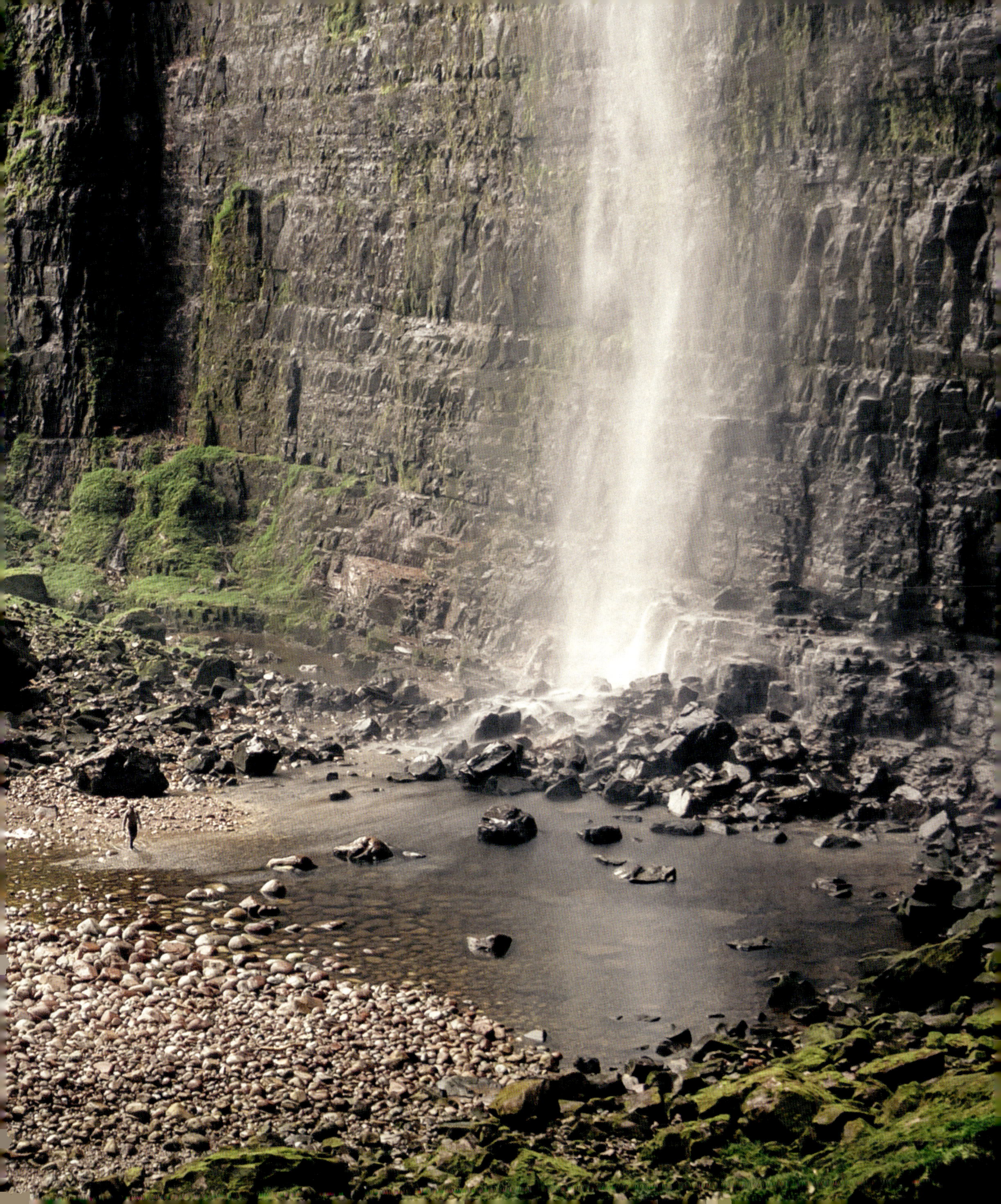

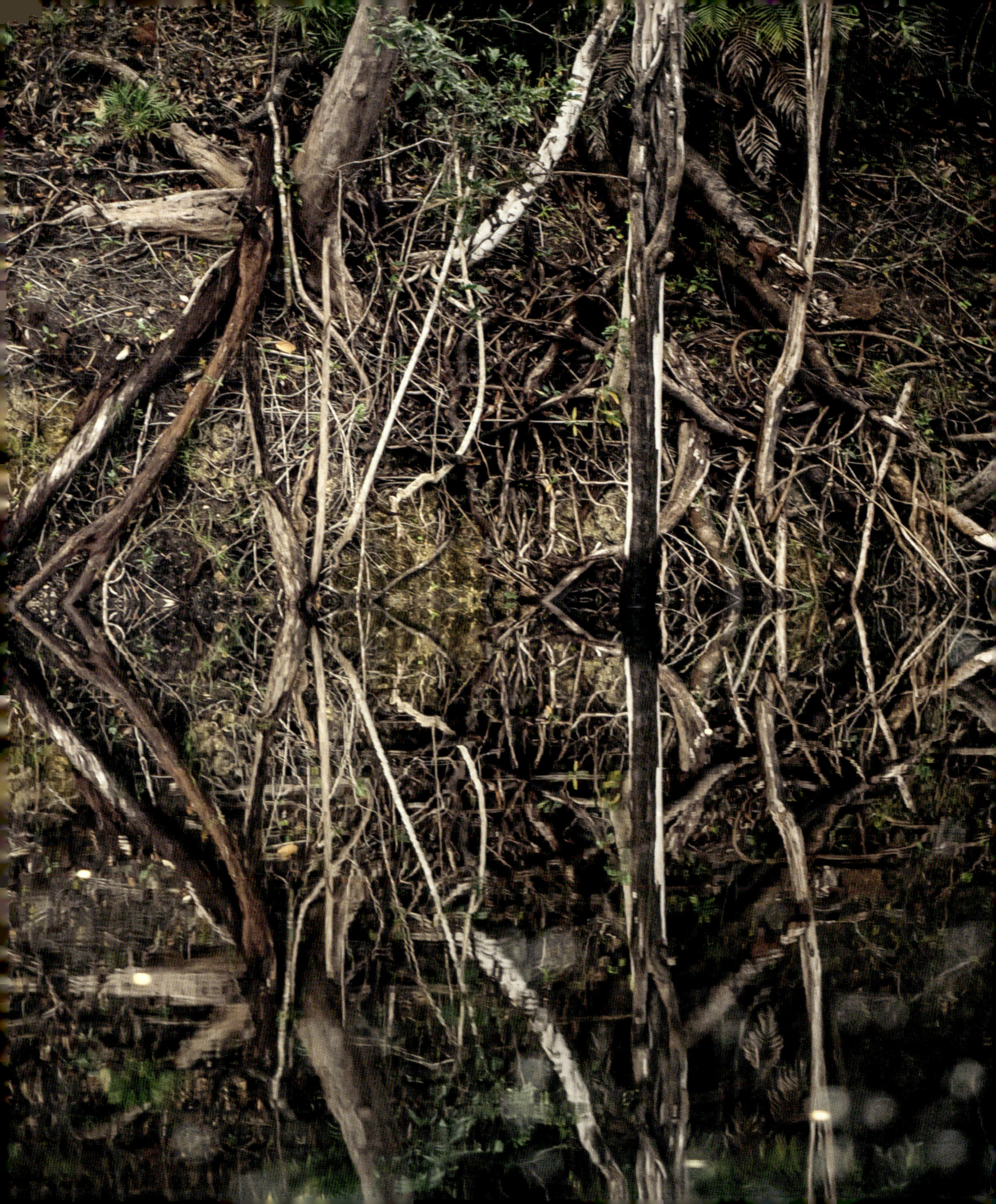

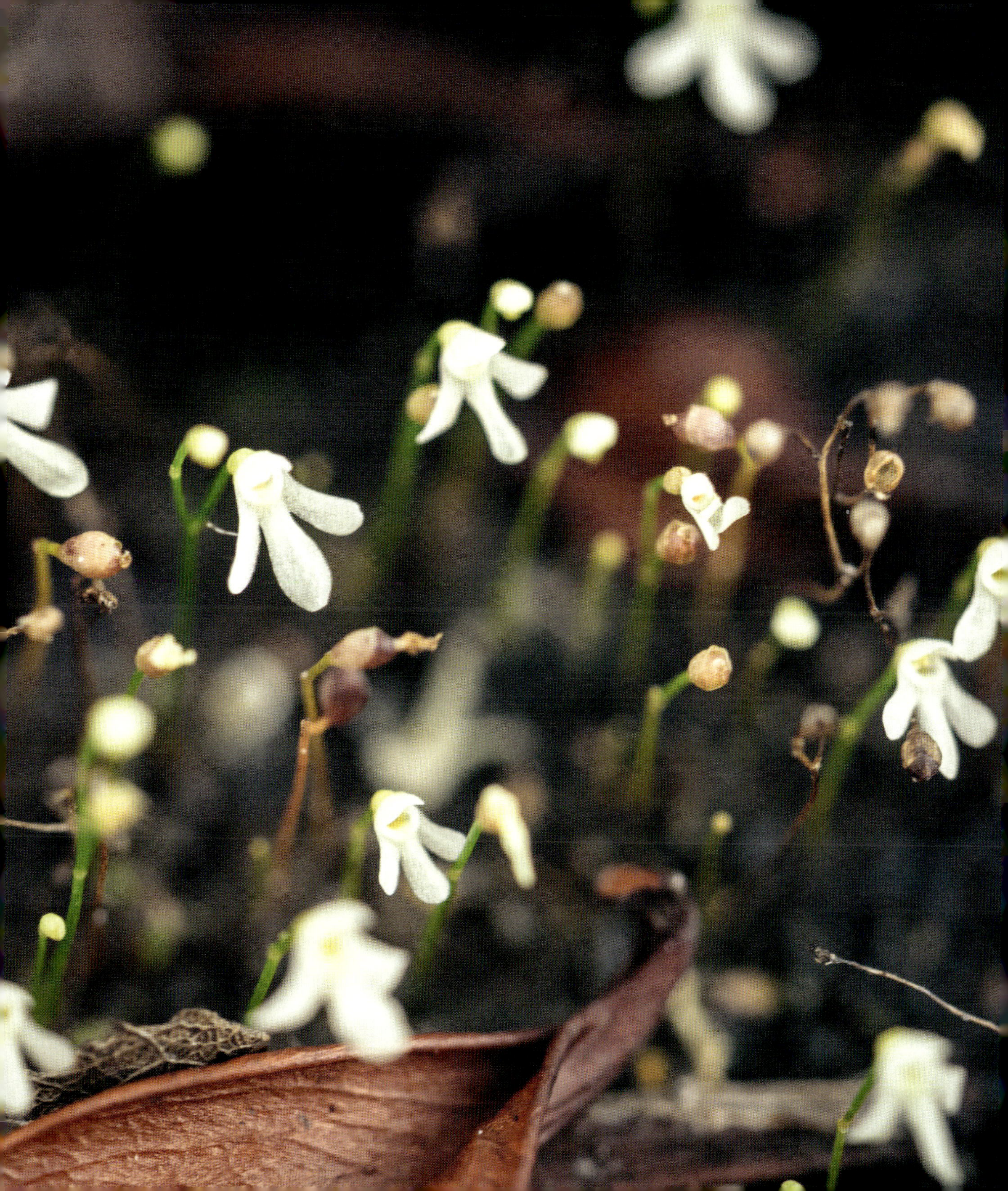

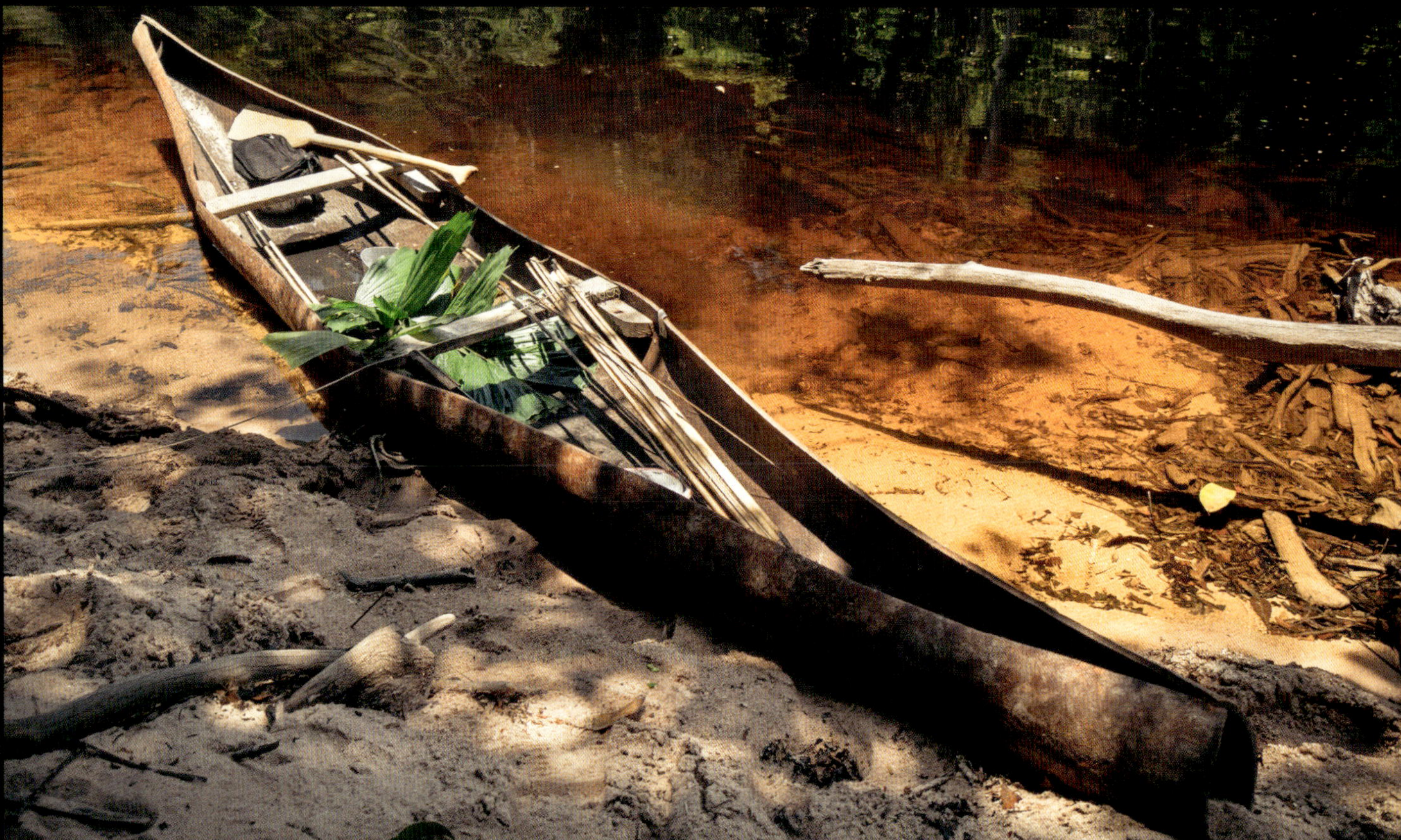

It's hard to describe just how refreshing it is to have an open sky overhead after days of imprisonment, constantly surrounded by impenetrable green walls. The wooden dugout glides peacefully across the amber waters, and I begin to feel like a passenger on a theme park ride, marvelling at the wonders that come our way. Pairs of colourful macaws fly across the sky, so magical they look almost like an artificial backdrop for the ever-increasing diversity of palm trees arching over the river, looking so perfect, as if they were part of a meticulously curated botanical garden display created by some nameless gardening prodigy. Suddenly, I grasp a blurry outline of a few pinkish figures moving underwater alongside the boat. These are the mysterious river dolphins, and just a few metres away... can it be? A pair of river otters staring in awkward silence at the unexpected visitors. Have they come to greet us, or just to take a look of disbelief at the foolishness of our endeavour?

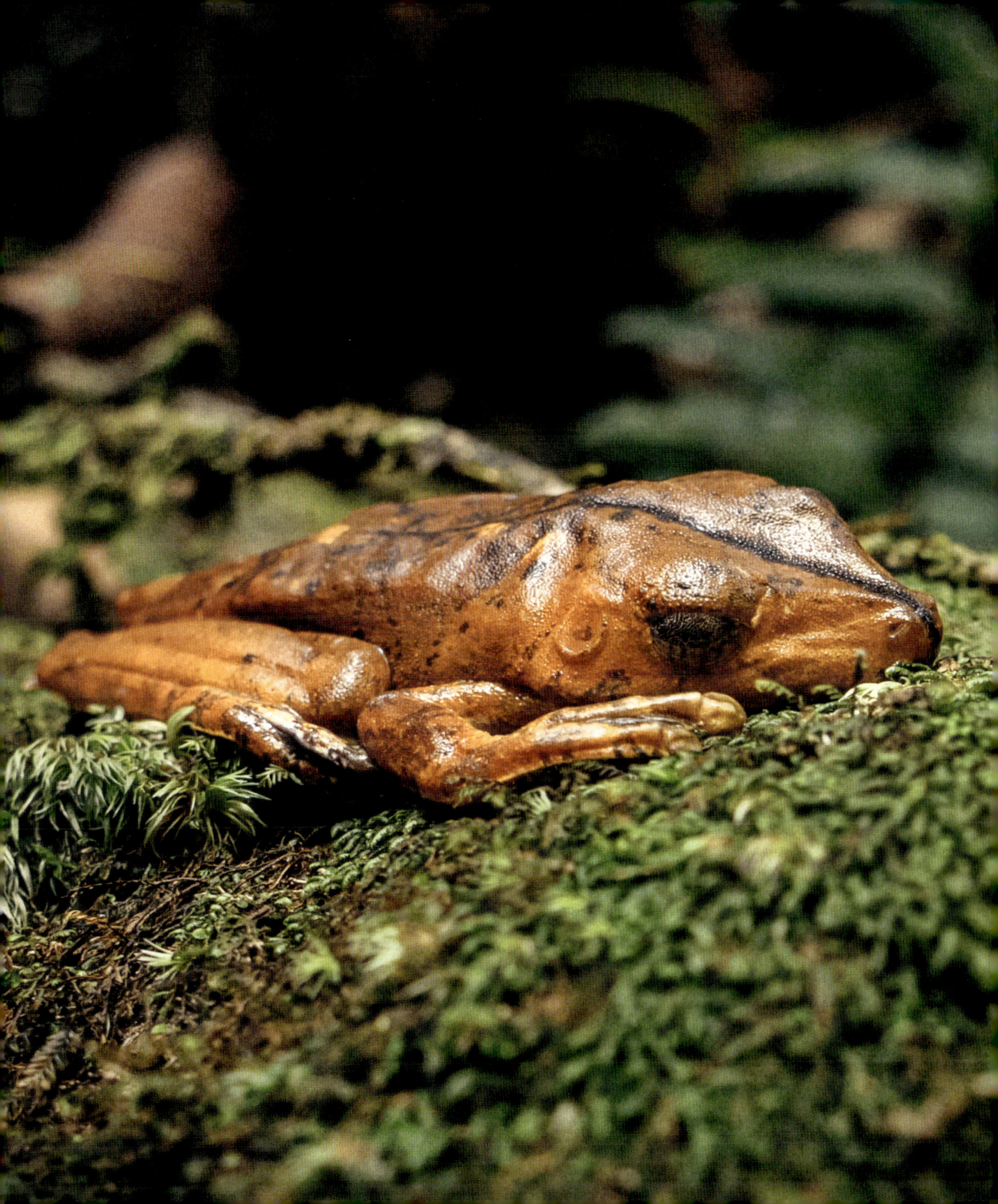

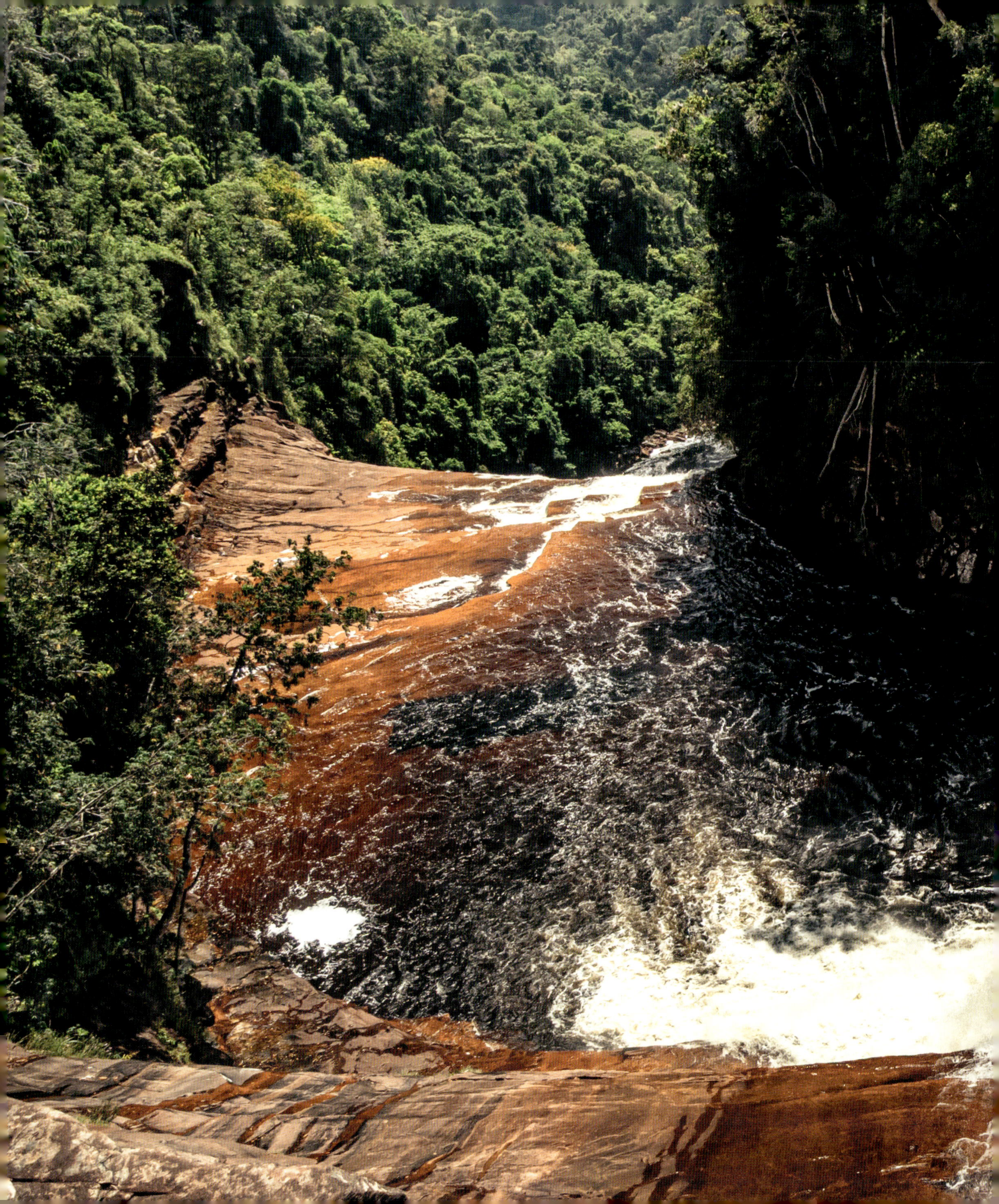

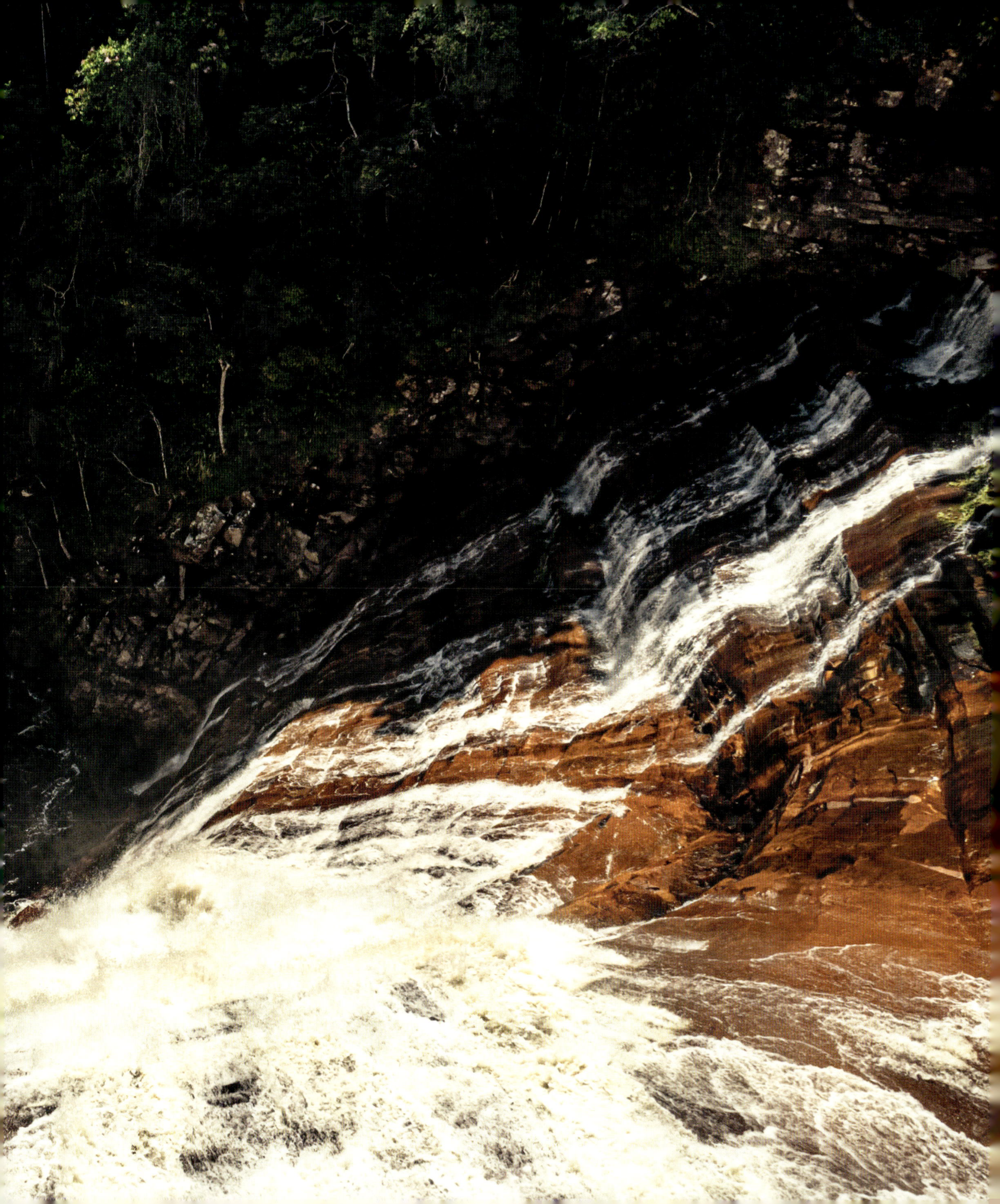

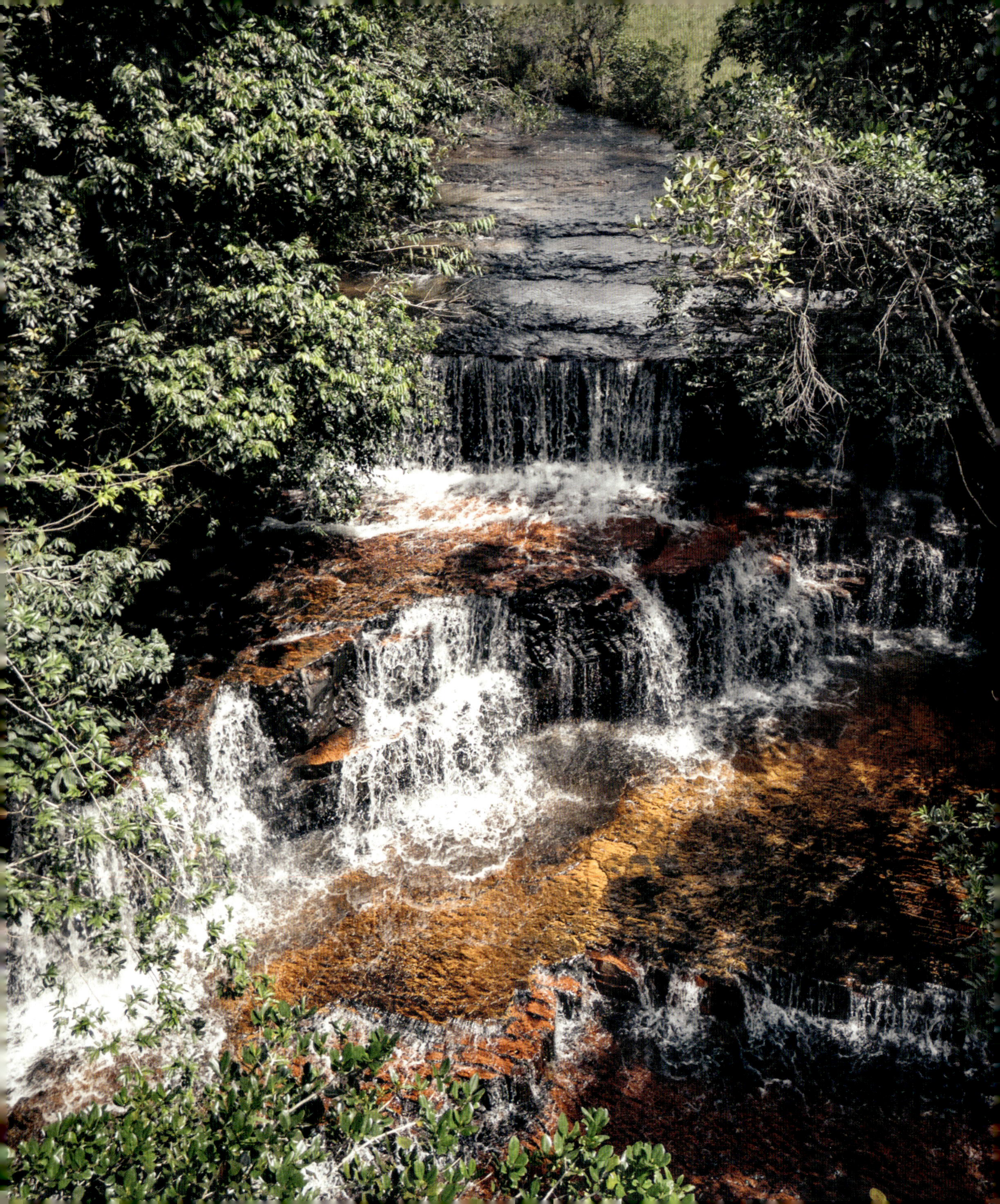

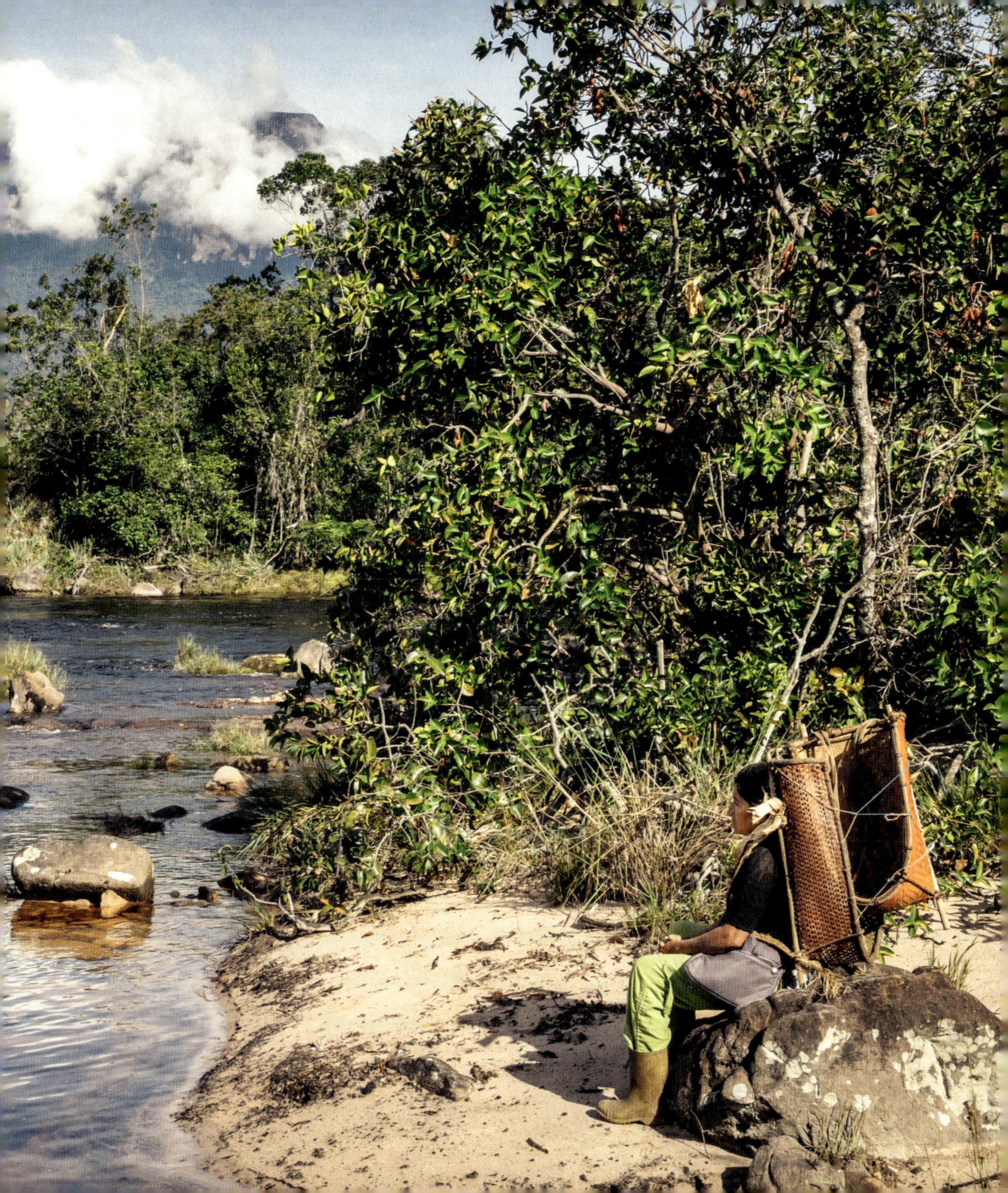

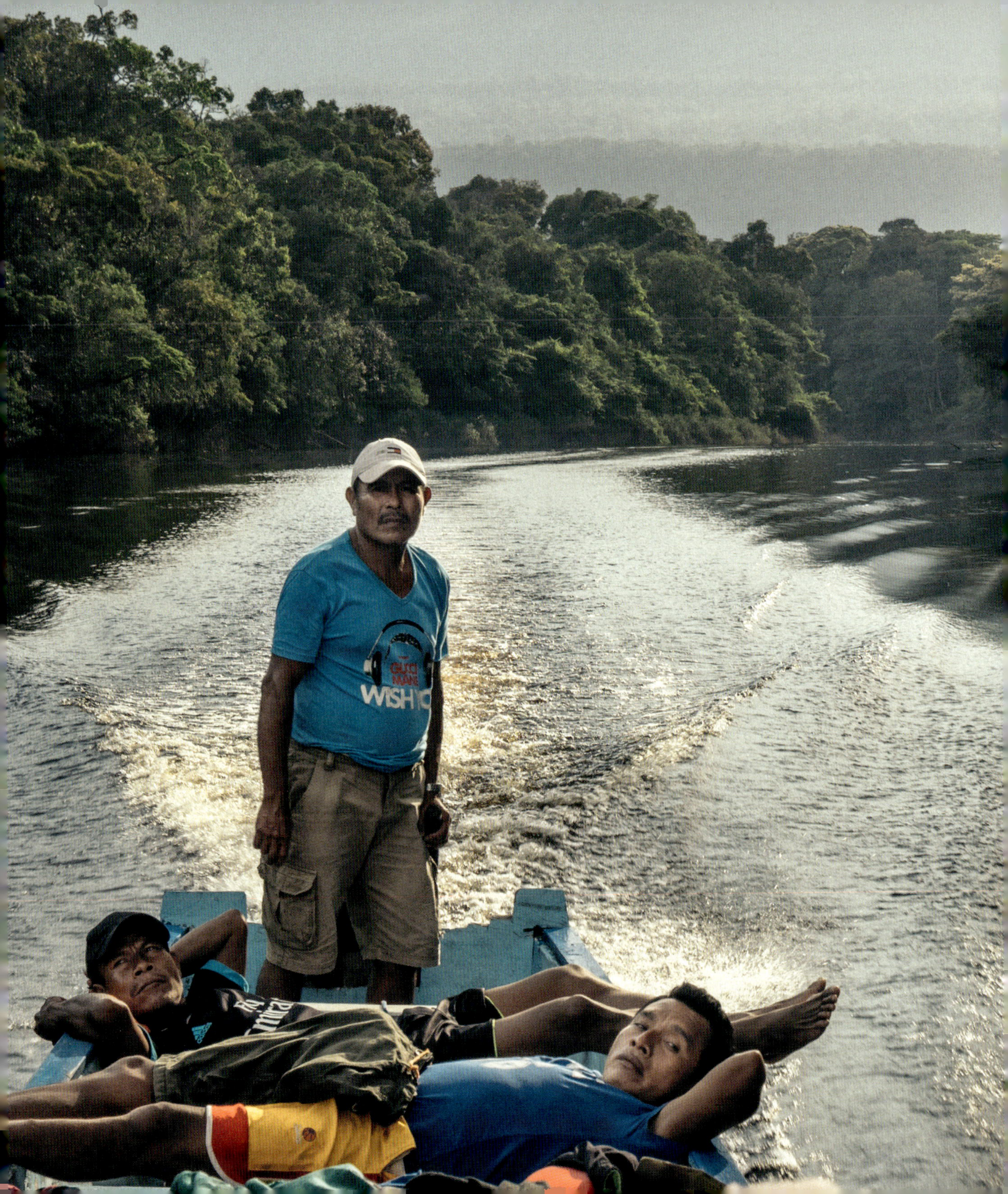

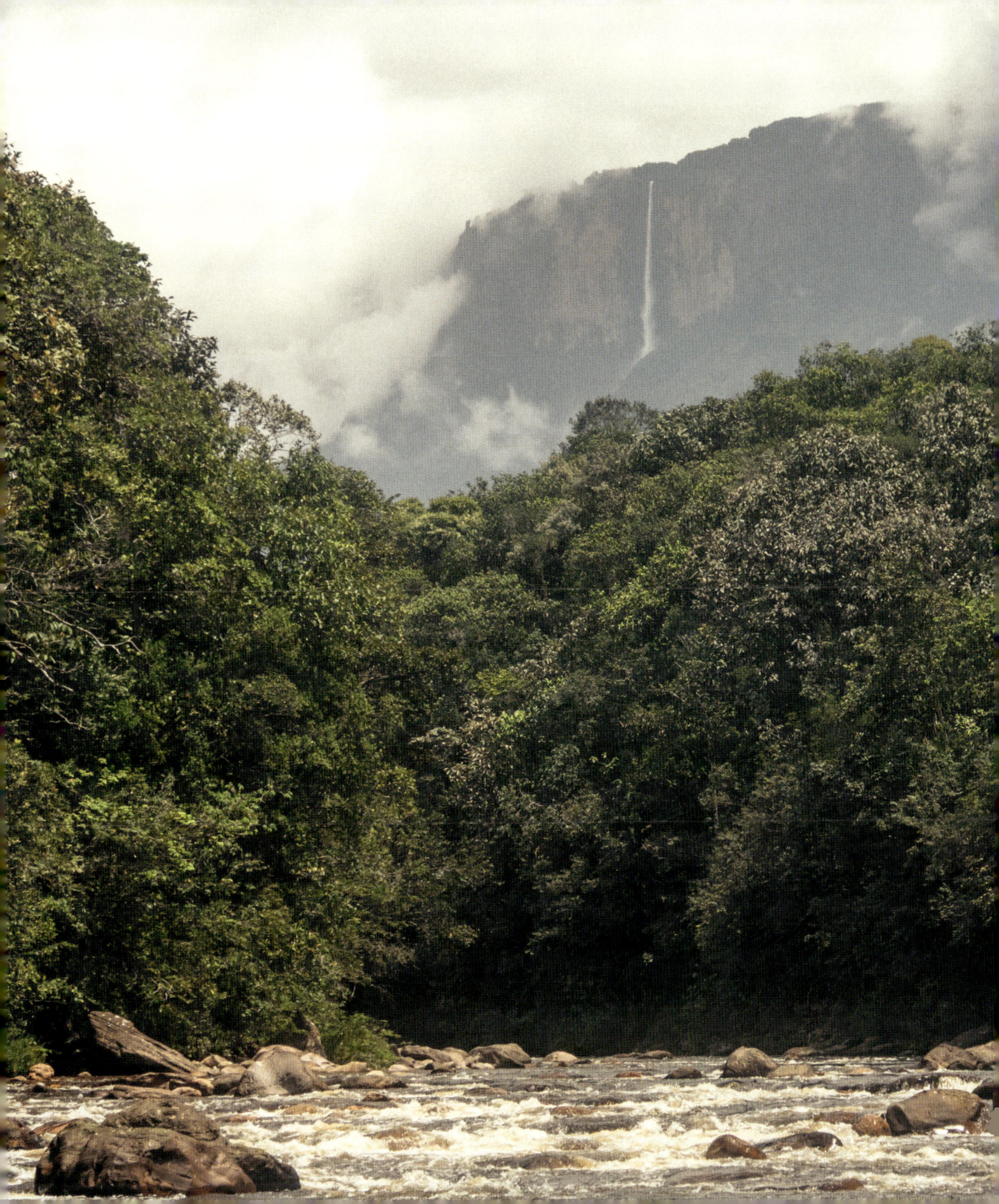

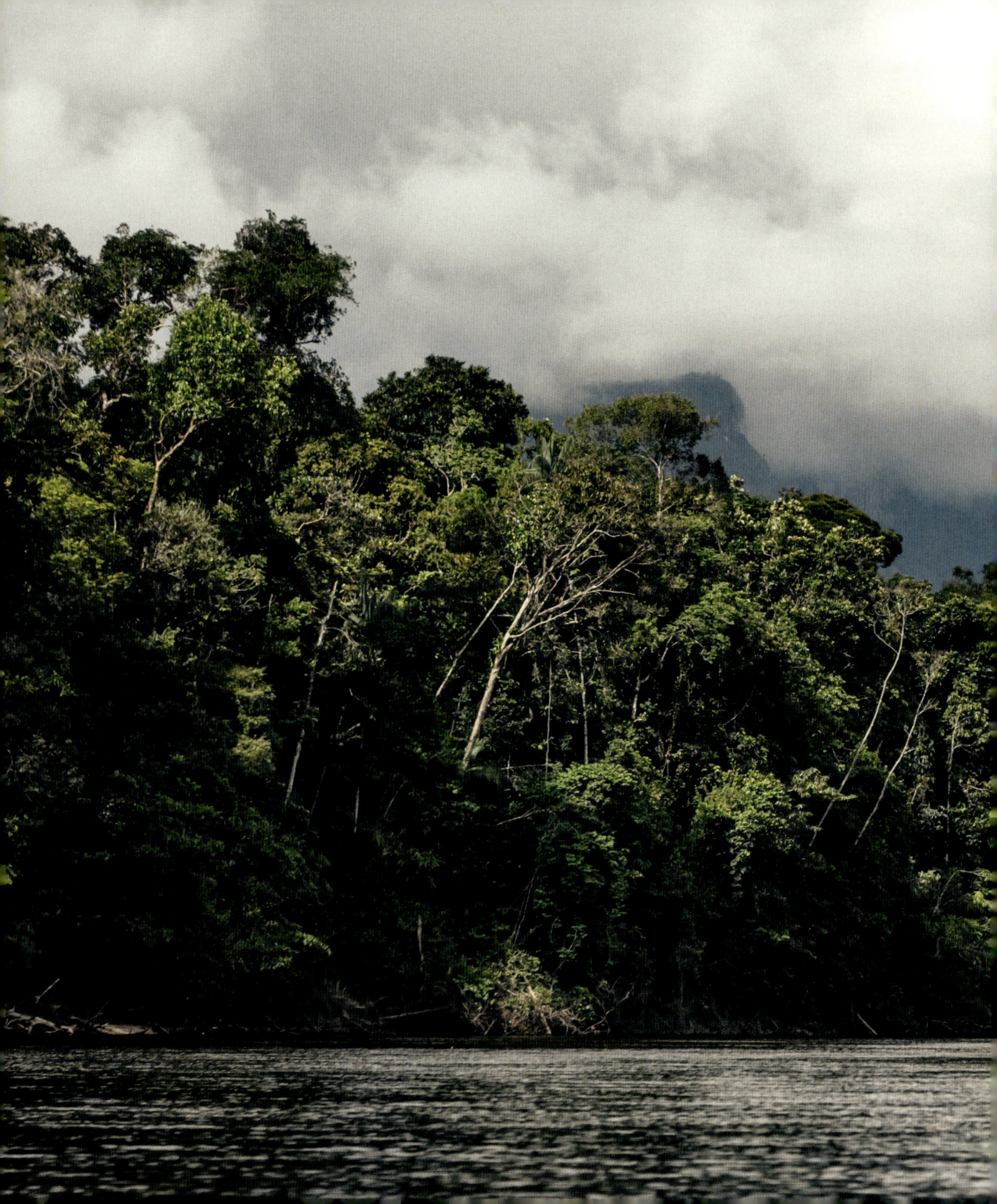

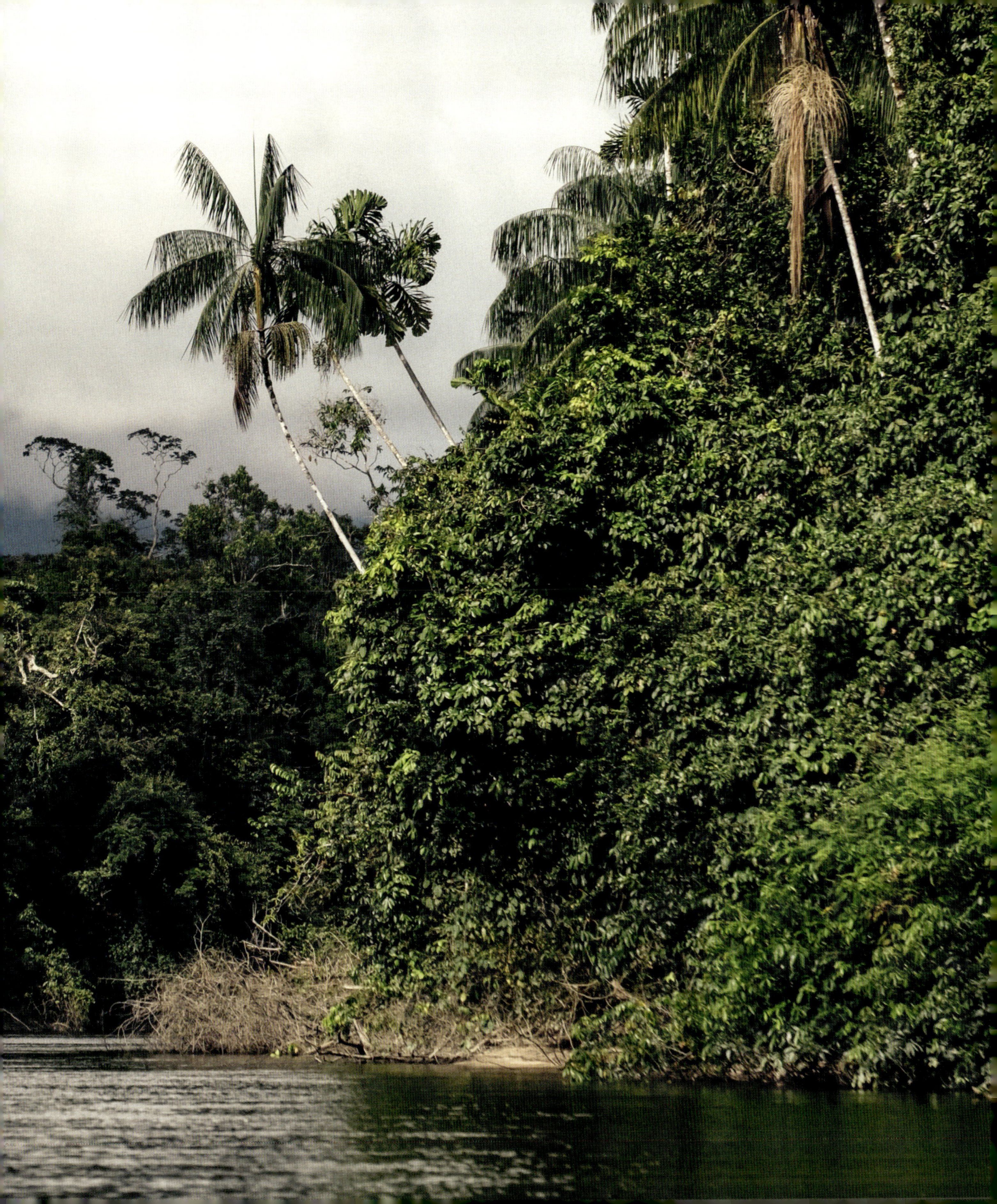

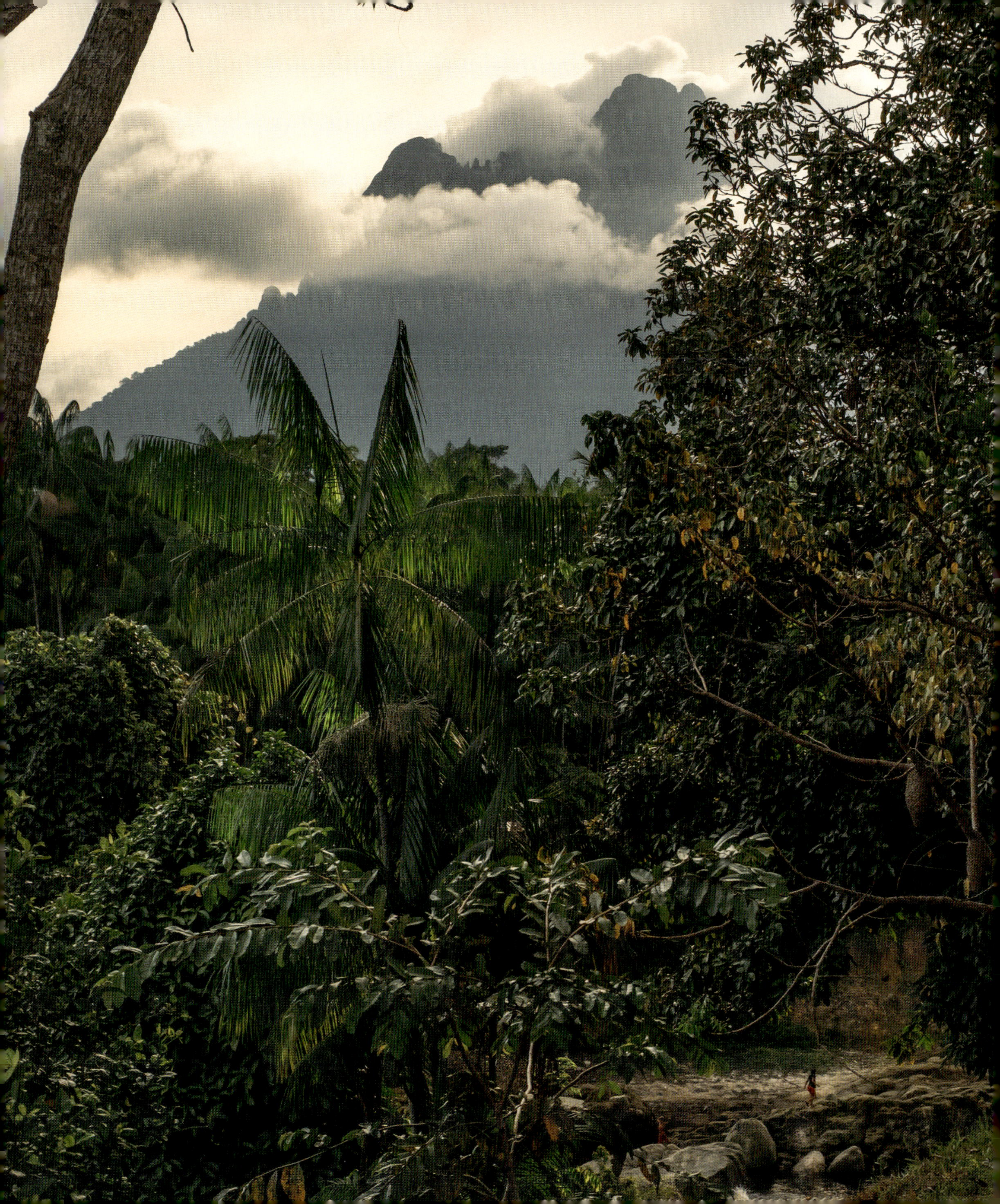

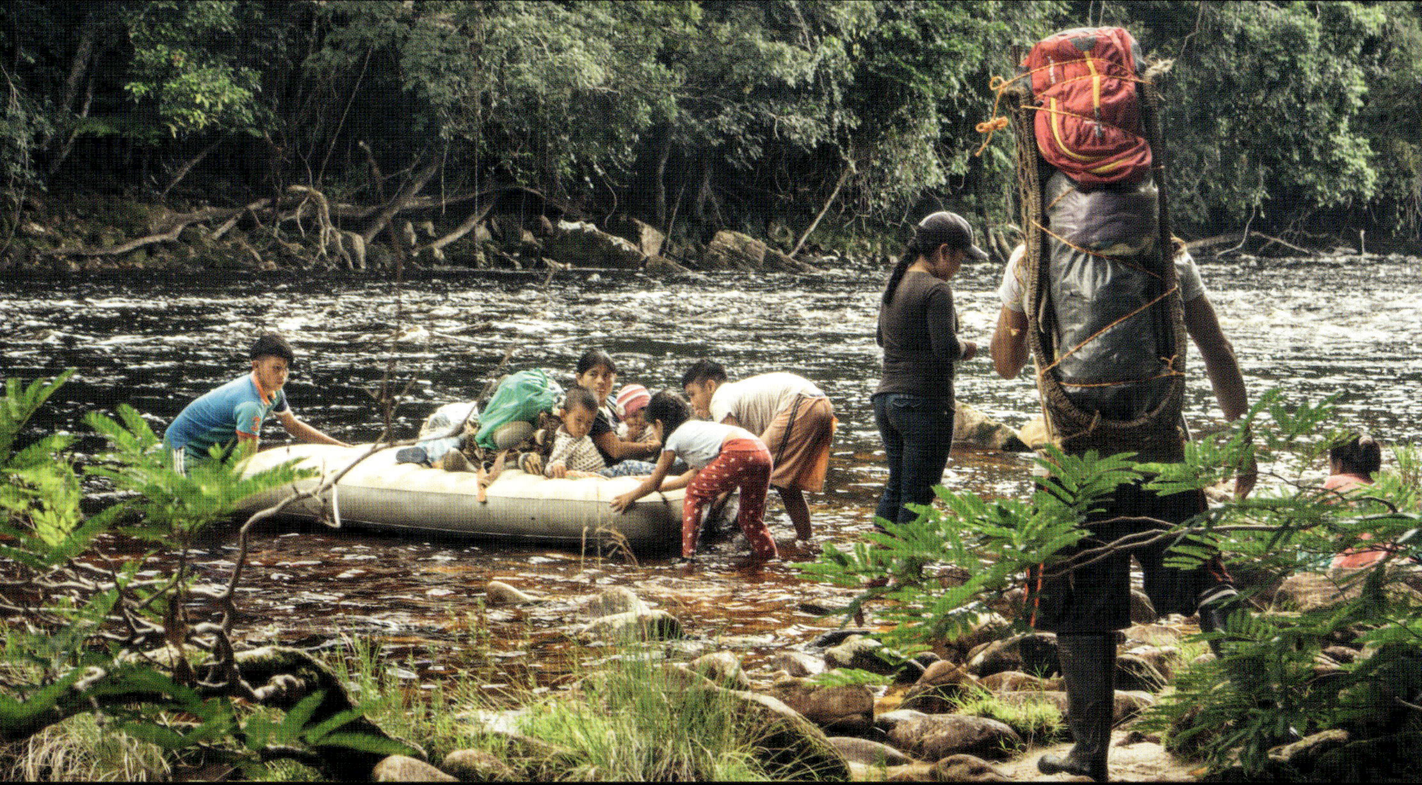

Hours spent by the rhythmic thrumming of the engine causes me to fall into a trance. Monotony and weariness creep back into my mind, and passing downpours washing over the dugout bring back that familiar sensation of a constant, damp chill that keeps piercing my thoughts, purging my senses and slowly reducing them into something almost animalistic. Dusk befalls us when we spot the thatched roofs of a village nestled atop a hill overlooking a shallow river bend. Greeted warmly by our hosts with a cup of kasiri and chunks of cassava bread, I suddenly stop at a sight that makes me gasp in disbelief.

Peering out from behind a layer of grey clouds in the distance is a gigantic cliff topped by a flat and seemingly never-ending summit, reaching all the way behind the horizon, fading into heaps of dark fog. From the cliff descend bright streaks, raging at the top, then dissolving gently into a spray of mist and disappearing behind the curtain of tree canopies below. Faded rumbles of the mighty falls carry down with surprising clarity from far away, blending seamlessly with the sounds of cheerful evening gatherings in the village. Is this even real?

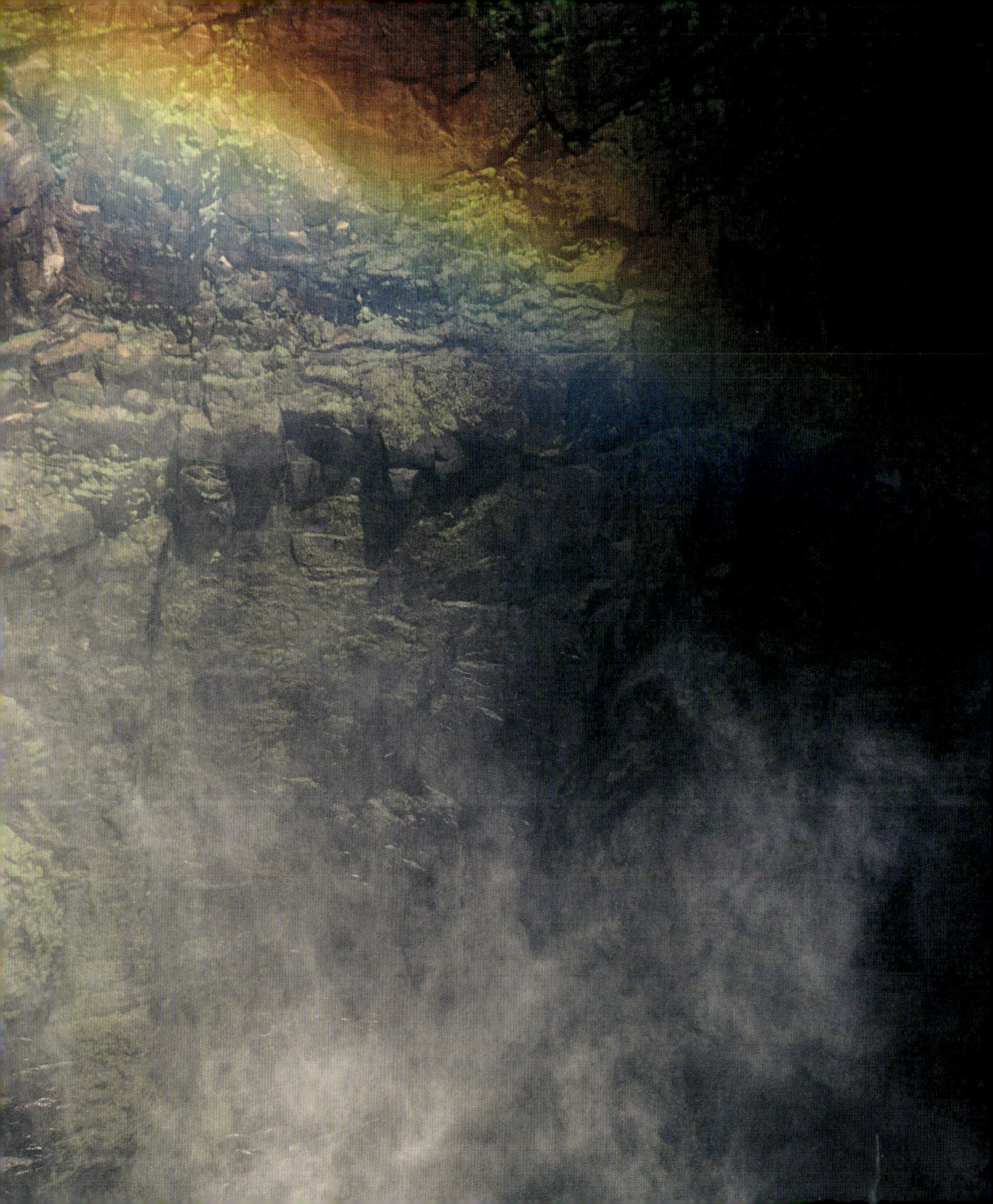

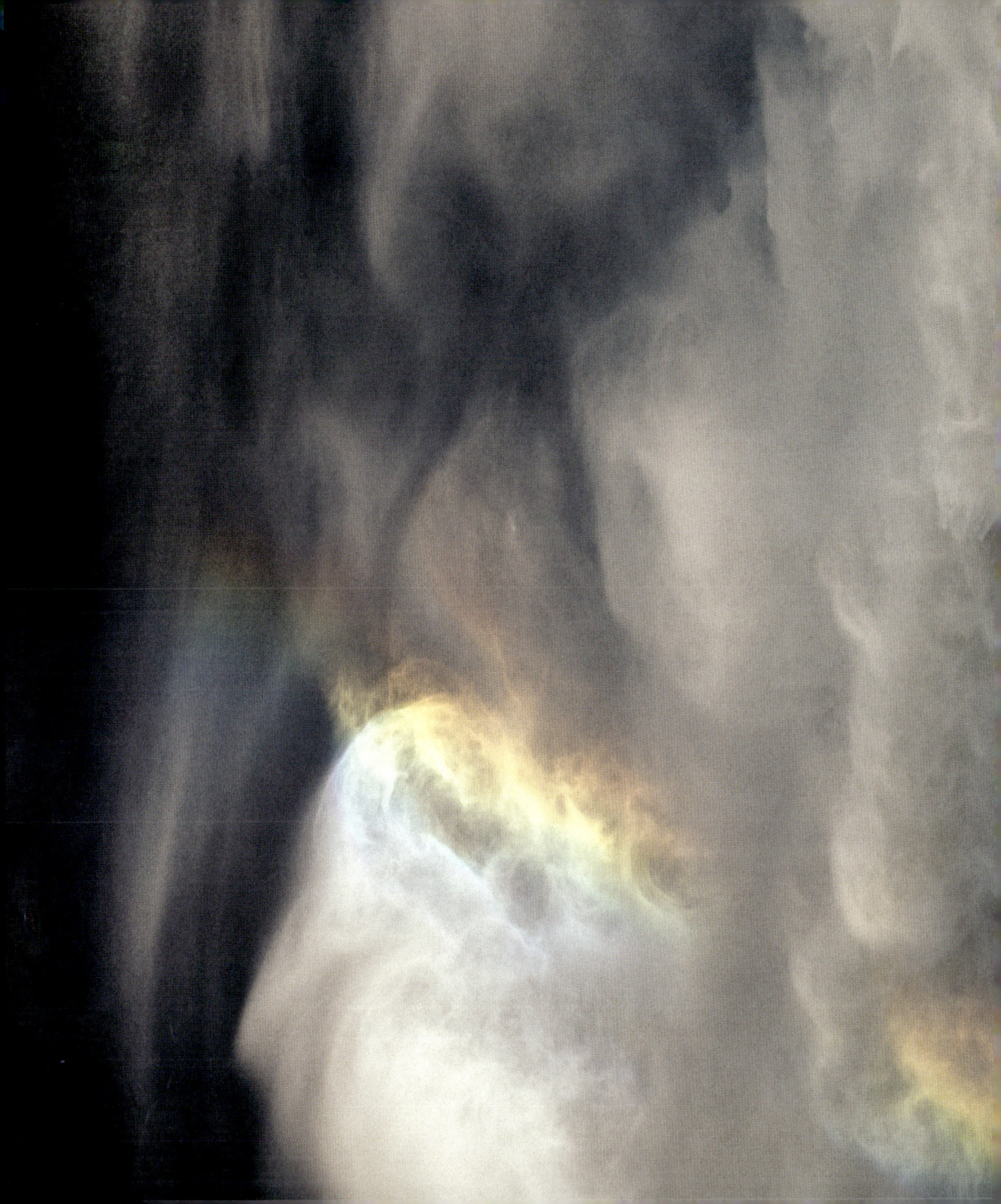

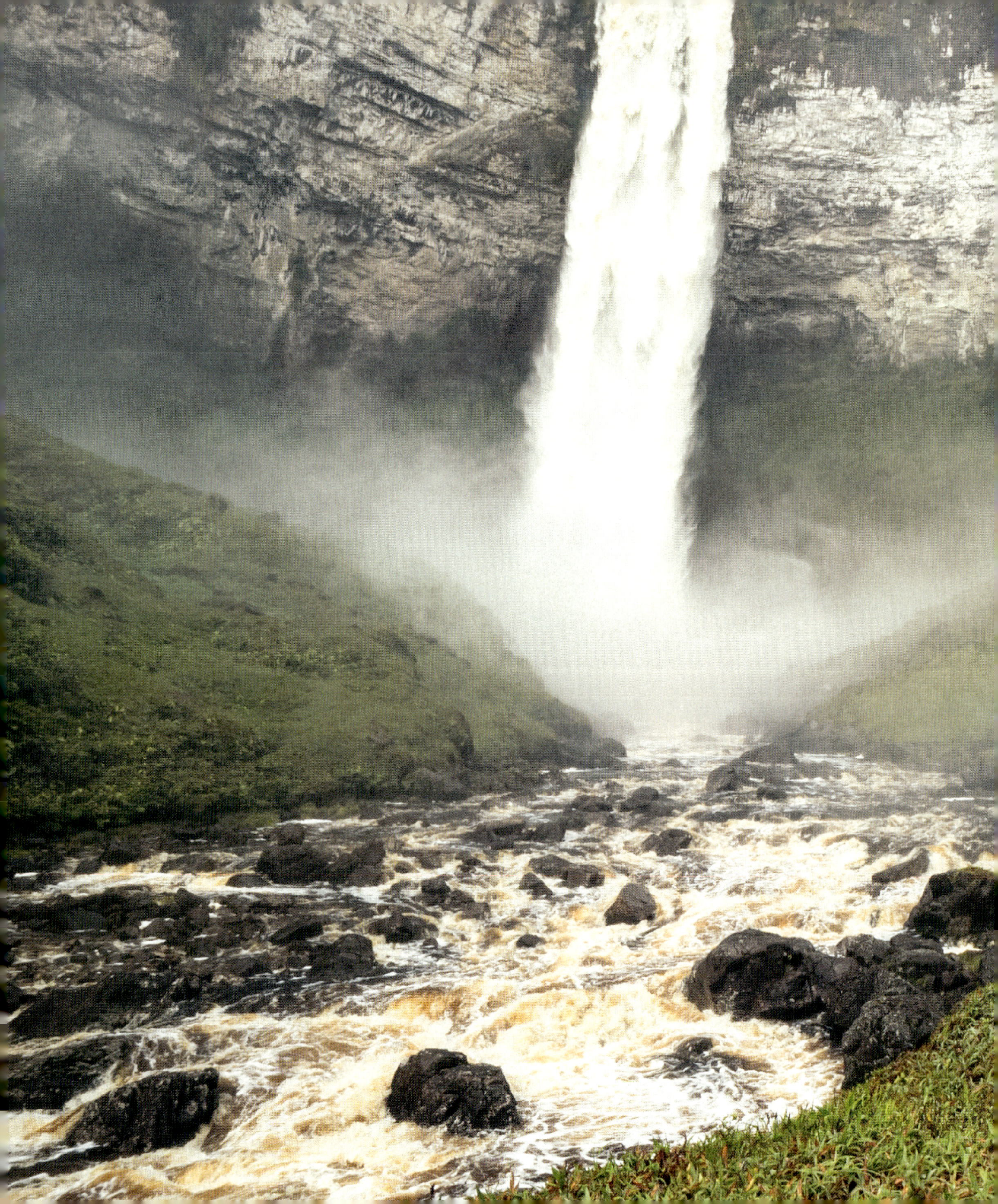

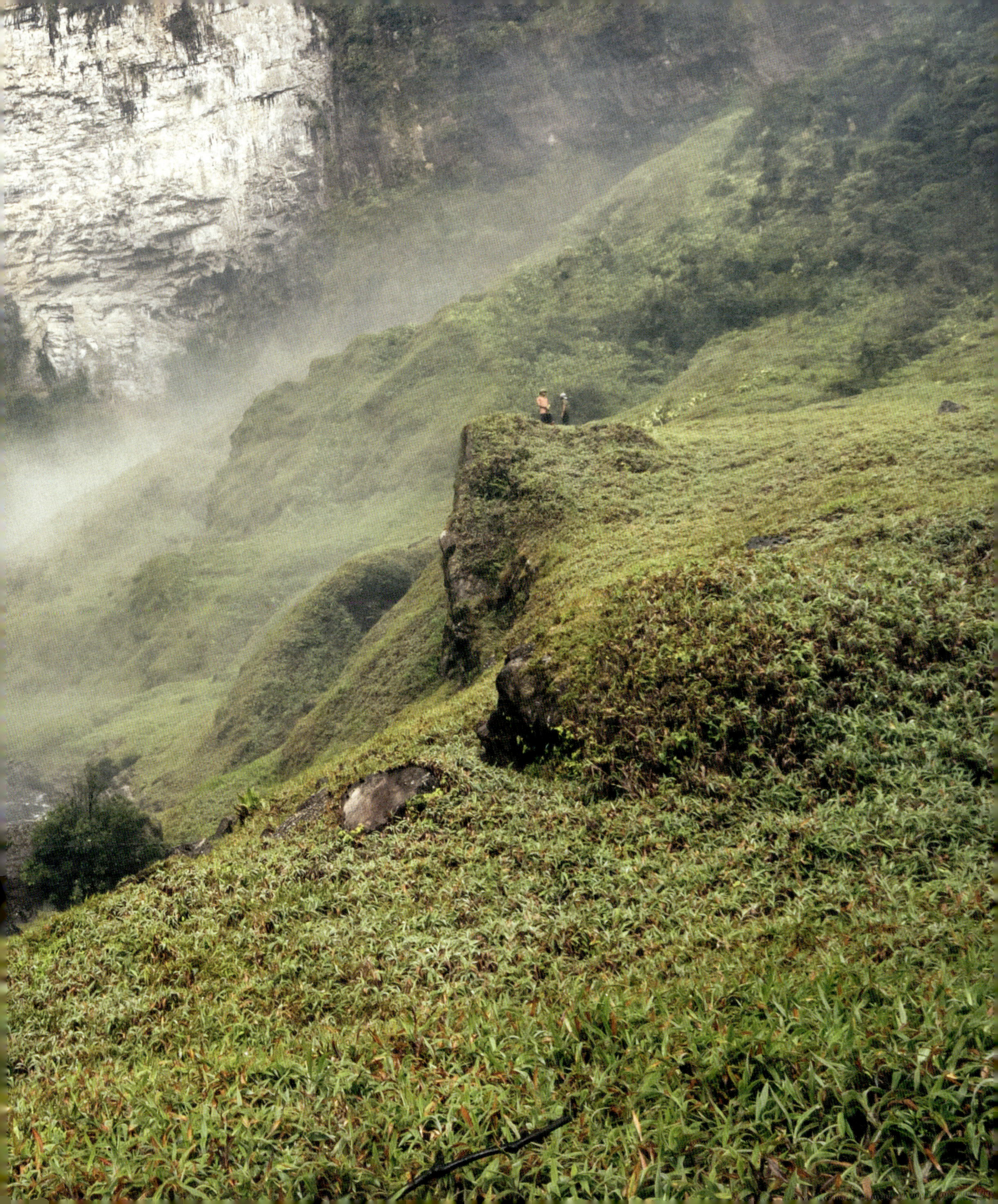

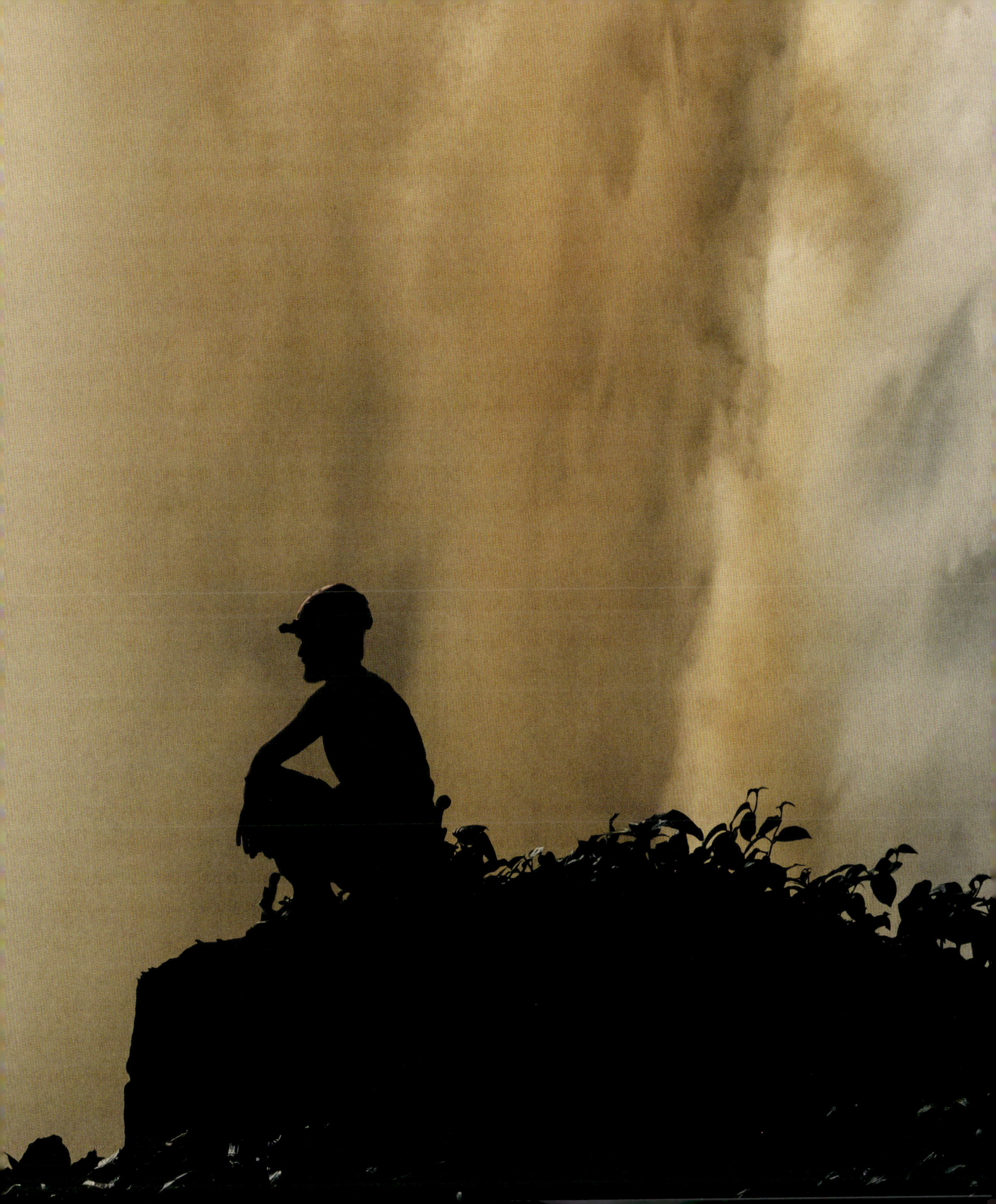

CHAPTER 3
Fire and Haze

"At sunrise we continued our journey through short, yellowish grass, damp from the night's dew. The cold, which was very perceptible, made us walk fast, when suddenly, on arriving at a precipice of the mountain chain, our eyes were enraptured by the view of a wide valley spread out below us. Was it illusion of the senses? Was it enchantment which thus transported us from a wilderness into a fairy land? A sea of mist was moving slowly and gradually over the valley, lying in ring-like circles on the luxuriant tops of the trees or on the summits of the low hills, which portion released from the envious veil were seen like islands rising above the white cloudy surface. Each glance discovered a new wonder; instead of the former ragged, sharp summits and peaks, a table-like belt of mountains rose above the mist in the north-east towards west ... Speechless with rapture we looked into the charming undulating valley, and across the sea of mist, which became more transparent every minute, and from which emerged a vegetation of the most wonderful tints, getting more attractive every moment."

Richard Schomburgk – *Botanical Reminiscences in British Guiana*, 1876

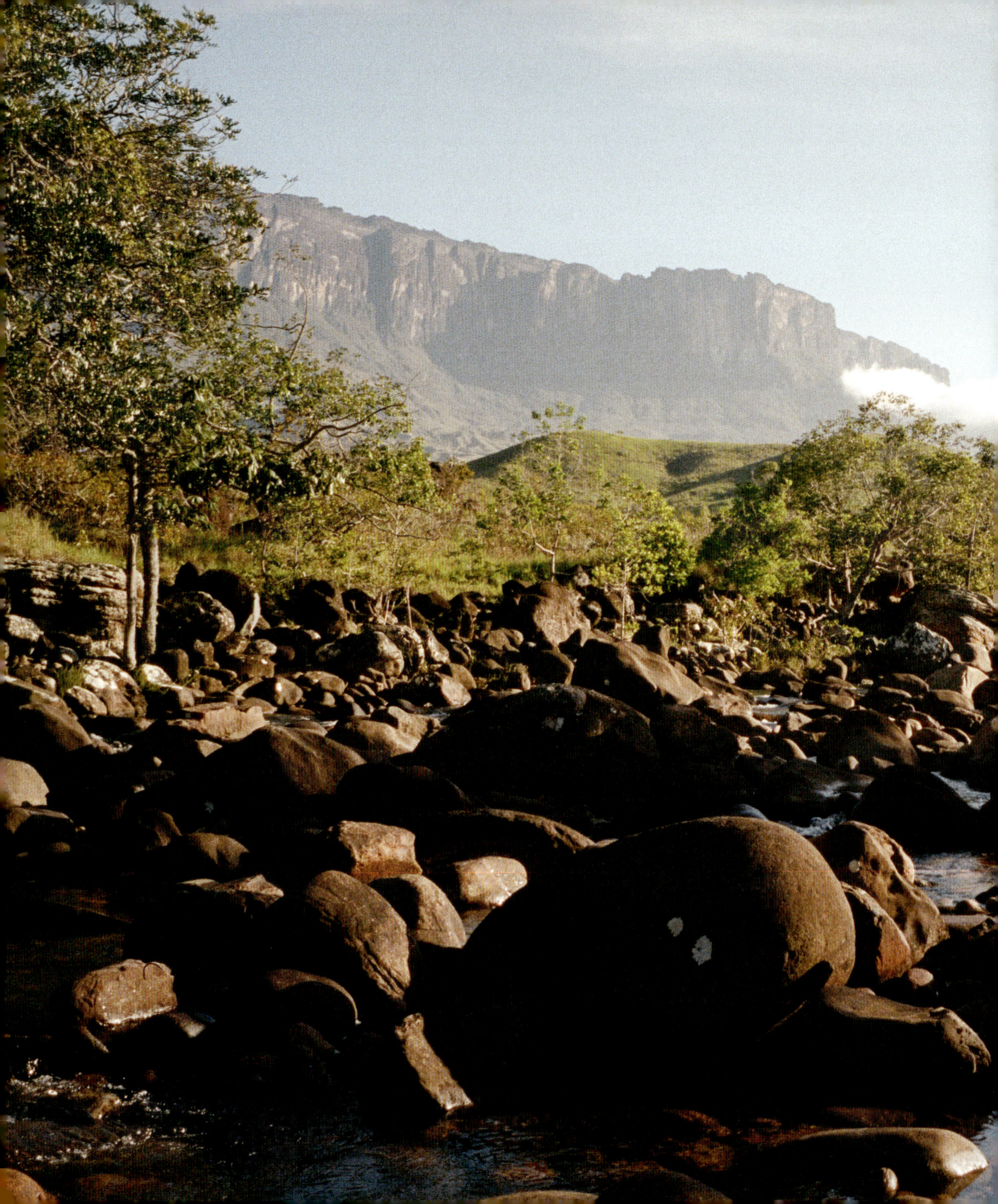

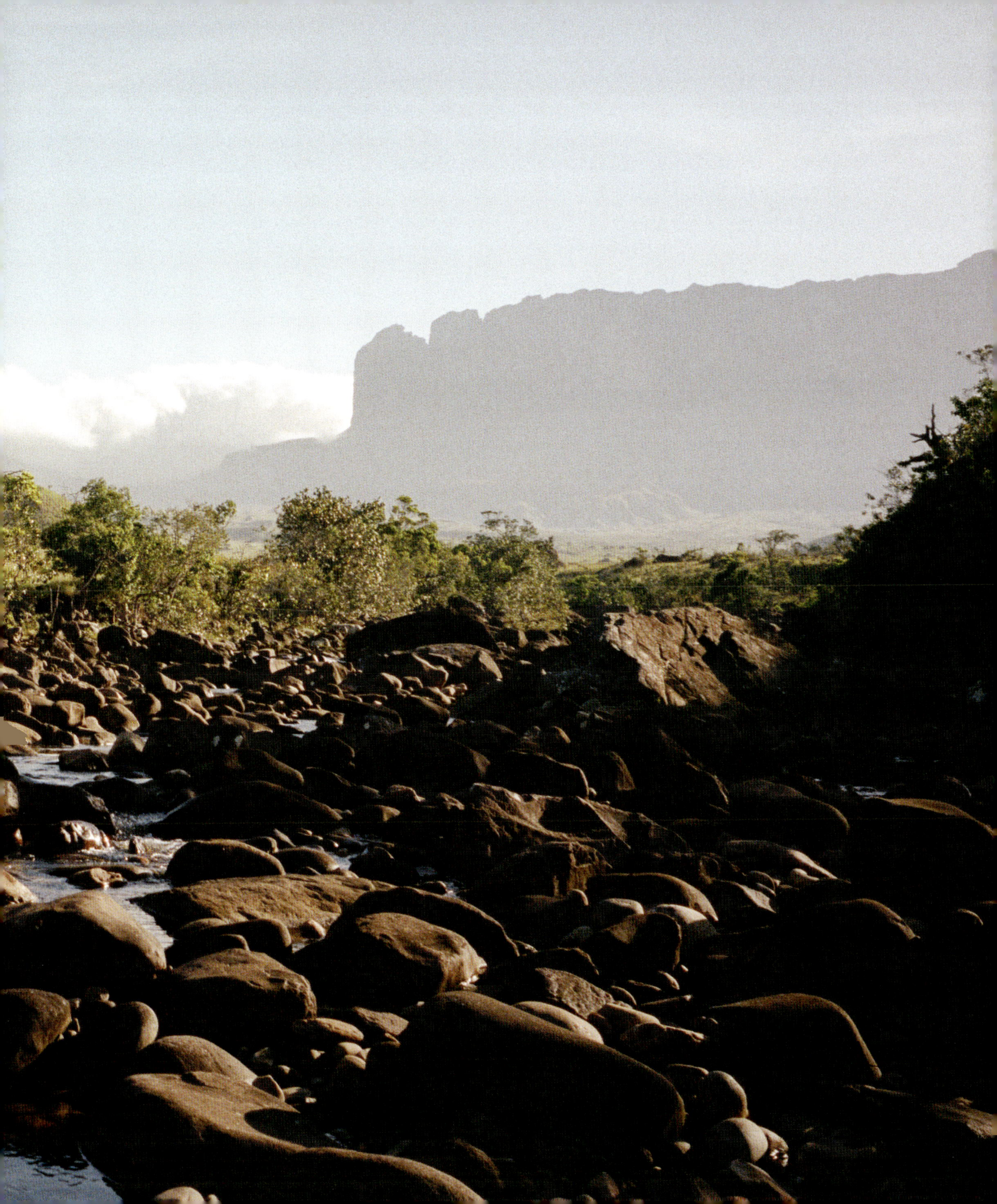

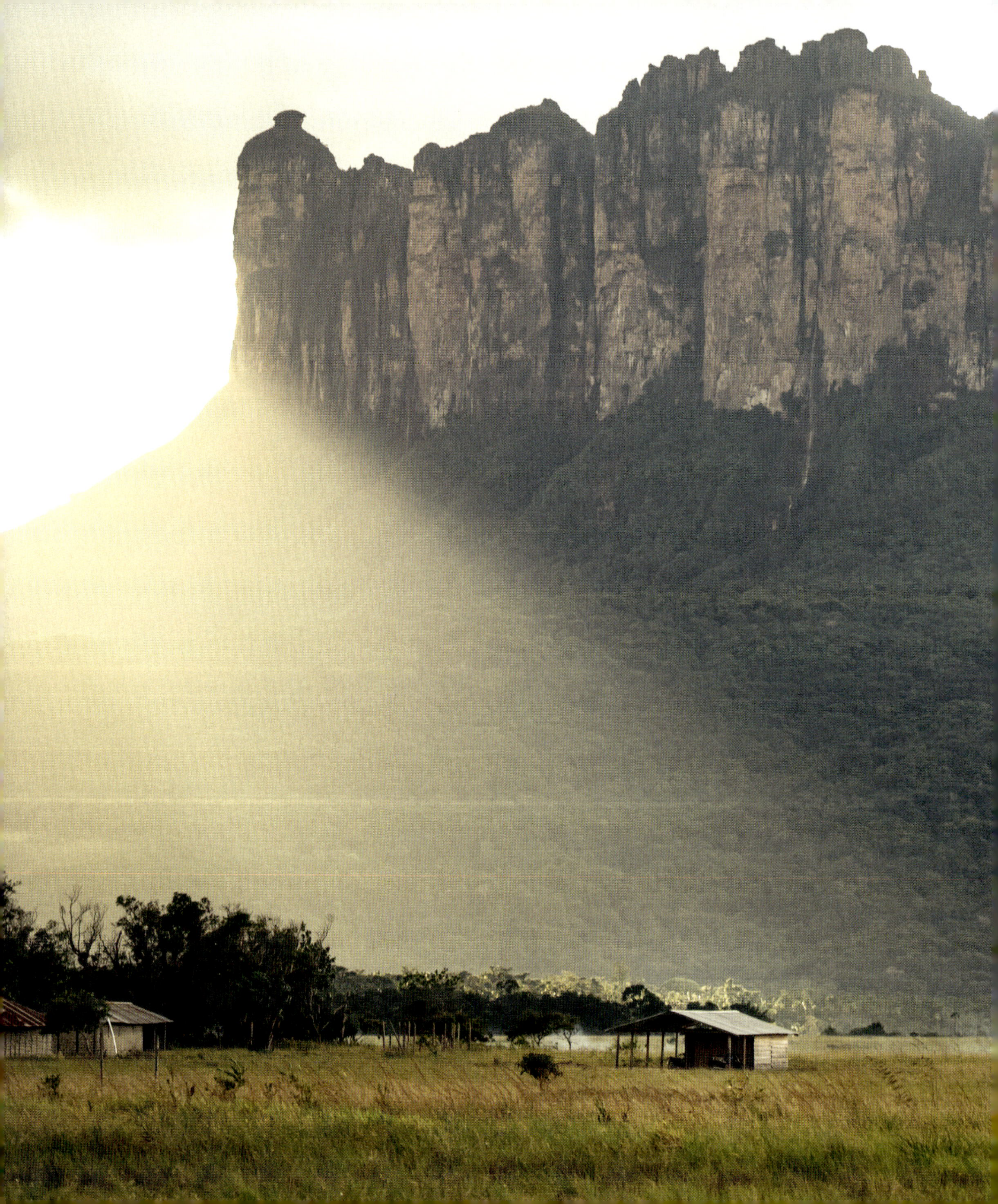

Right up to the very end, the forest seems reluctant to let me go. In the final stretch of the river, the sound of the engine is being drowned out by the wooden bottom of the dugout grinding against piles of jasper pebbles hidden in the water, forcing everyone to jump overboard and pull it through the shallows. Soaked and exhausted, the moment finally comes to leave the boat on an exposed area of a sandy bank and prepare for the night's rest, only to return into the embrace of the dark, emerald abyss in the morning.

I have to make my way up a steep slope, so exhausted that I barely notice how the air begins to turn dry and warm, and how the forest is becoming covered subtly in an ever-thicker coating of golden light. I'm tripping over the endless tangle of roots again and again, driving me to the point of insanity. Protruding from the ground like giant tentacles, they remind me of some primordial beast trying at all costs to hold me prisoner in its muddy misery. I hasten my pace and reach my hand out to brush aside a curtain of foliage, when a violent flash of light blinds me completely, making me fall to the ground.

As I slowly get back up, I indulge in the sudden warmth of the afternoon sun, relieved by how it finally purges the moisture off my body. From behind my half-closed eyelids, the silhouettes of monumental rock walls slowly begin to take shape in a distance, like fortresses towering over folds of golden hills striped with black bands of scorched grass and topped with gentle plumes of grey smoke.

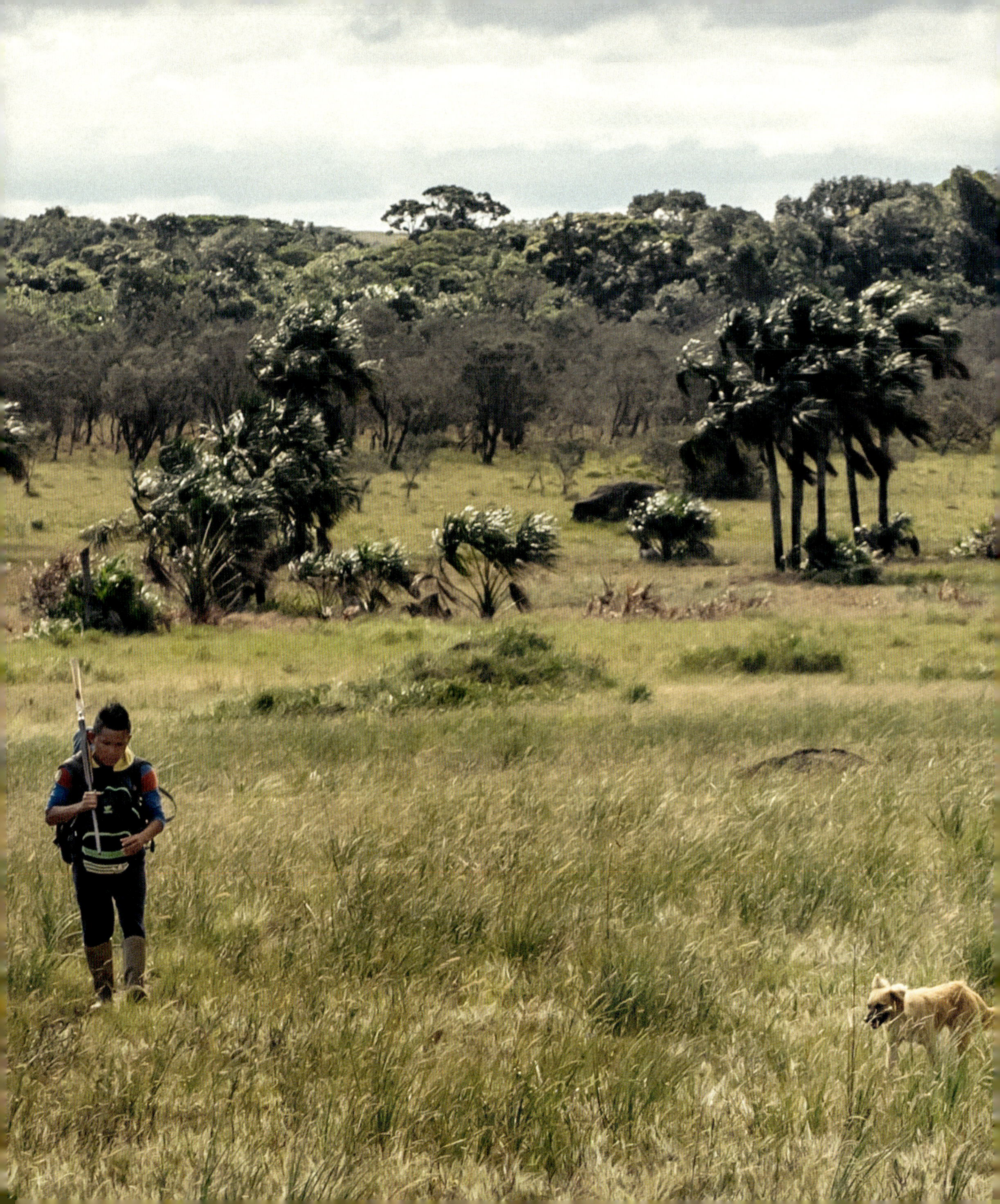

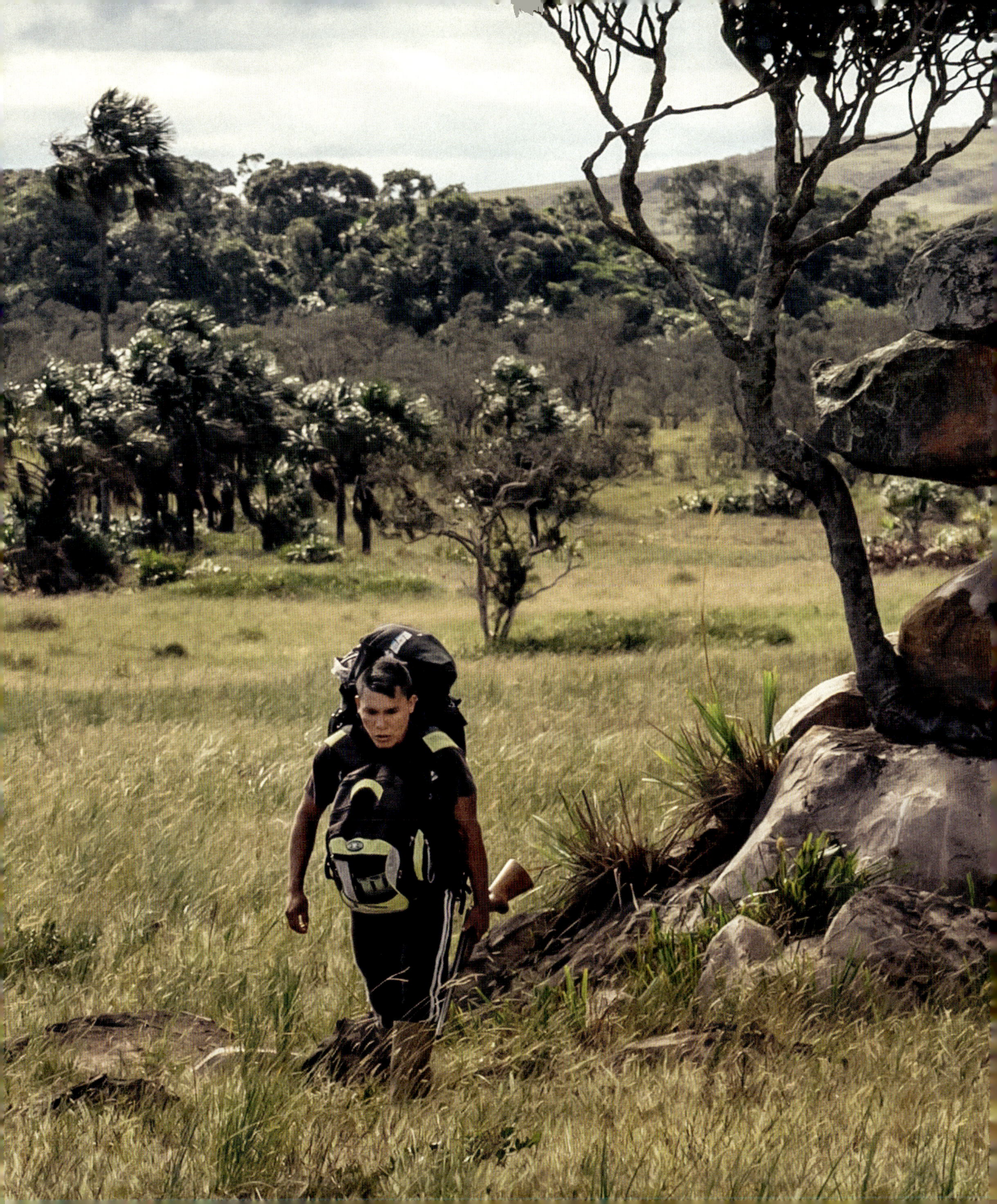

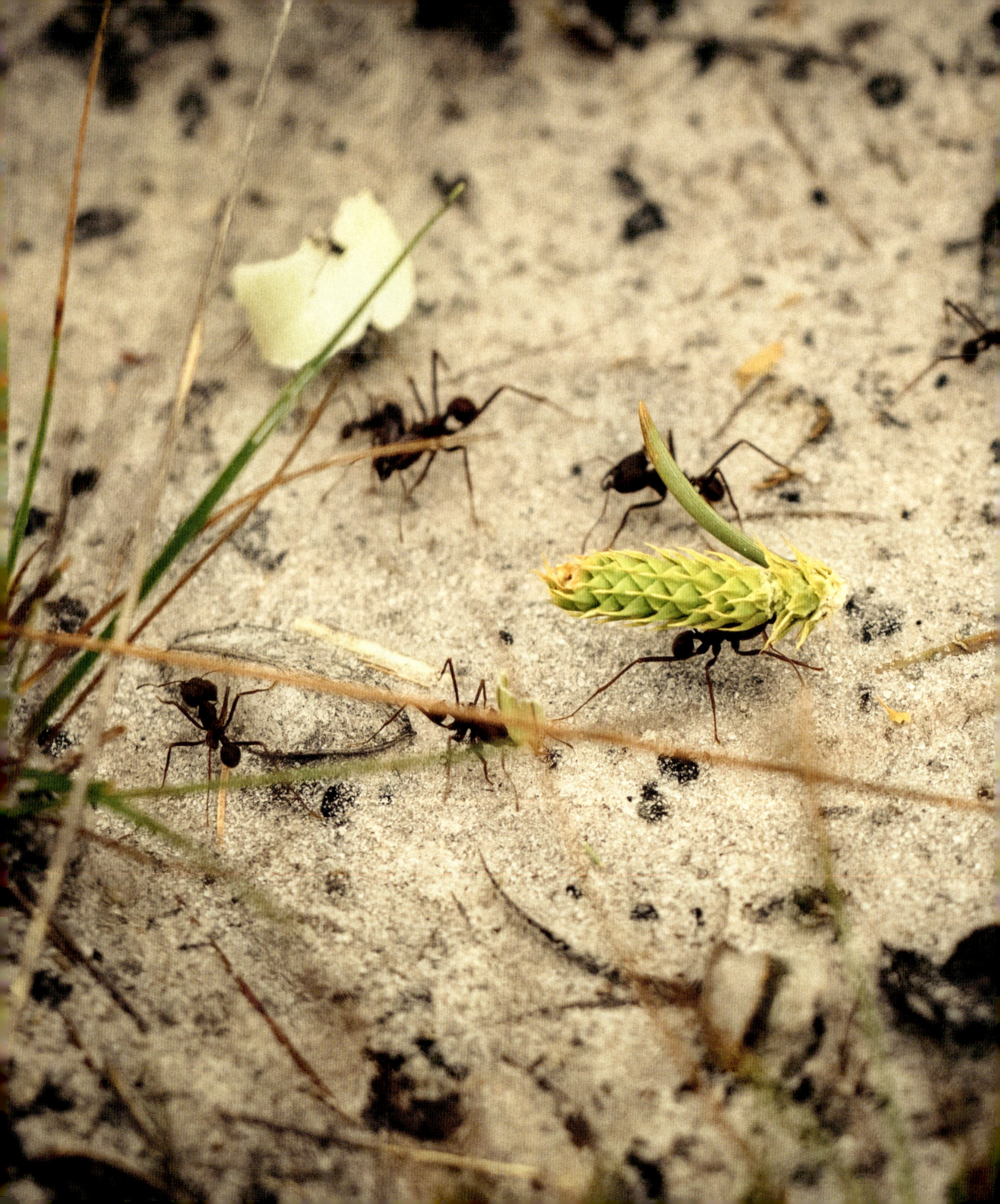

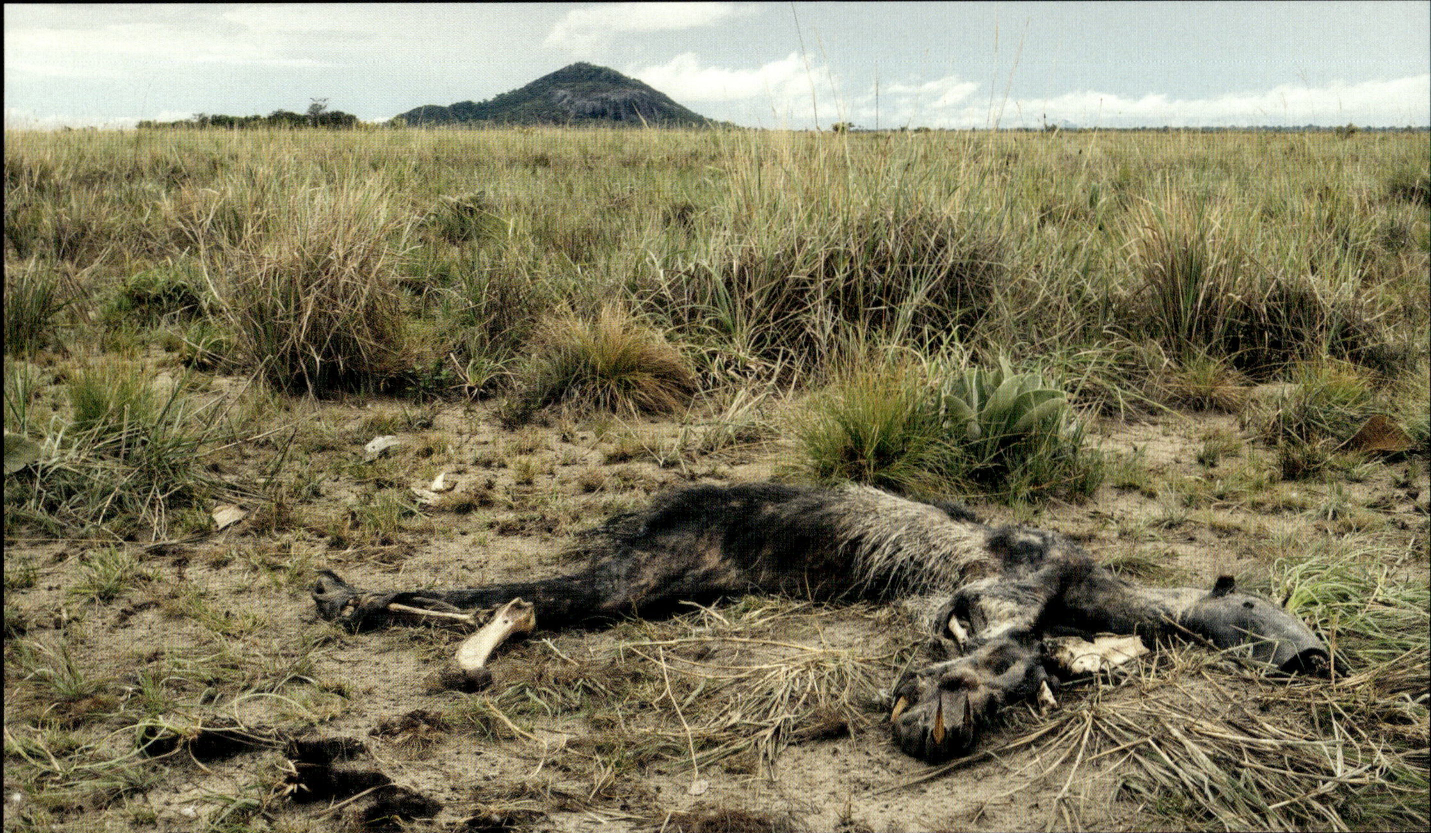

I try to enjoy the long-awaited change of scenery, but my naive excitement is quickly dampened by endless swarms of tiny, thirsty puri-puri flies trying to get on to every exposed inch of my body, including my eyes, nose and ears, leaving behind itchy dots of blood on my skin. Brief gusts of wind are the only thing that appear to ward them off, bringing but fleeting moments of relief. I follow a narrow, trampled path towards the stone giants, at times pausing to rest at groves of moriche palms, their vigorous leaves rustling in the warm breeze.

At one point, I spot a dark, crumpled figure on the ground. It's the remains of a giant anteater, its carcass slowly desiccated by the relentless heat pouring from the skies. I notice it being viciously consumed by a busy swarm of ants feasting on the remains of their nemesis, as if revelling in some grotesque act of revenge. Its sharp claws are pointed at the sky – like an empty echo of its past formidability.

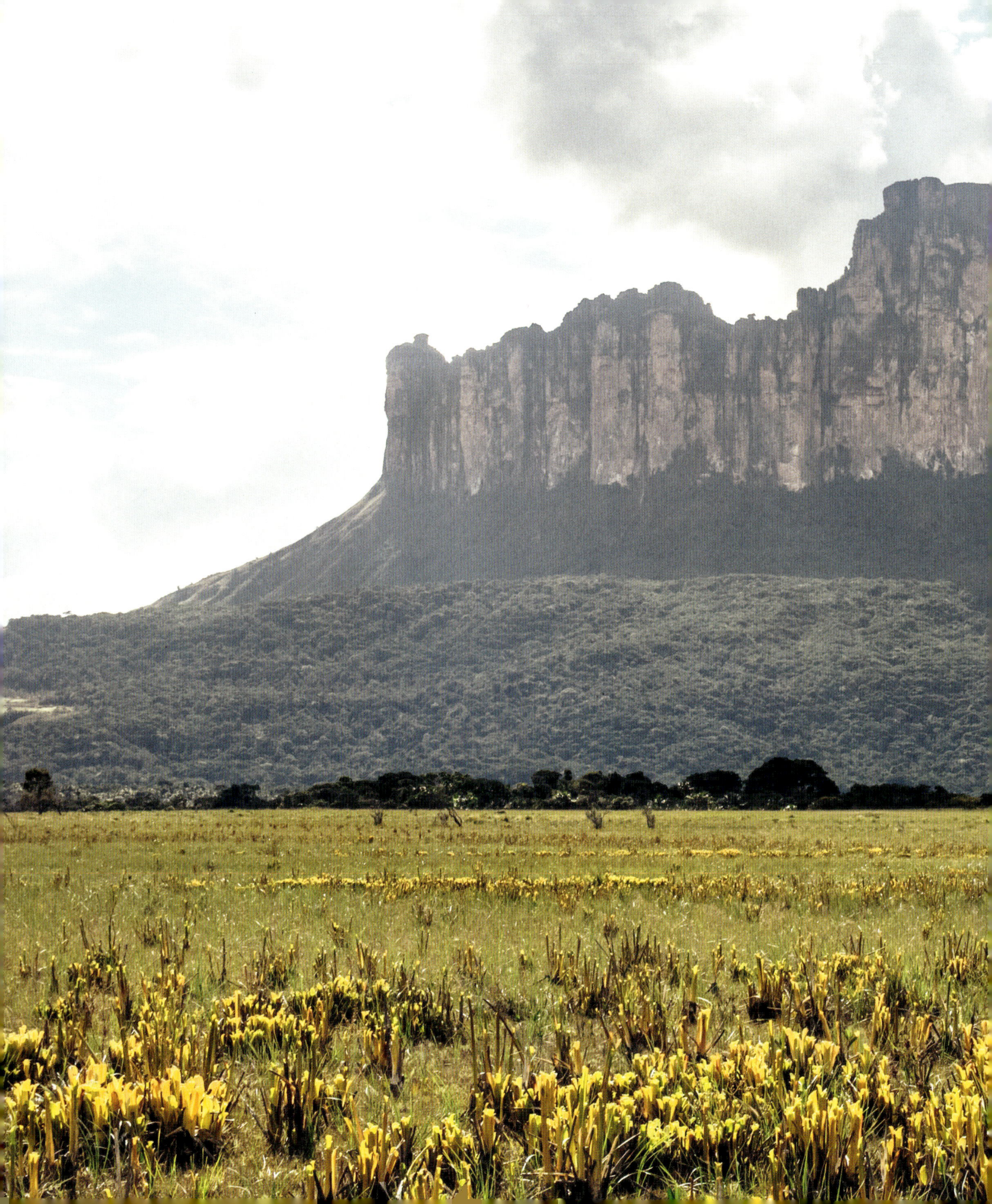

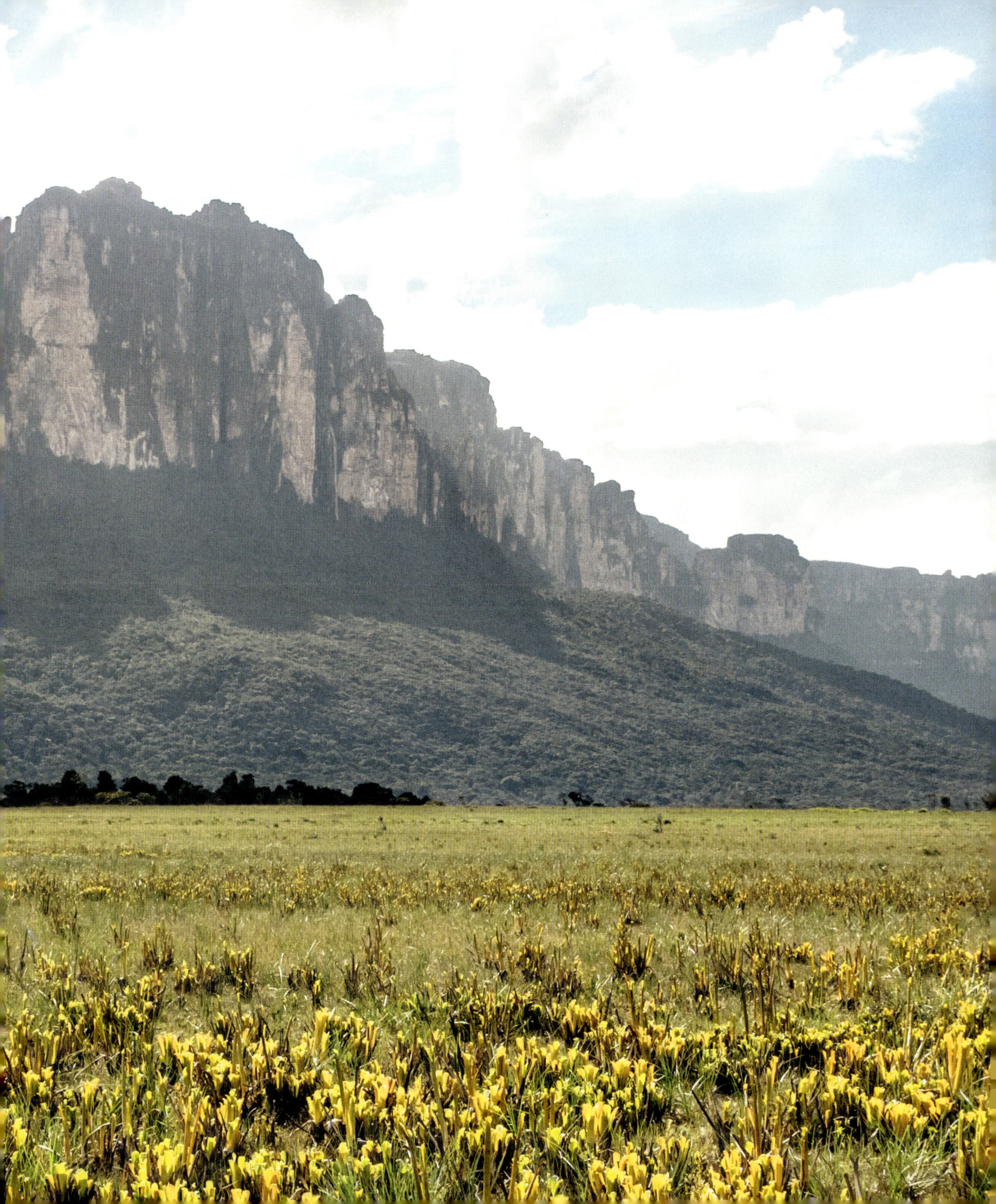

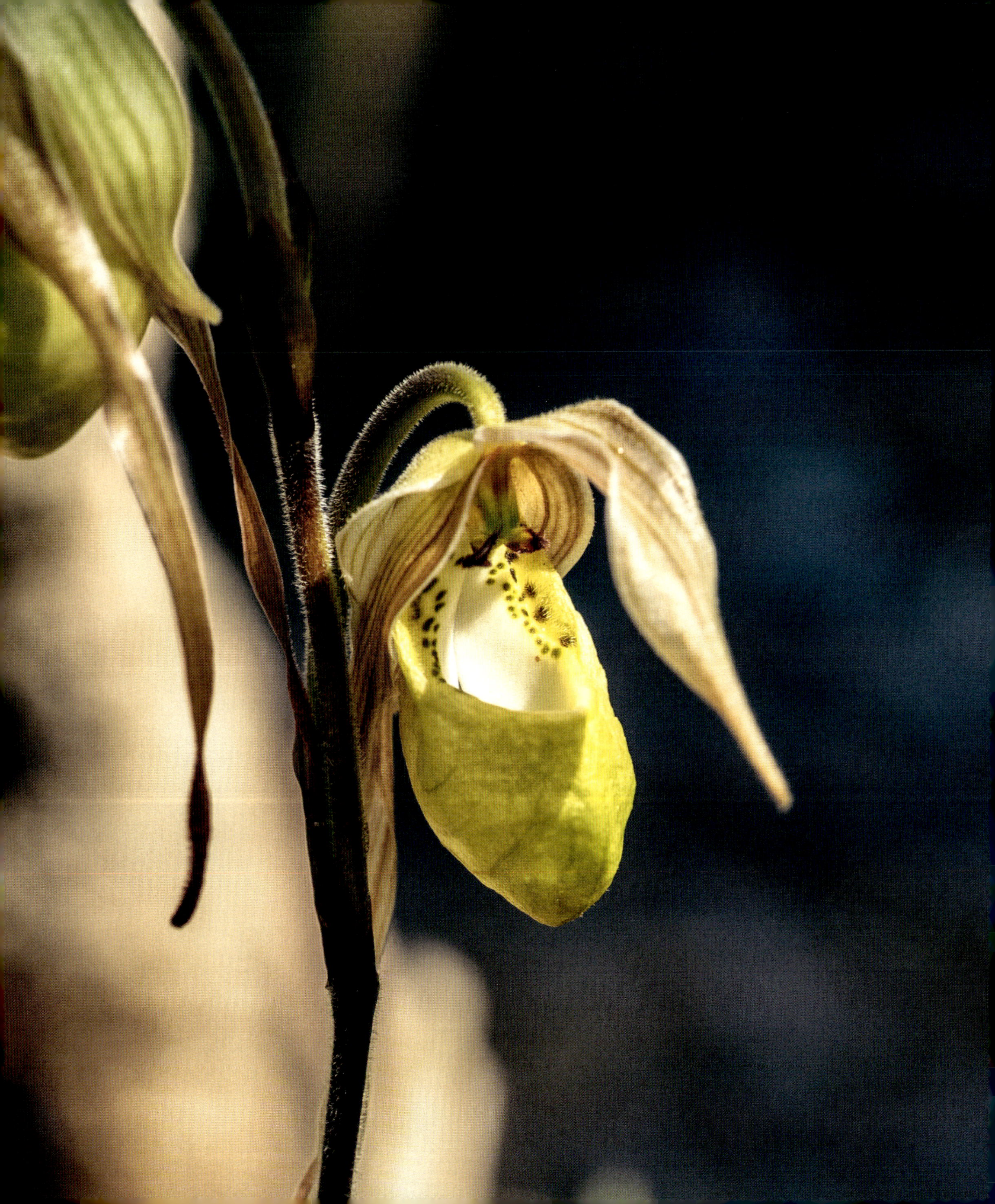

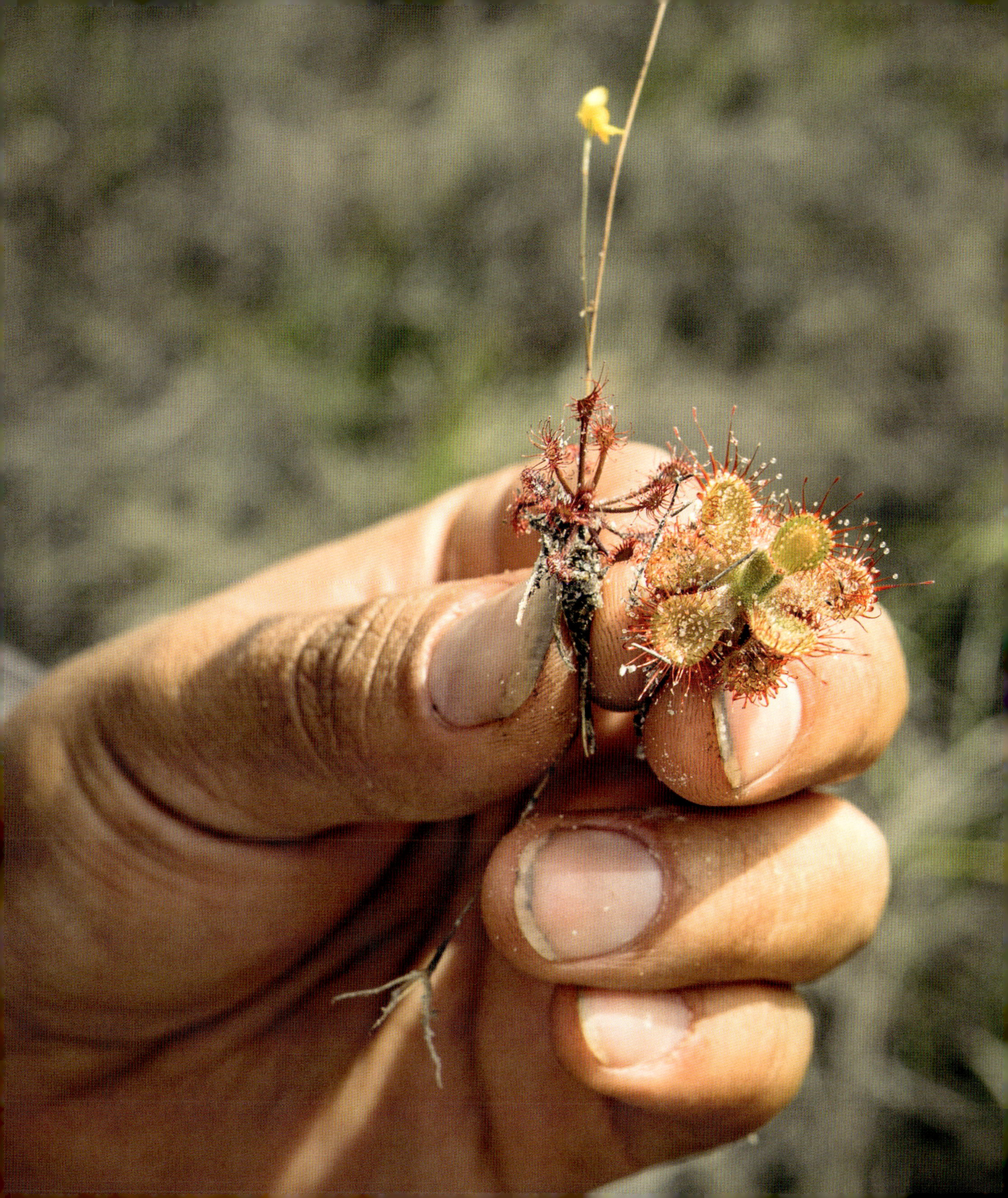

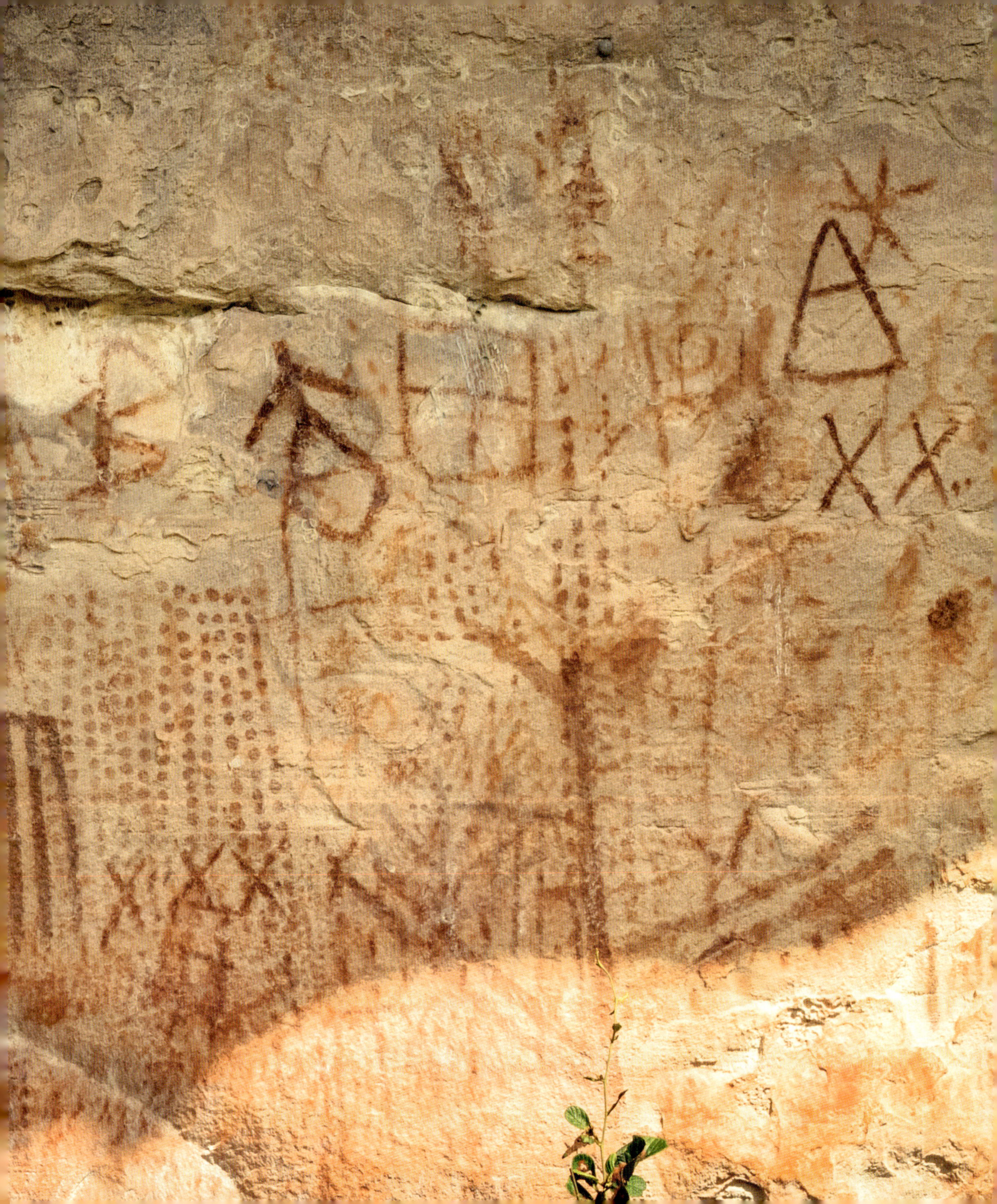

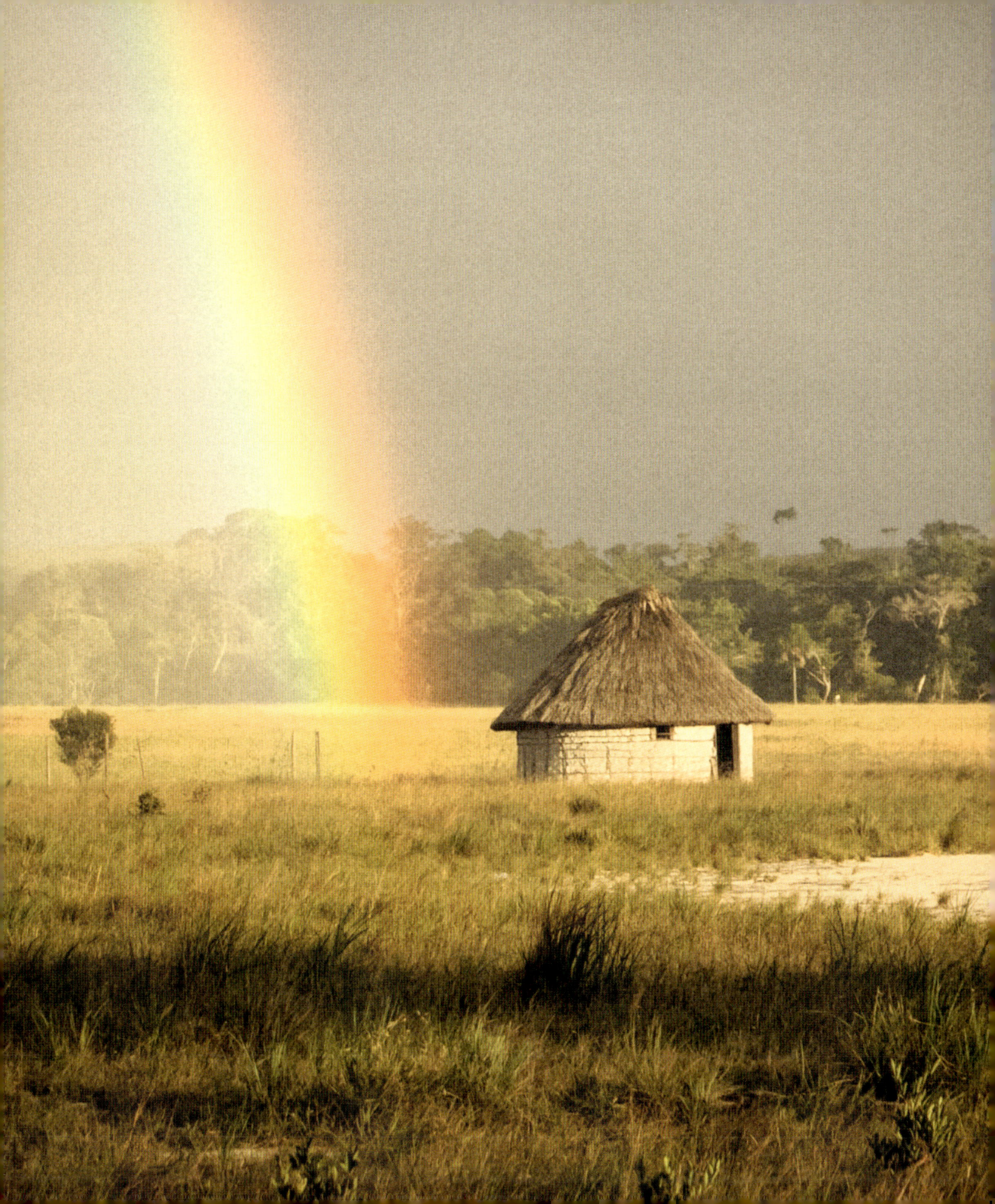

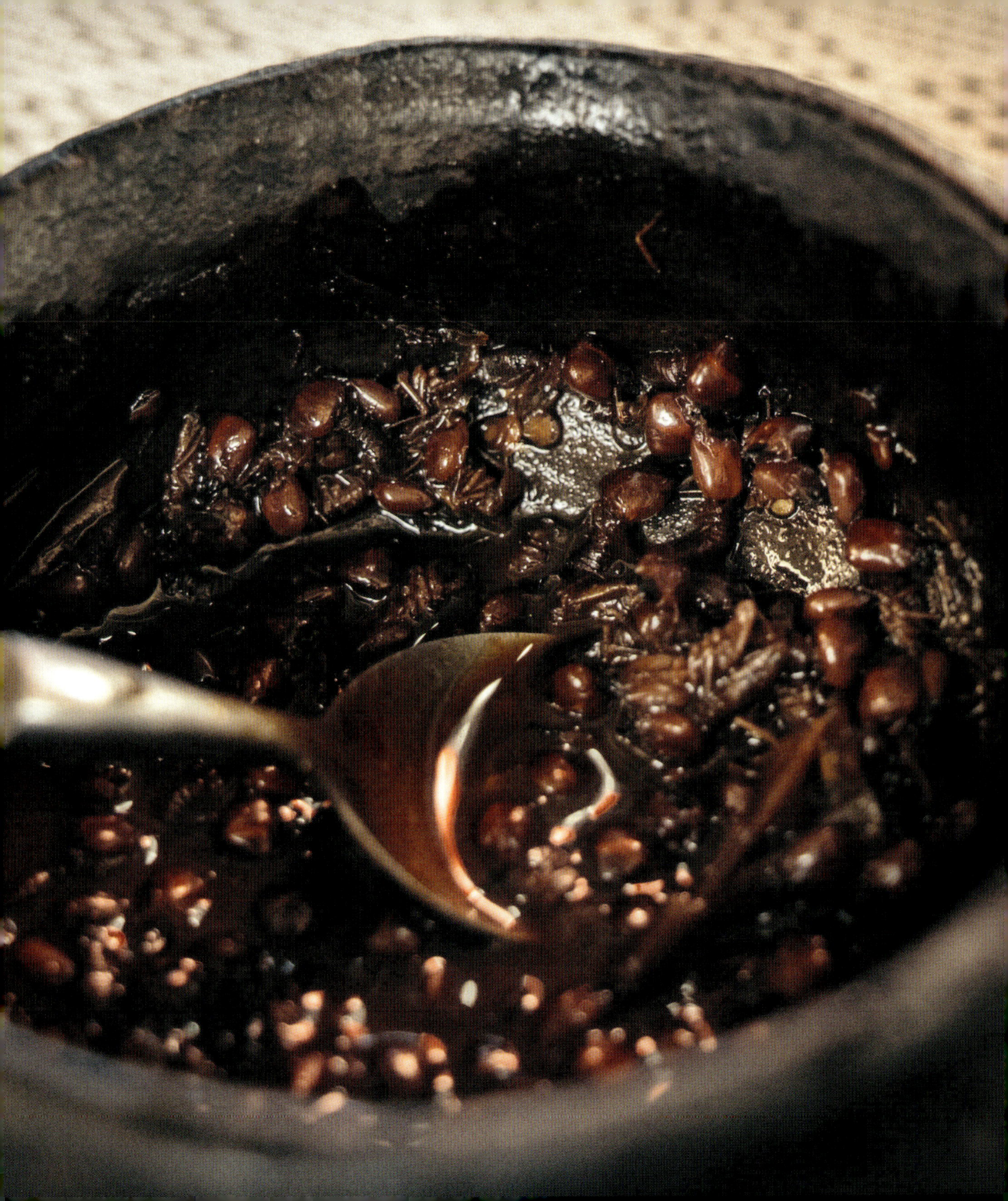

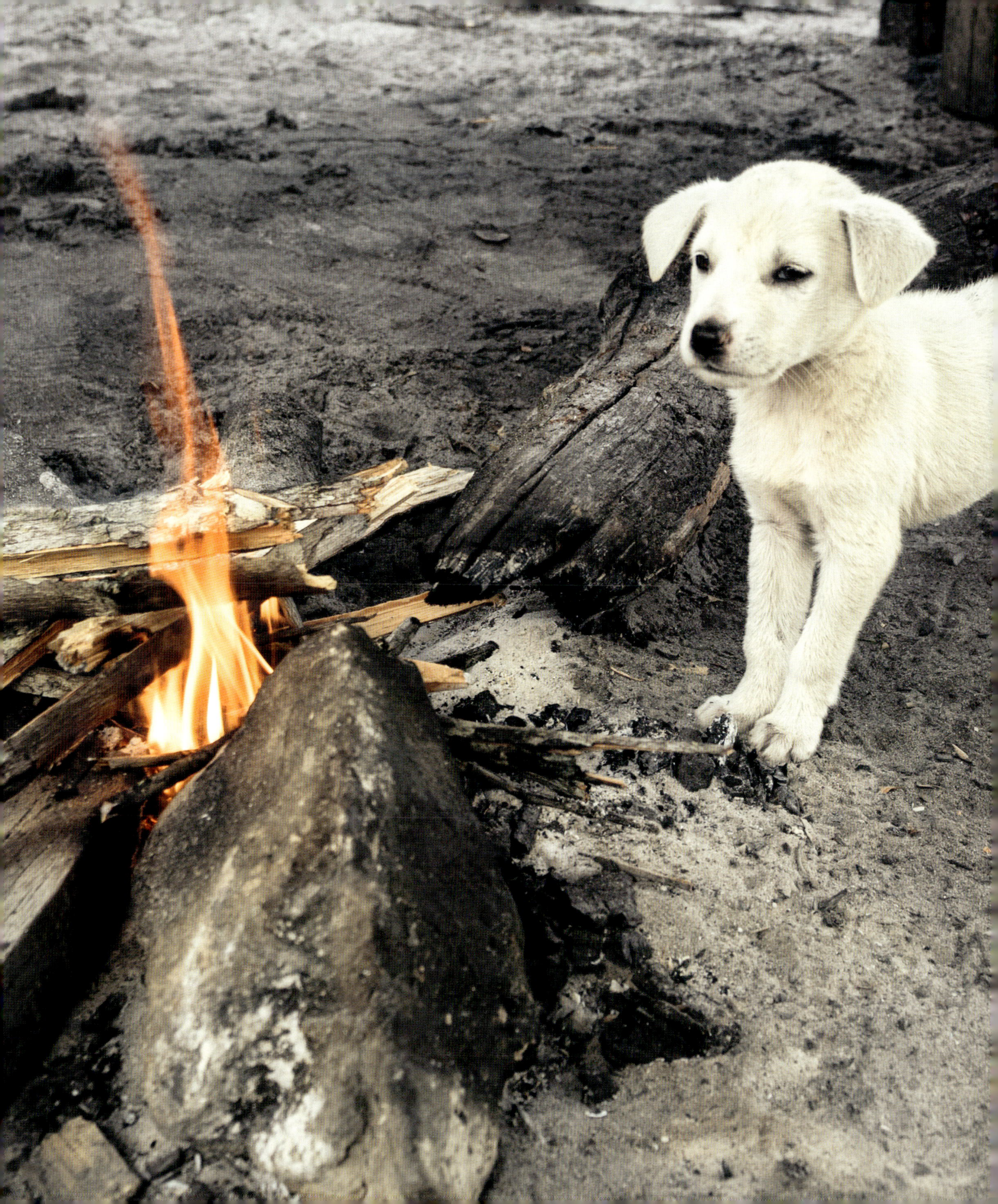

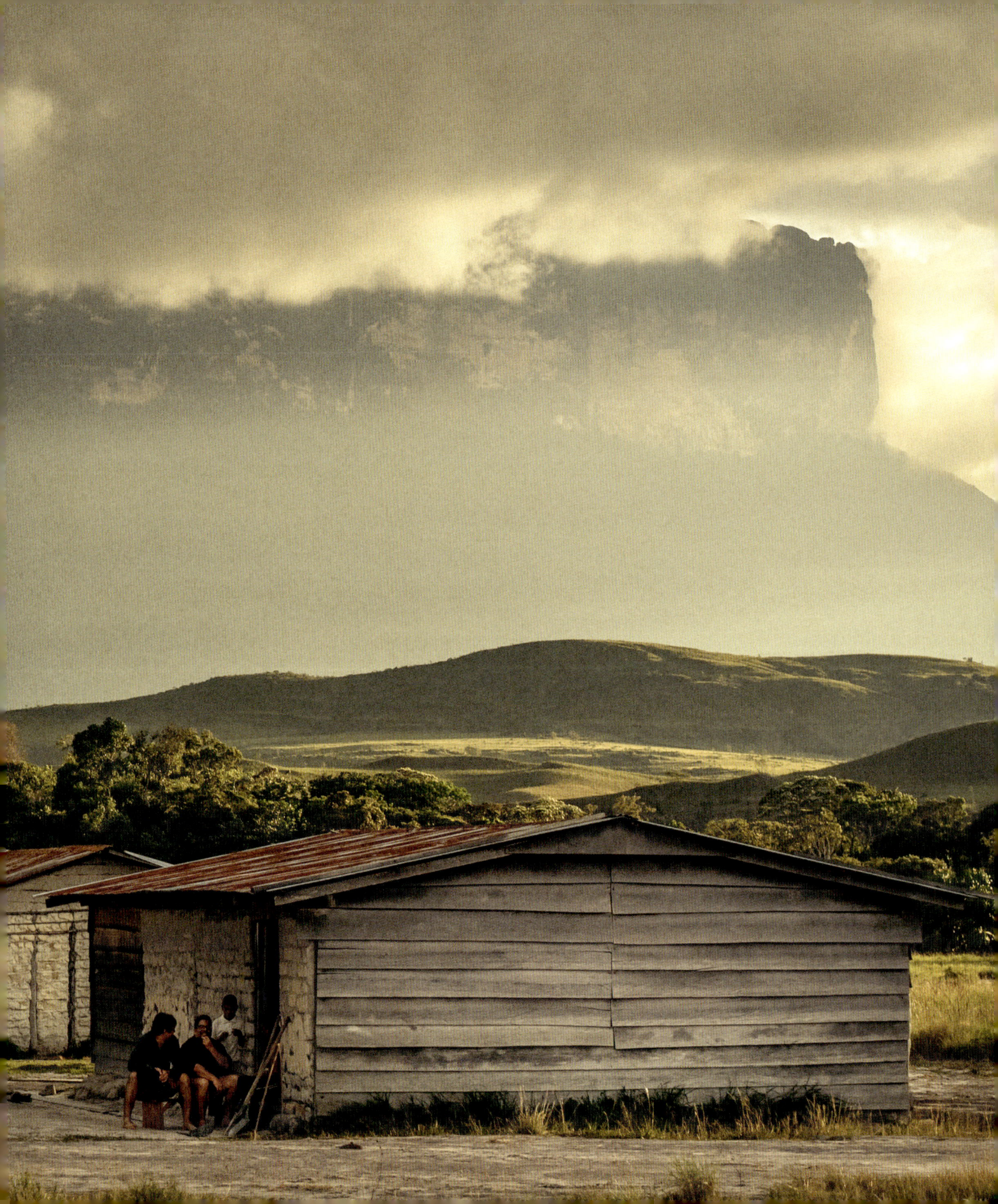

When I reach the top of a nearby hill, the landscape changes in the blink of an eye. An outline of the imposing rock wall has vanished completely behind a curtain of dark grey clouds, providing a backdrop to a group of round, clay-walled houses scattered along an amber-coloured vein of a shallow, meandering river. From a distance, I can hear children playing, blending with the sounds of thunder and passing rain, whose ghostly streaks, visible from afar, move slowly over the hills like a painter's brush on a canvas, leaving behind dark bands of vibrant vegetation. The downpour meets me as I descend the hill towards the village, washing the dust off my face and soaking my clothes yet again, only to then disappear as quickly as it arrived.

I walk through a field of shimmering, yellow bromeliads when the rhythmic splash of wet earth is interrupted by a crunch of shattering glass beneath my feet. I look to my side and see the wreck of a small aeroplane, its nose pointing towards the sun as it sets behind the horizon, as though gazing at it in a hopeless gesture of defeat. I notice the tail had been severed during the impact, leaving behind a jagged hole in the back of the hull. I crawl inside and brush the shards of glass from the pilot's seat to rest for a moment. Looking from behind the lens of a cracked windscreen, the most extraordinary scene begins to take shape, as though I were looking through a kaleidoscope. The cliff reveals itself from behind the grey curtain of thick storm clouds, bearing dozens of perfectly vertical streaks of waterfalls formed by the evening rains. Stripes of rainbows suddenly begin to descend upon the village nestled beneath the mountain slopes, so numerous and so lucid that I can't decide whether to take them for reality or a mirage caused by a long day marked by heat and fatigue. Was this the last thing the poor pilot saw before he met his fate here?

The evening engulfs the village in a wave of cold. I hang up my hammock under the thatched roof and join my hosts by the fire, gathered around a steaming pot of spicy tumá soup. I pour myself a bowl, grab a piece of cassava bread, and go out to sit on top of a large sandstone boulder behind the hut. The skies are dotted with thousands of stars, and the Milky Way stretches like a glowing arc above the endless savanna, astonishingly clear and bright in the crisp mountain air.

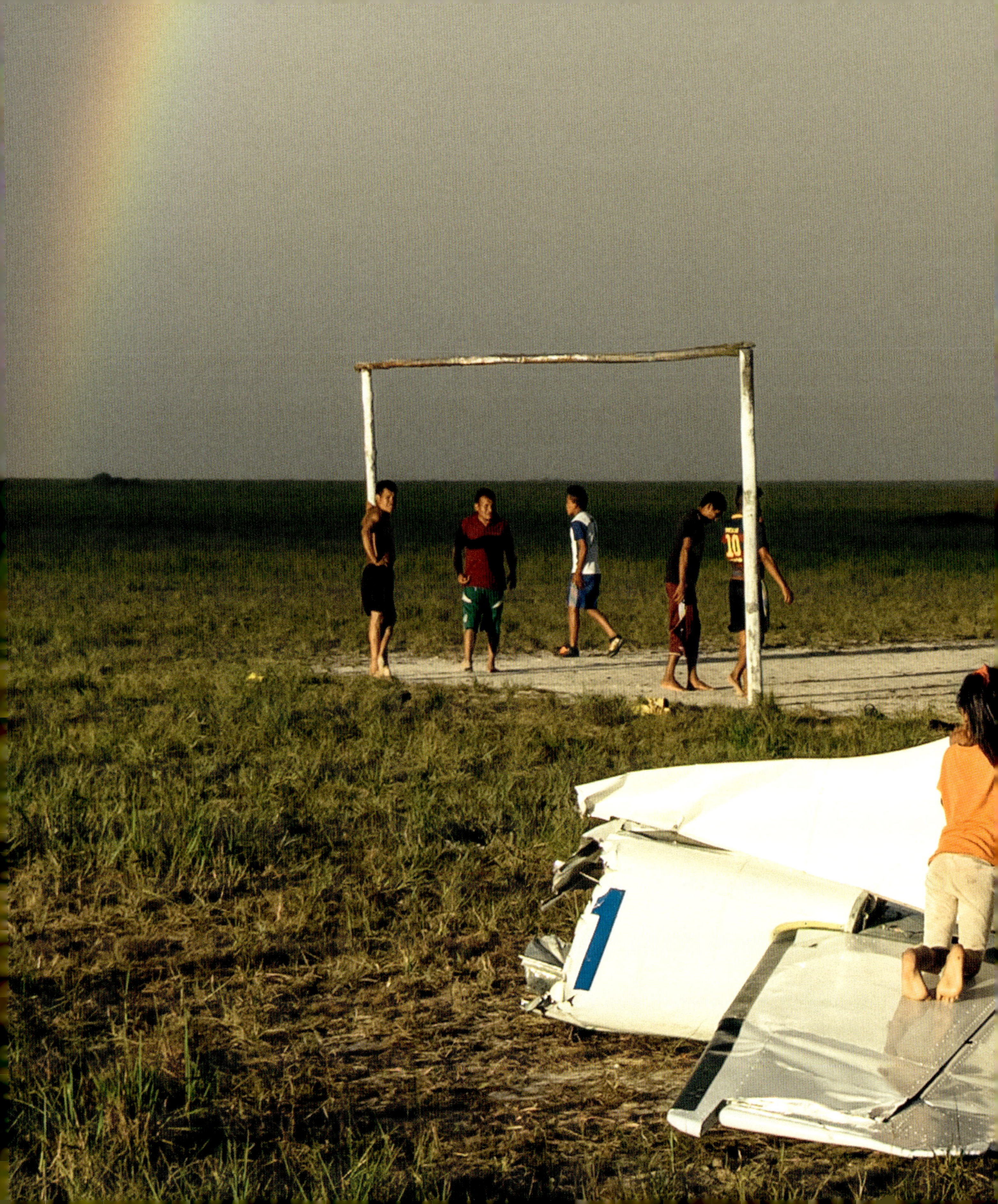
10
1

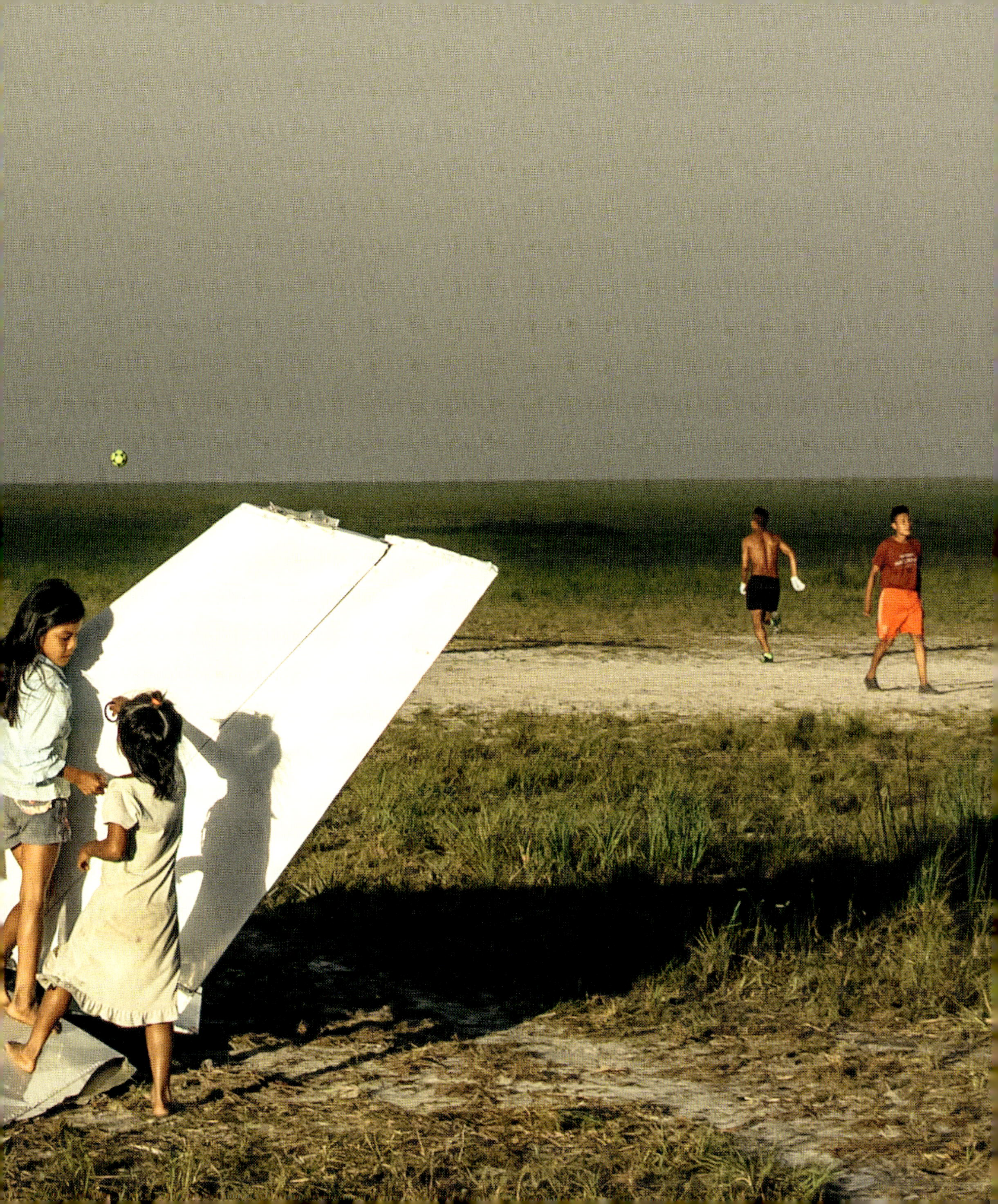

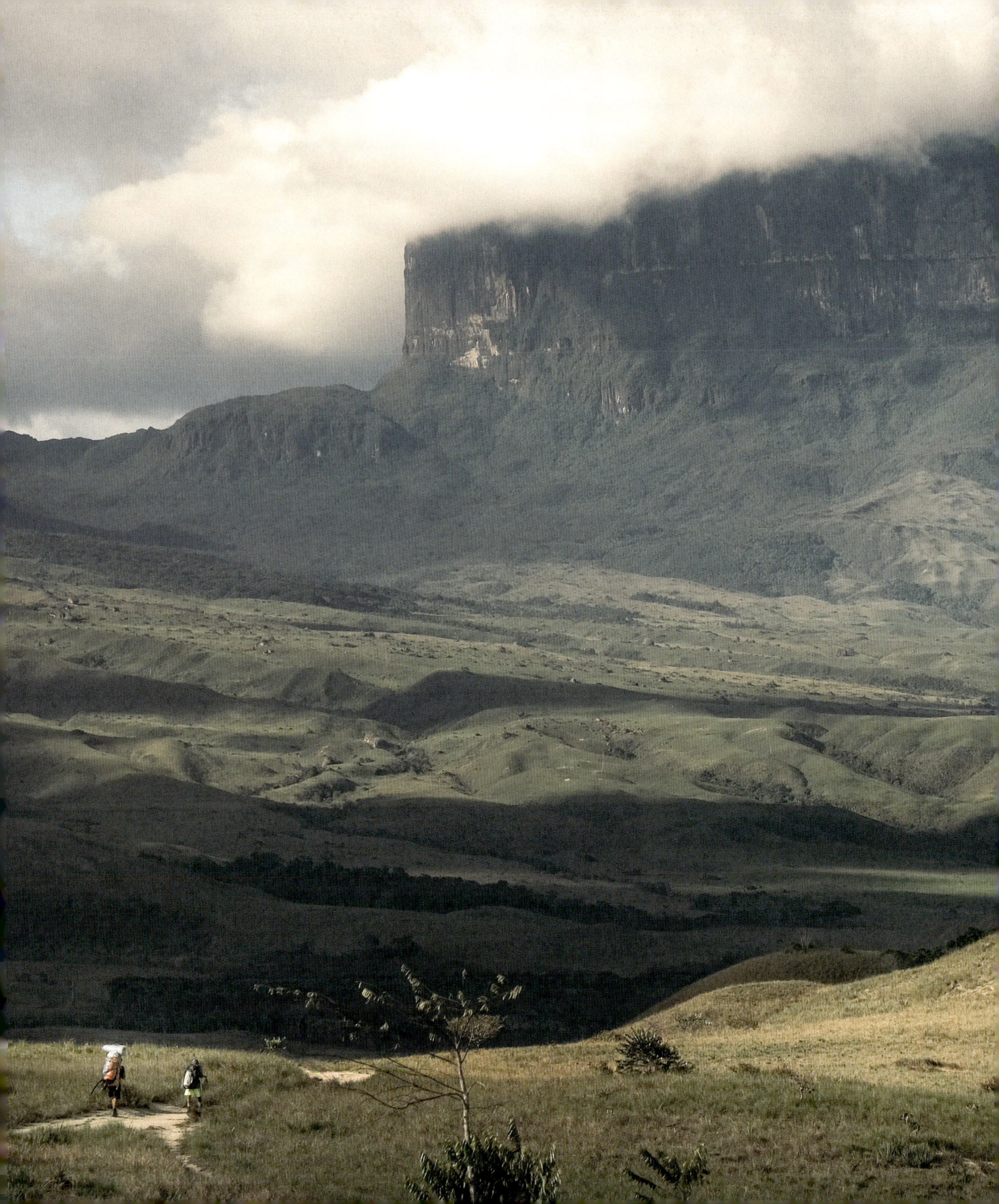

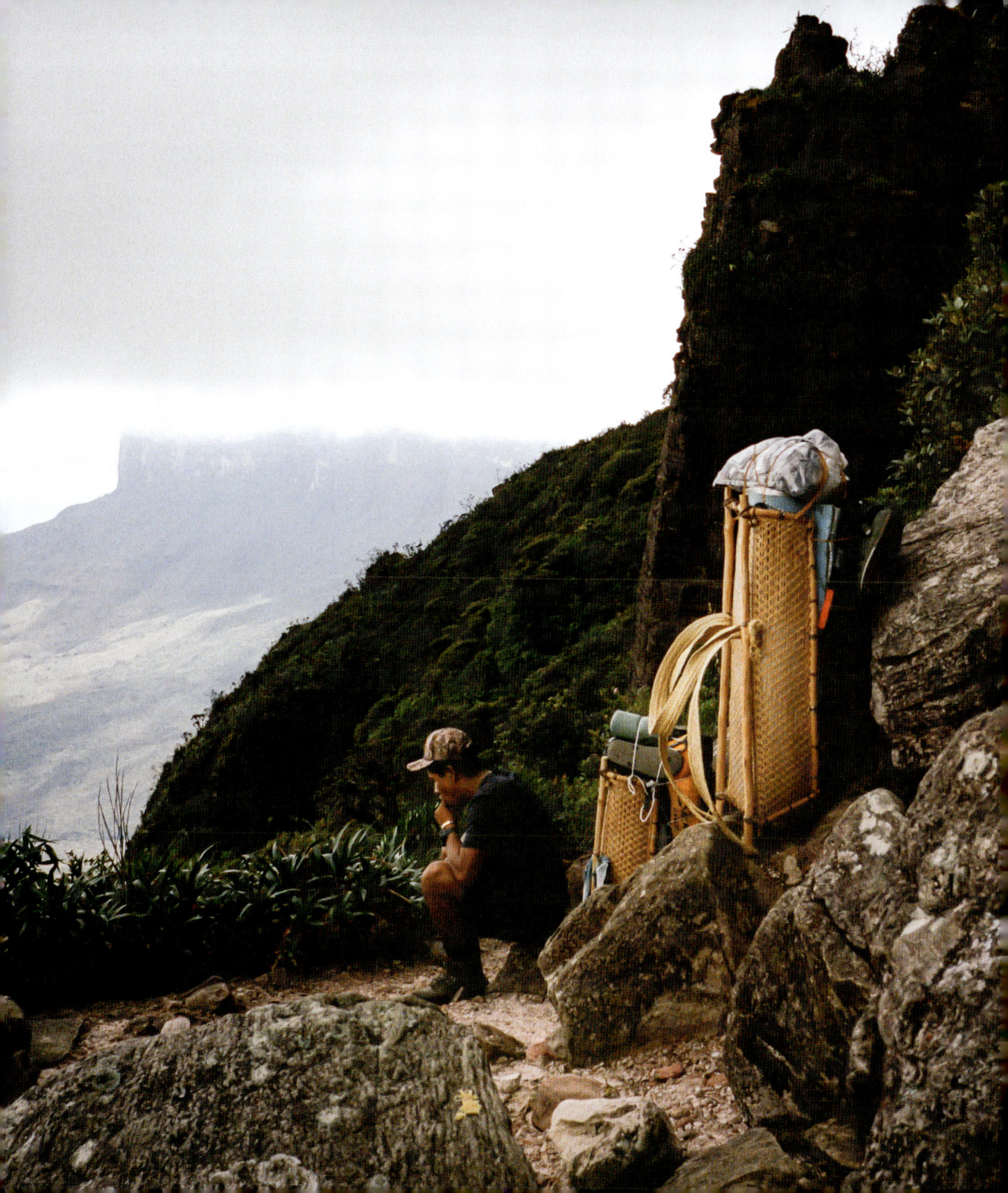

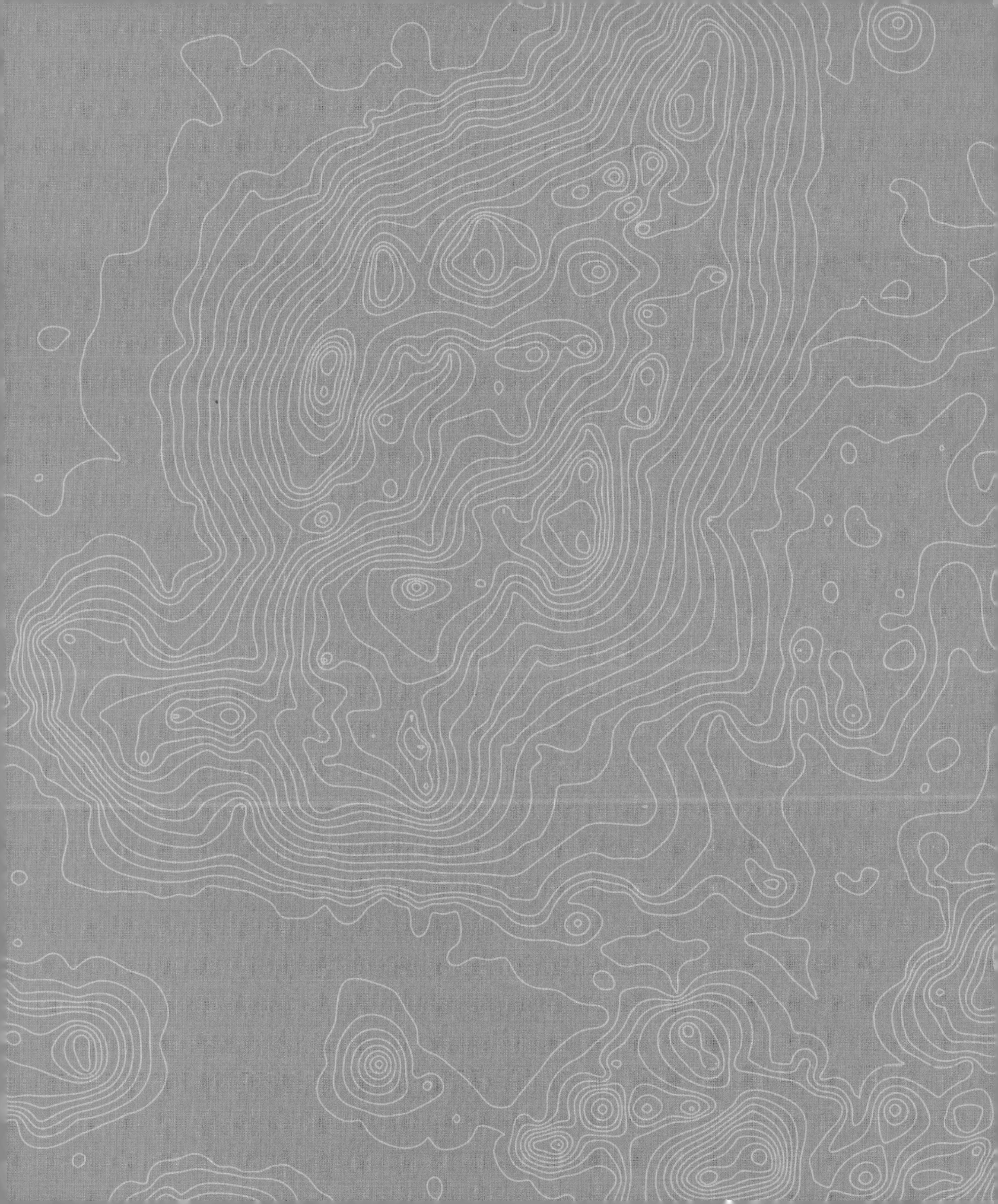

CHAPTER 4
Some Strange Country

"Lying always in the shadow of the mountain, saturated with moisture at every season, forms have evolved here which are unique. It was a wilderness of dark, bamboolike turubanas, towering ferns, plants with flapping flag-fronds and small drooping orchids; lianas writhed in every direction like endless snakes, and every possible surface was covered with cankerous growths of sponge mosses or hung with a sinister long greenish hair gorged with ice-cold water, which would stream from it as I gripped a turubana stem to help me up the path. The path was composed of mud, moss and low fern, and for long stretches it was overgrown with slippery lianas and roots which we had to clamber over, our feet sometimes slipping through the interstices to the earth some yard or two below. Everything was ice-cold and wet, and we too, before long, were saturated with cold moisture."

Michael Swan – *The Marches of El Dorado*, 1958

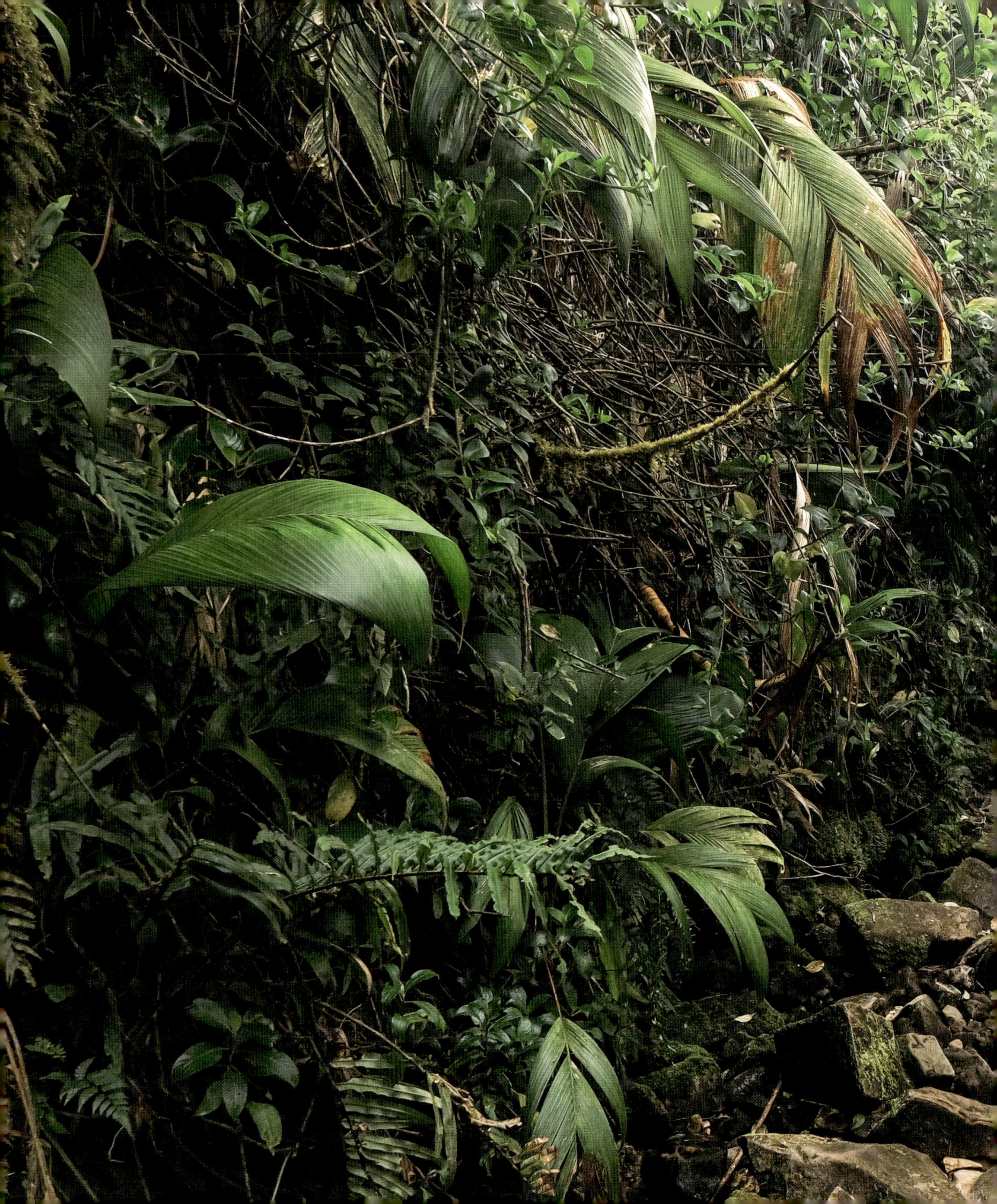

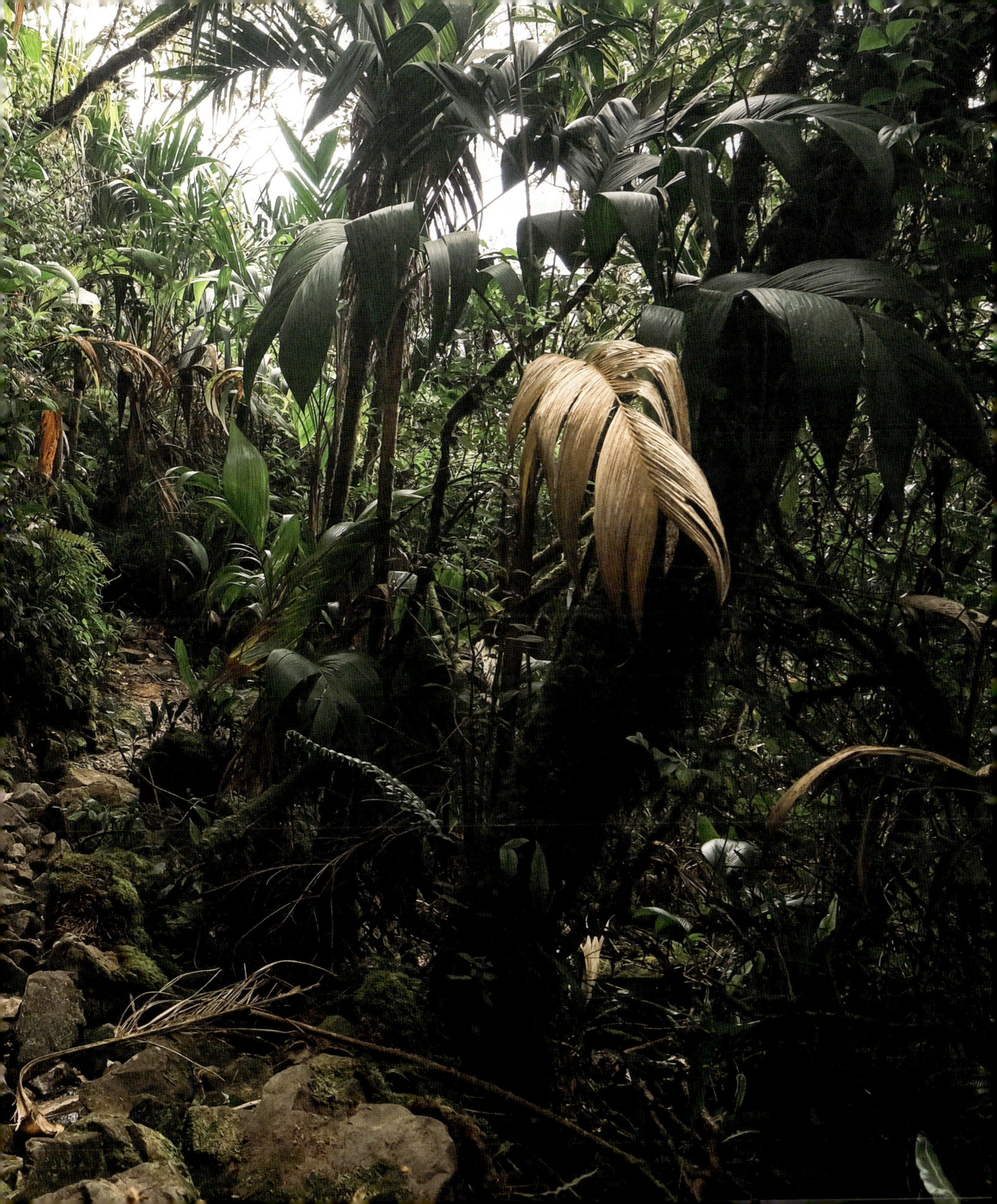

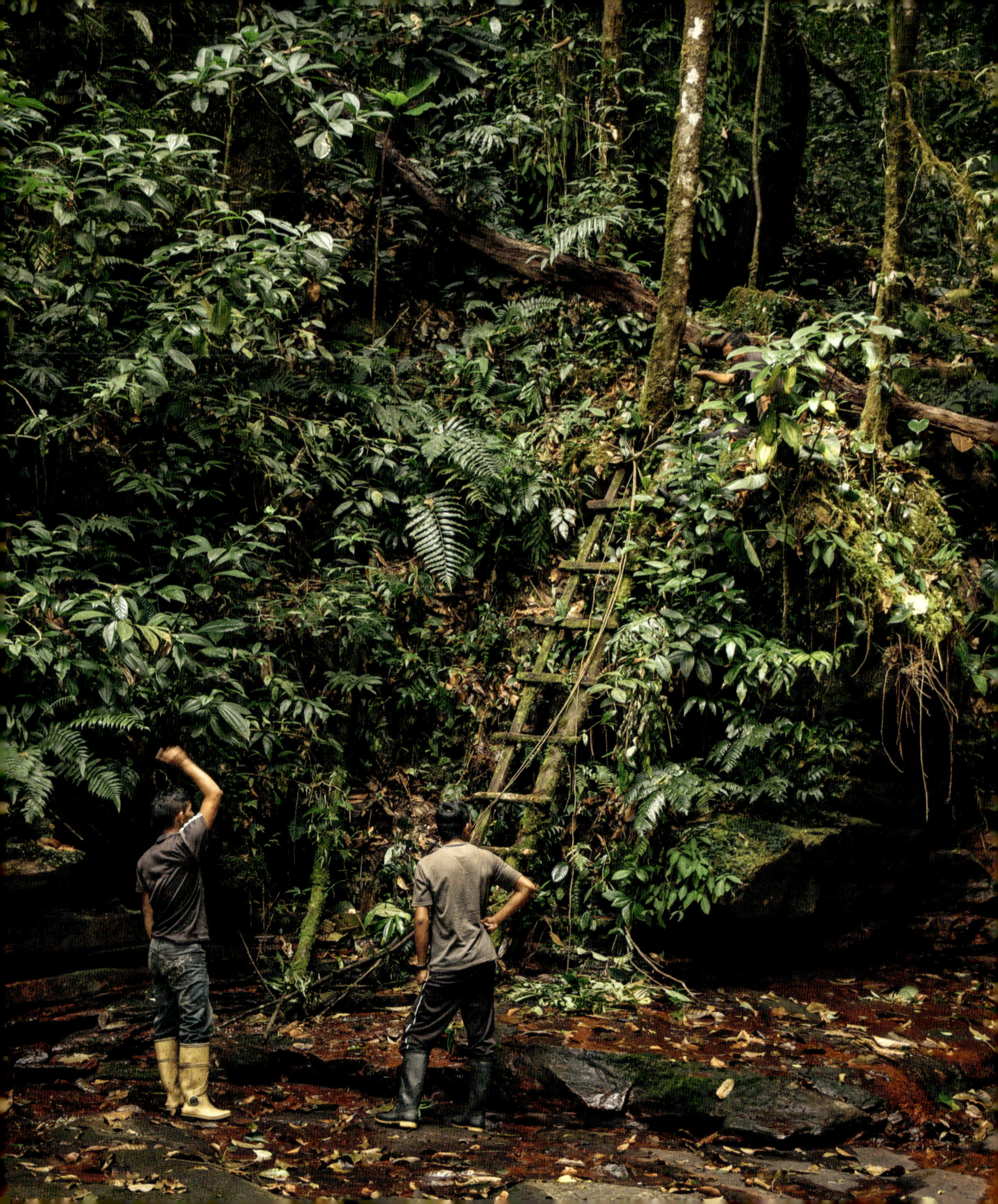

The time spent on crossing the sun-scorched savanna has made me look like a different person entirely. My lips are dry and chapped, and with every step I take, the dust rising from underneath my feet powders my clothes, my face, and leaves of grasses and short bushes around. I follow up a path descending from the massif, which has already grown to obscure most of the landscape ahead. Most of the day, when illuminated from behind it looks like a giant, featureless dark monolith. But when the golden evening sun touches its surface, it reveals intricate patterns of colours and textures, as though covered in lines of indecipherable ancient pictograms and petroglyphs left by a long-forgotten culture.

Gentle folds of grassy hills have given way to dense shrubs. Finally, I reach a sight that brings back memories from days ago. Once again, I stand before a wall of tangled green branches and vines, in which I notice only a small, barely visible opening. Through it emerges a narrow strip of light-brown clay, marking a steep path up the slope. The opening exudes a steady stream of damp, cold air and drifts of delicate mist. It doesn't look like an entrance into a dark forest, but more like a rift, a narrow rupture offering a glimpse into some different dimension. I'm staring into the void, and the void is staring back. This time however, I feel no fear. I've never been here before, but for reasons completely unknown to me, the place seems strangely familiar. I even notice something inexplicable within me like a call, hastening me to go into the shadows.

When I finally take my first step up the track, pulling myself up against the trunk of a short palm tree, I feel a drizzle on my face, as cold droplets fall from its leaves.

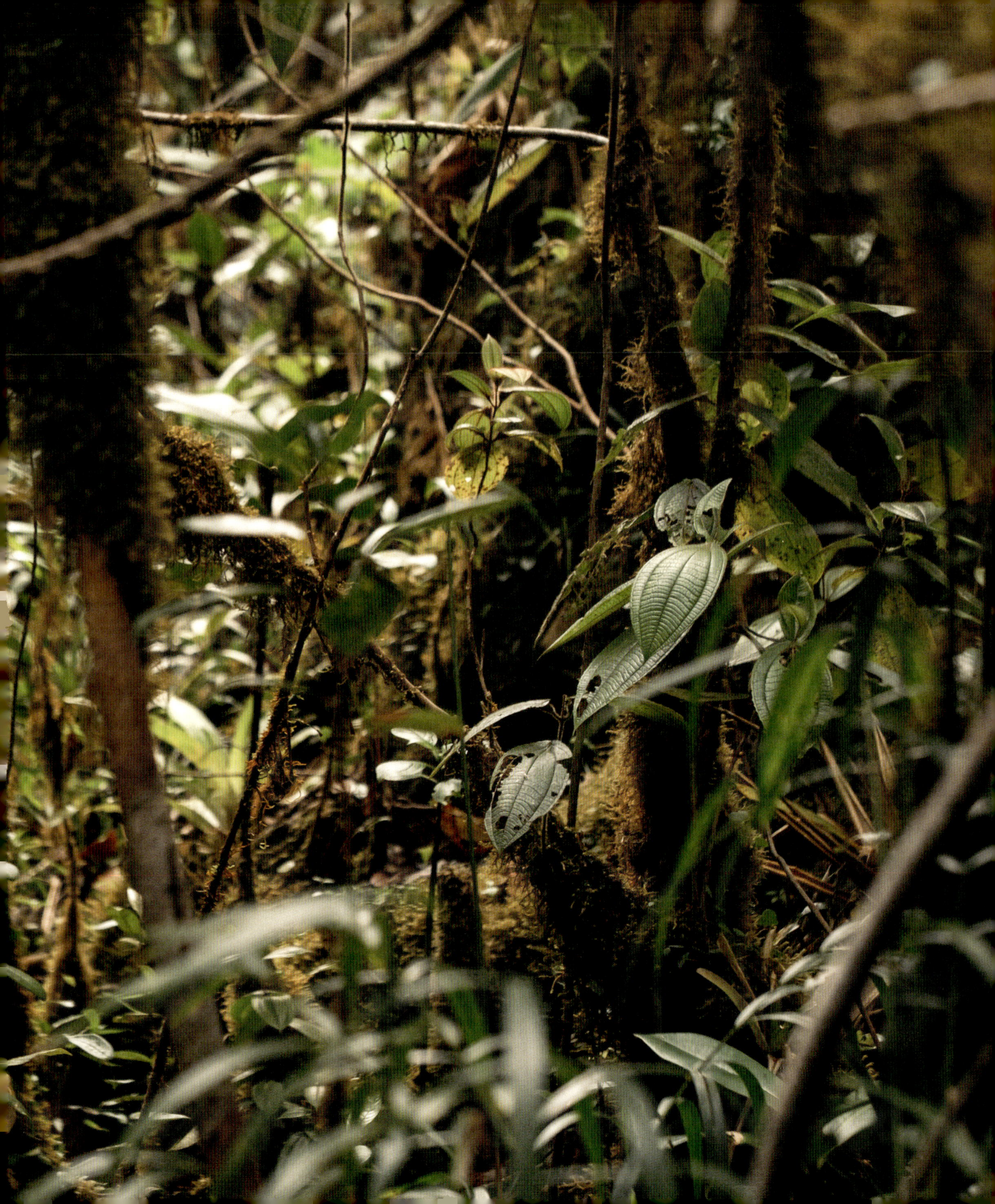

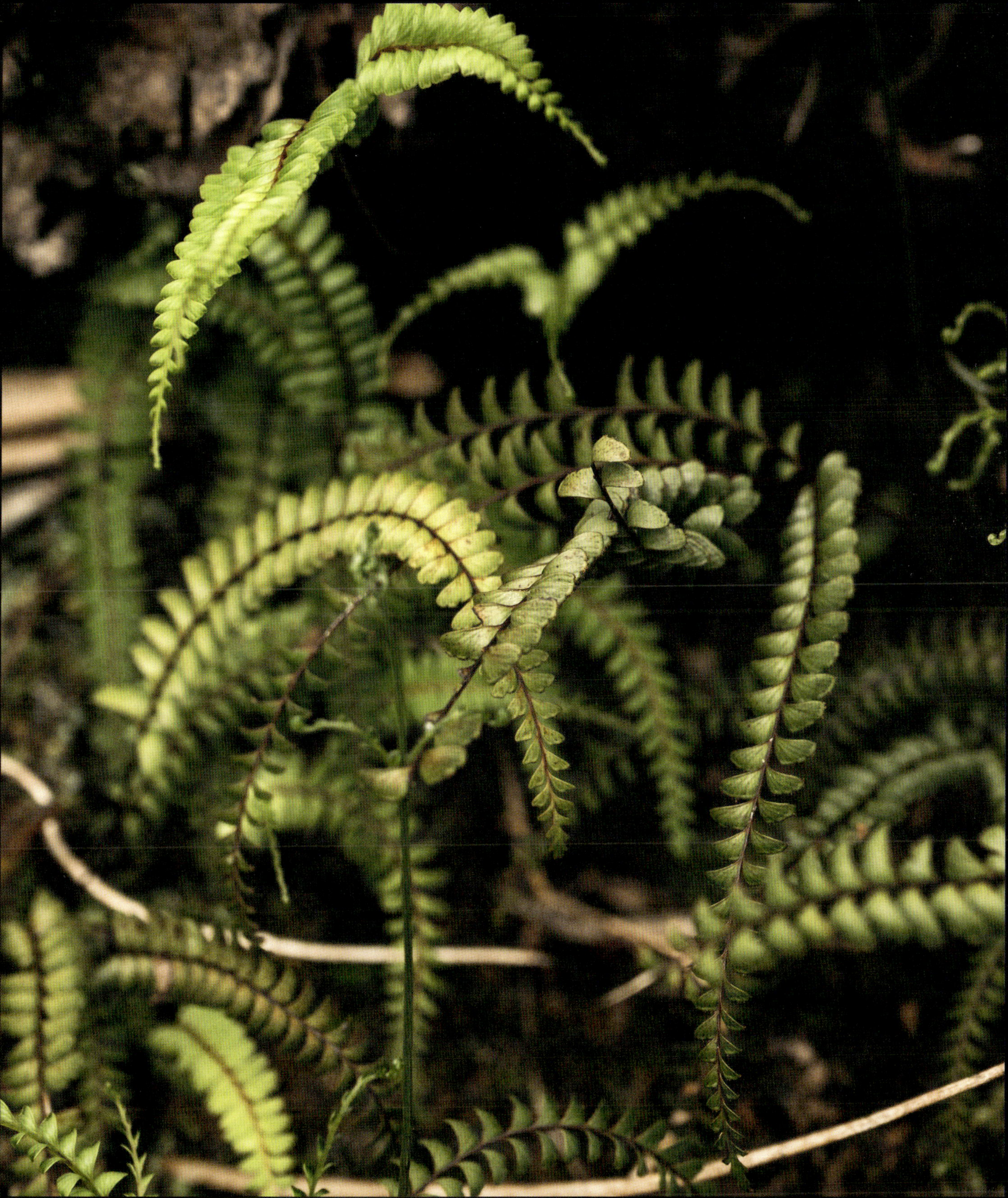

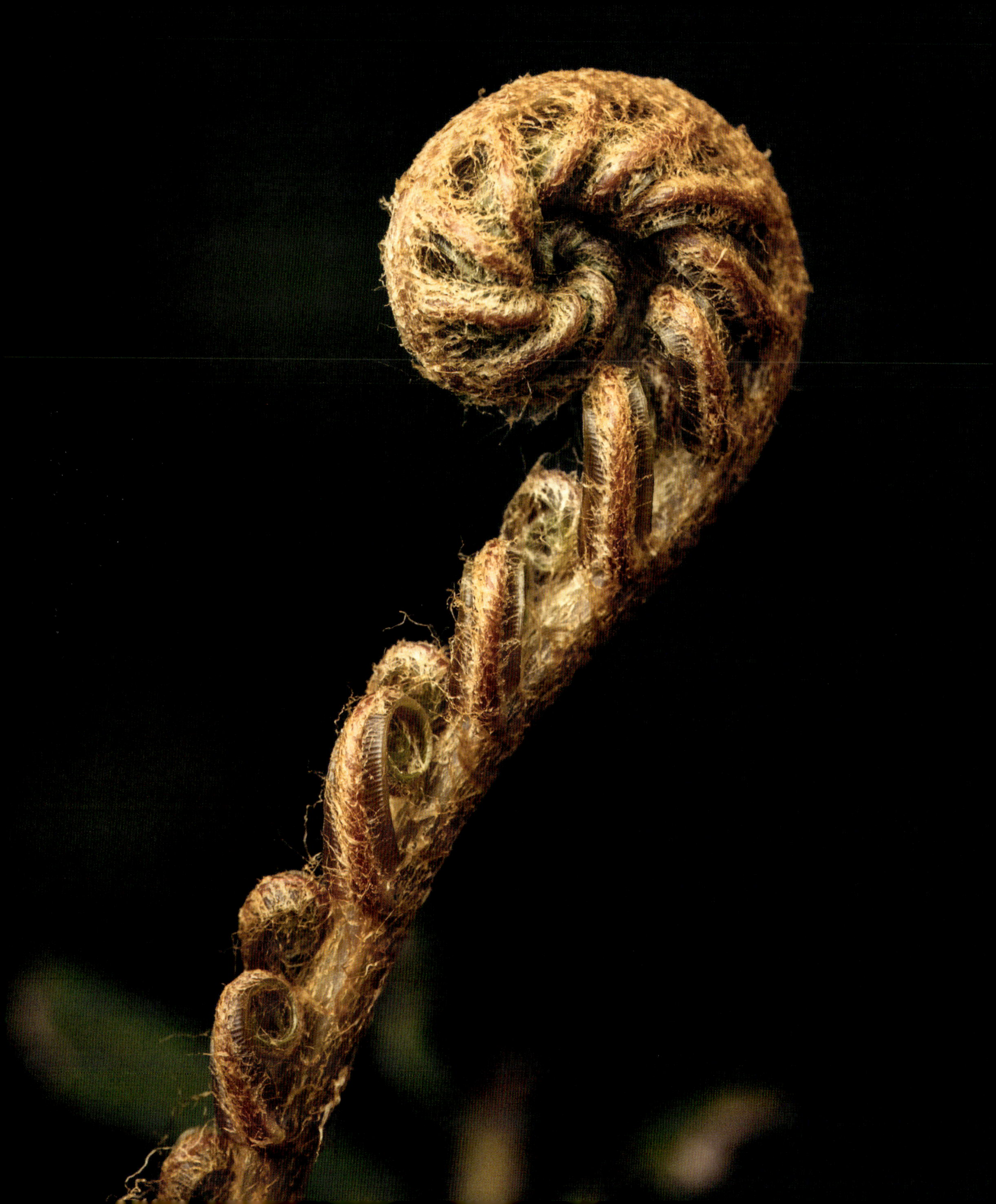

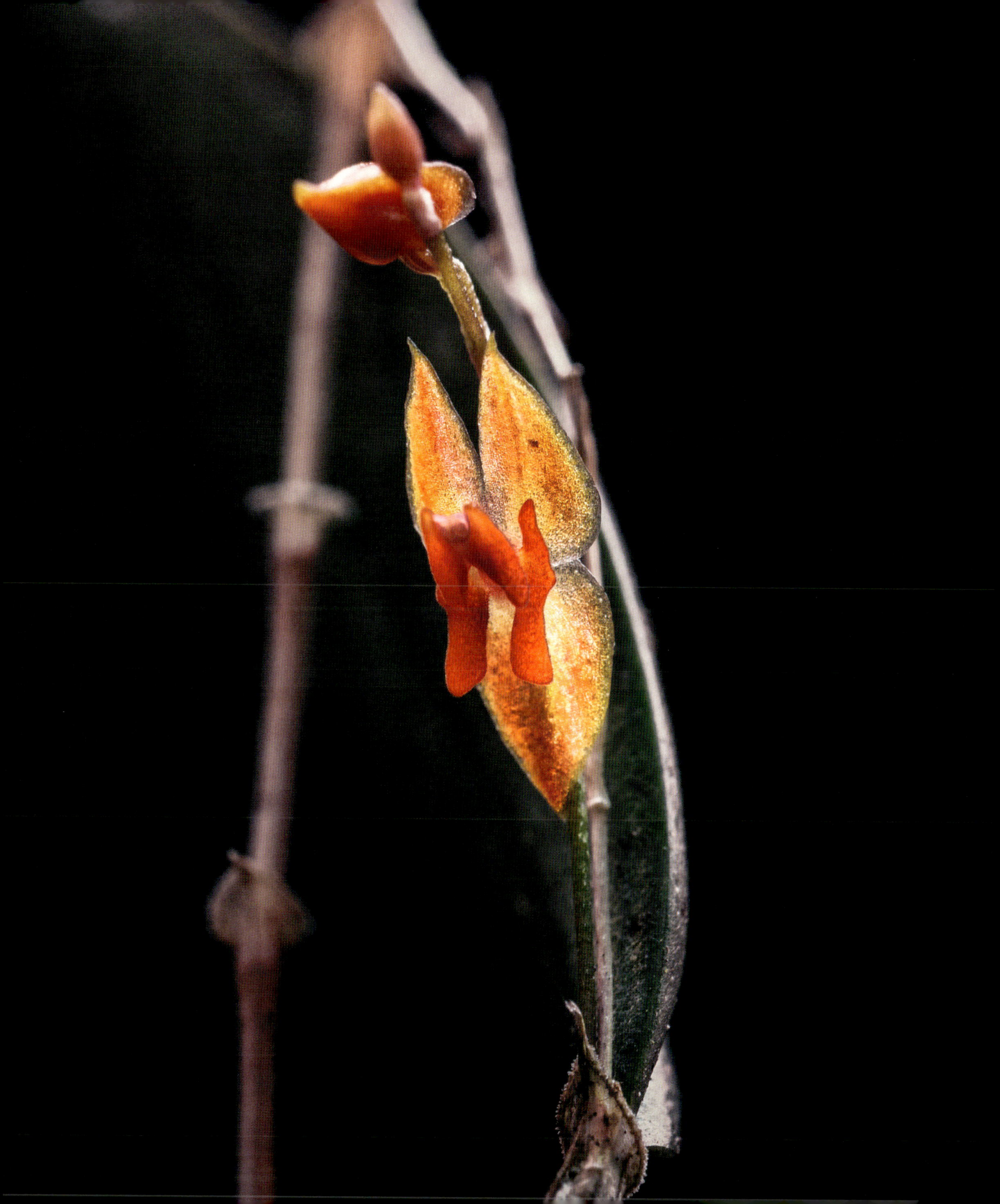

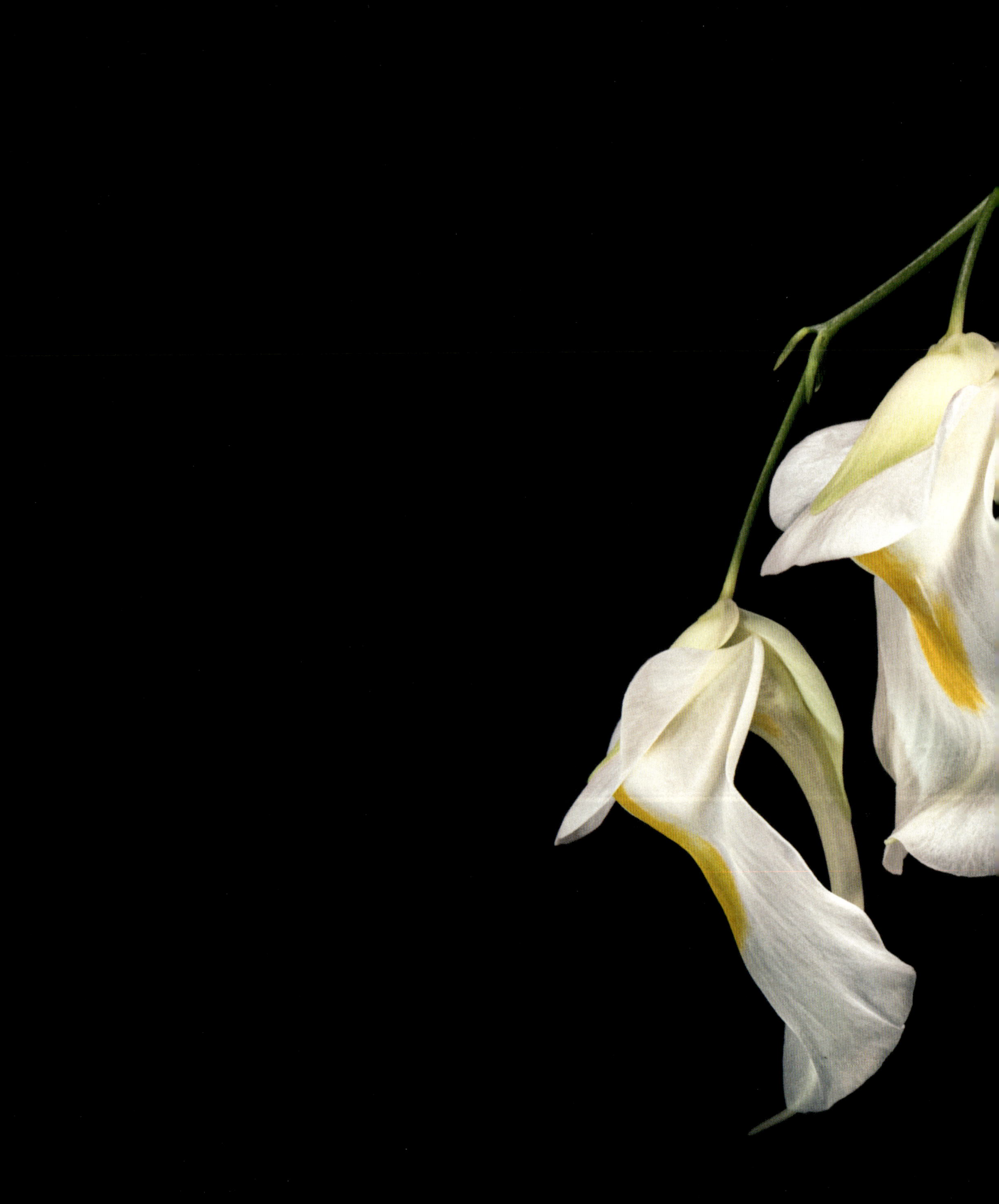

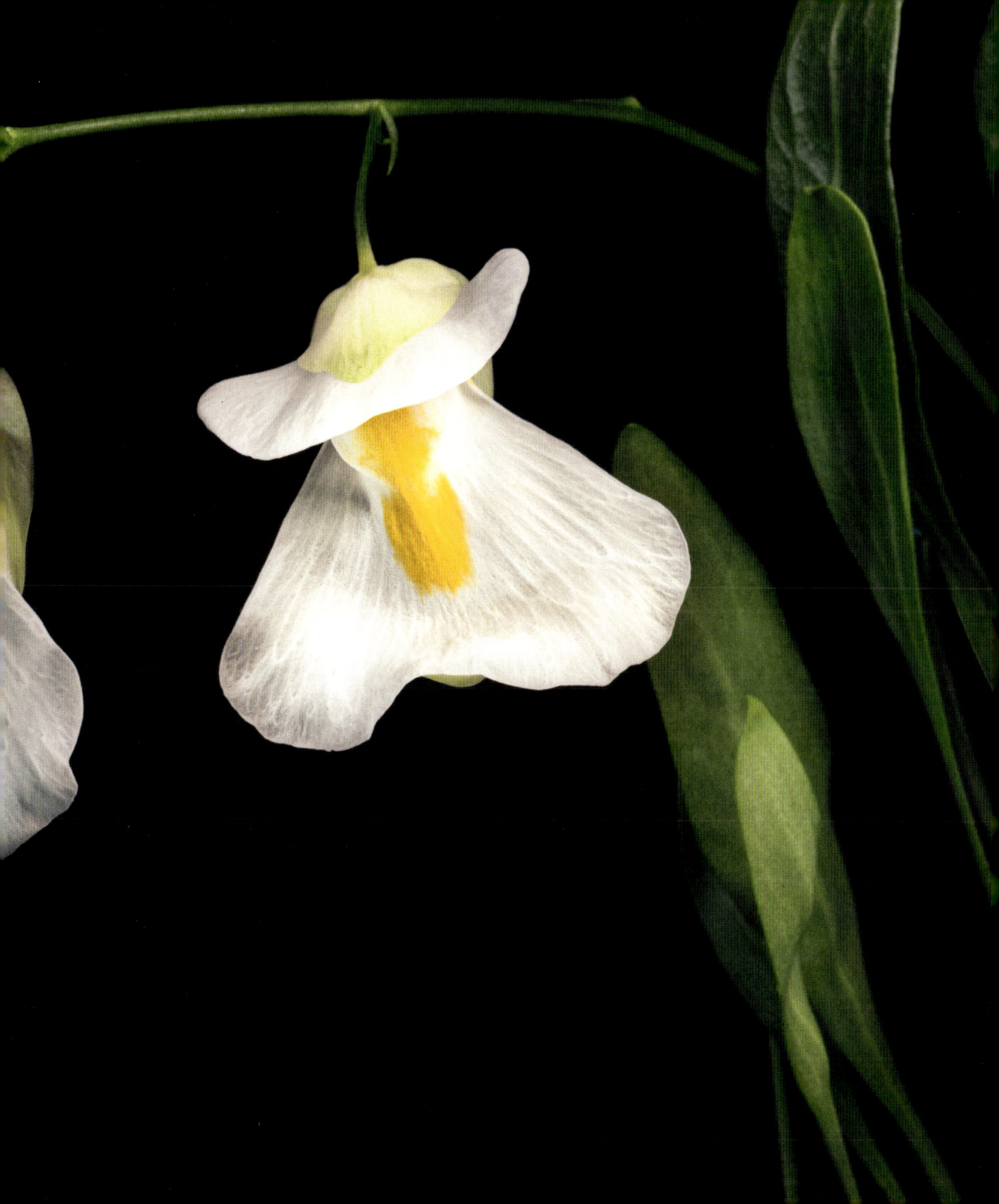

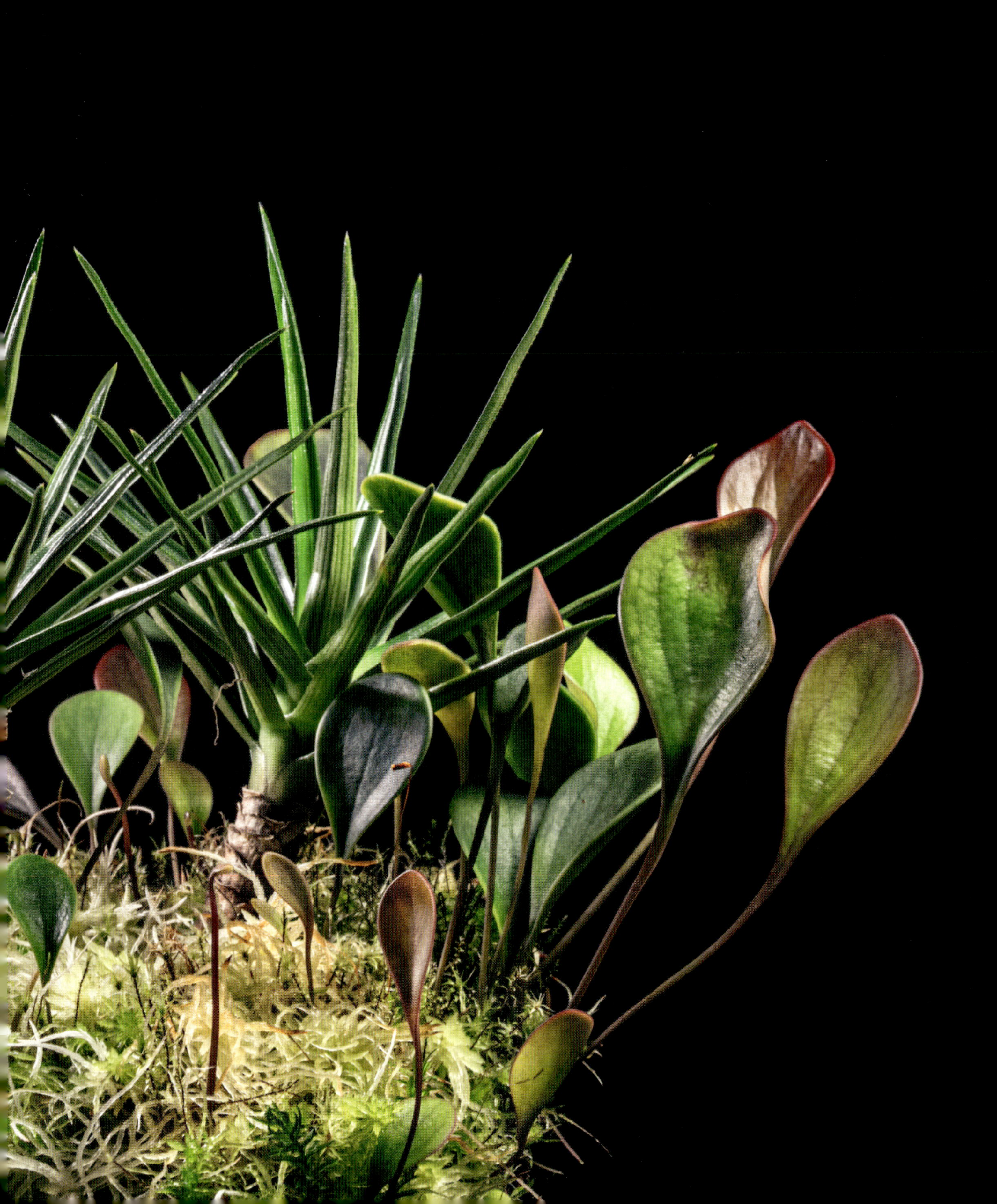

What is this place? I can't decide if it feels more cursed or enchanted. Everything is shrouded in a veil of cold mist, enveloping the surrounding vegetation in a peculiar, mysterious aura. This forest... whispers. It speaks to me through the rustling of leaves stirred by the moist breeze and water dripping from layers of moss all around, like in some ancient, extinct language. And for some reason, it's a language I can understand. It's clearer than anything I've ever heard before. And I think – I know – that it carries more meaning and substance than anything anyone's ever told me.

I scramble my way up the path, stumbling over slippery rocks beneath my feet. I'm surrounded by shapes, forms and colours of the most extraordinary nature. Not a single inch of space is wasted here. Everything is alive, so vividly and furiously alive that I have no words to describe it. Even stones on the ground look as though they were breathing, covered in pillows of dark-green mosses and electric-yellow crusts of lichens. Trees become ladders for clusters of epiphytic bromeliads climbing all the way to the crowns, their tanks providing shelter for curious frogs that stare at me from the surface of their waxy leaves. The forest is filled with fresh, unfurling fern fronds that climb upwards, forming fibrous trunks. On one of them, I spot a clump of blood-red flowers and shiny, oval leaves attached to strange bulbous objects embedded within the fibres. I decide to take a closer look, narrowly avoiding crossing paths with a pit viper. It pauses briefly, looks me dead in the eyes, then continues on its way, crawling underneath a layer of brown, fallen leaves.

My senses are amplified so much that I feel like an overstimulated wild animal thrown into an unknown territory, and experiencing this feels like the most delightful thing imaginable. I'm wet and I'm cold... and never in my life have I felt any better.

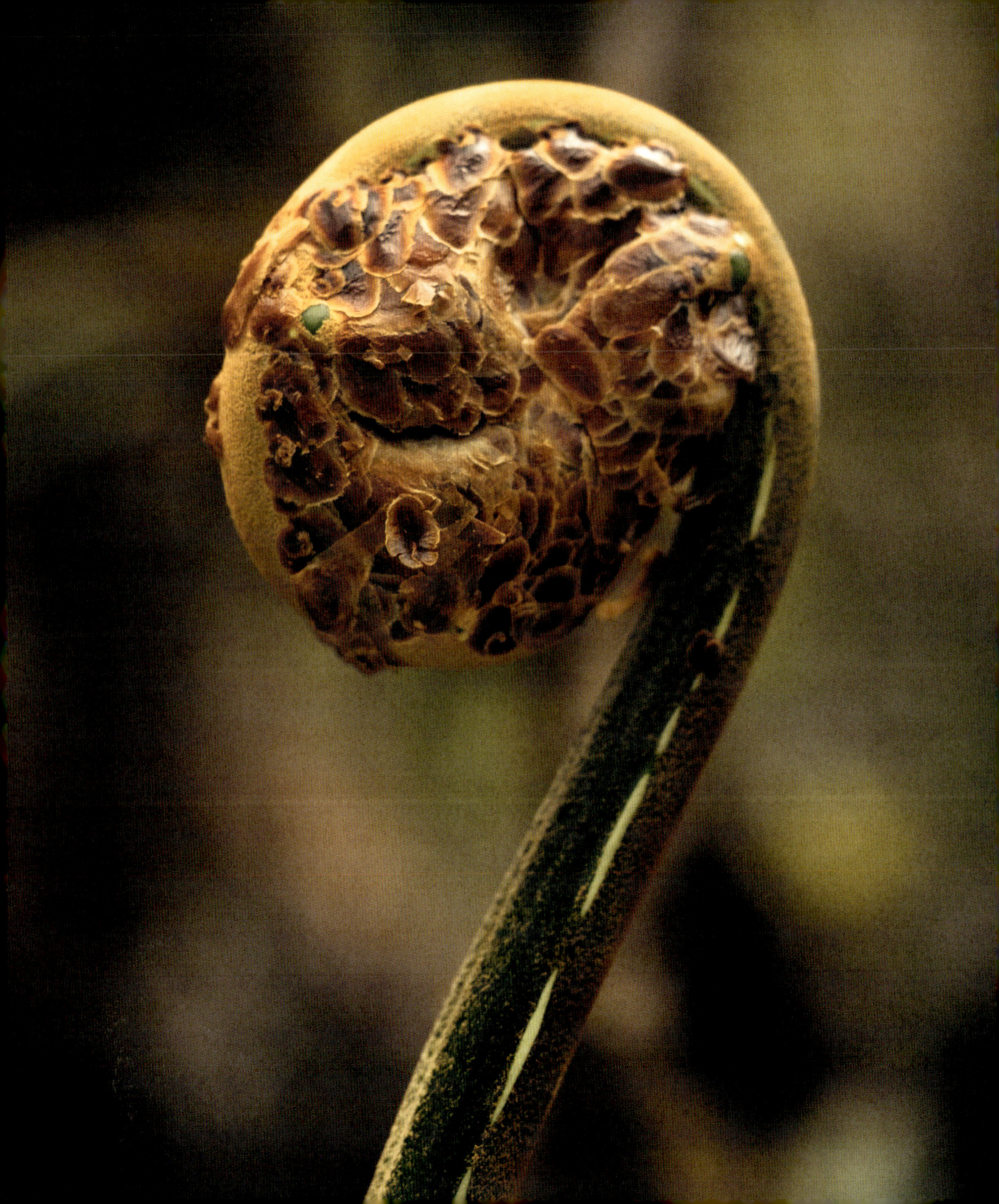

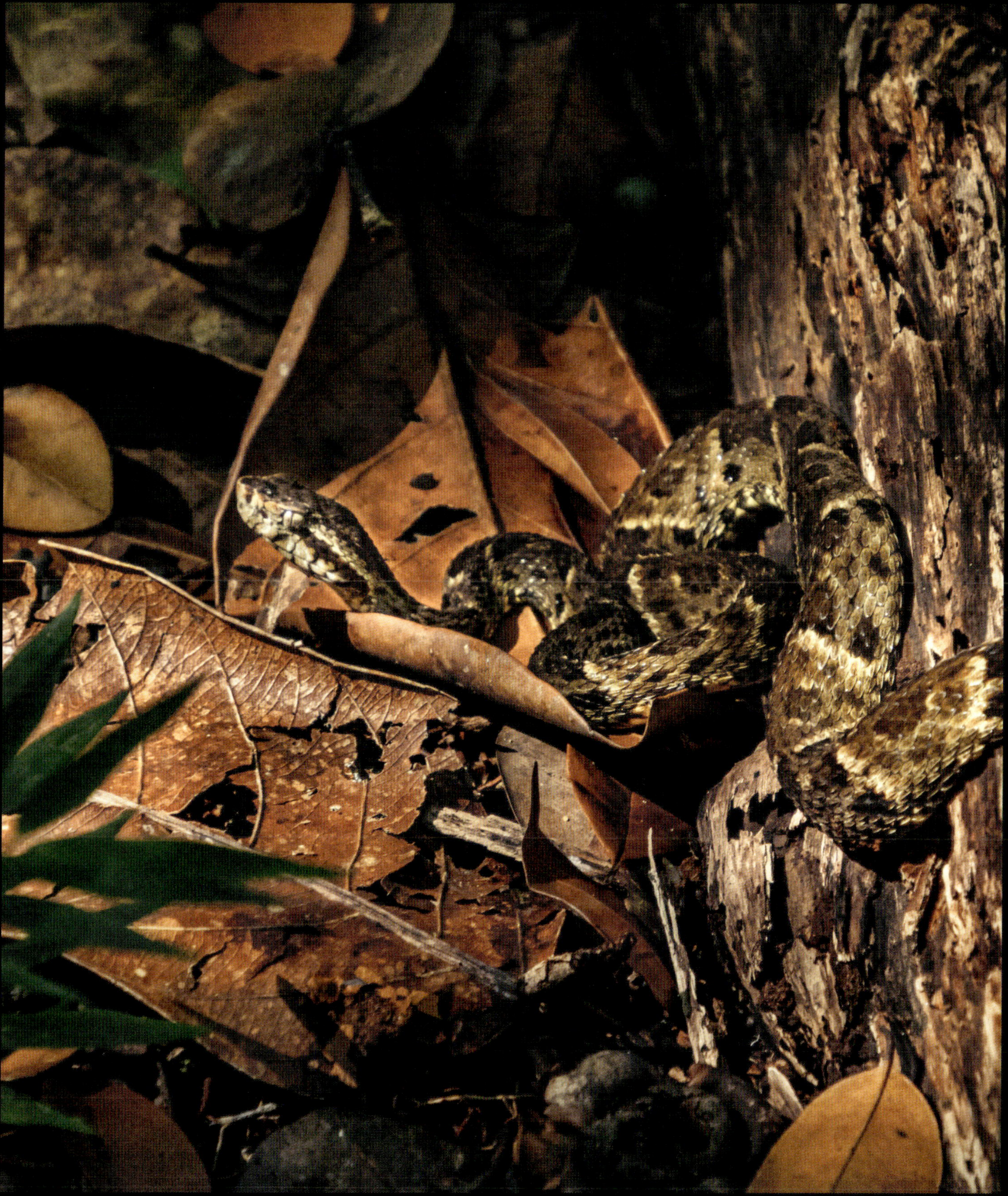

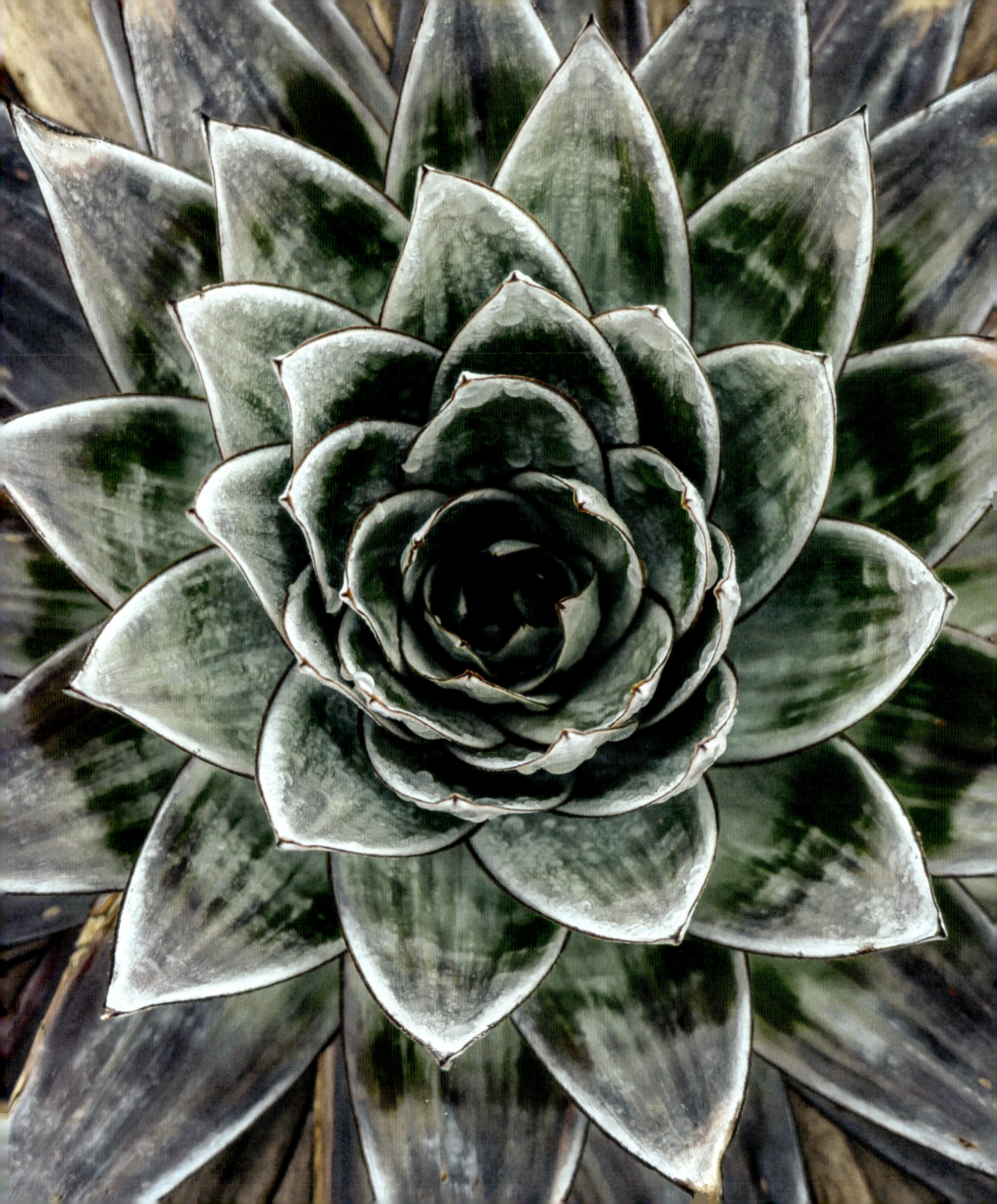

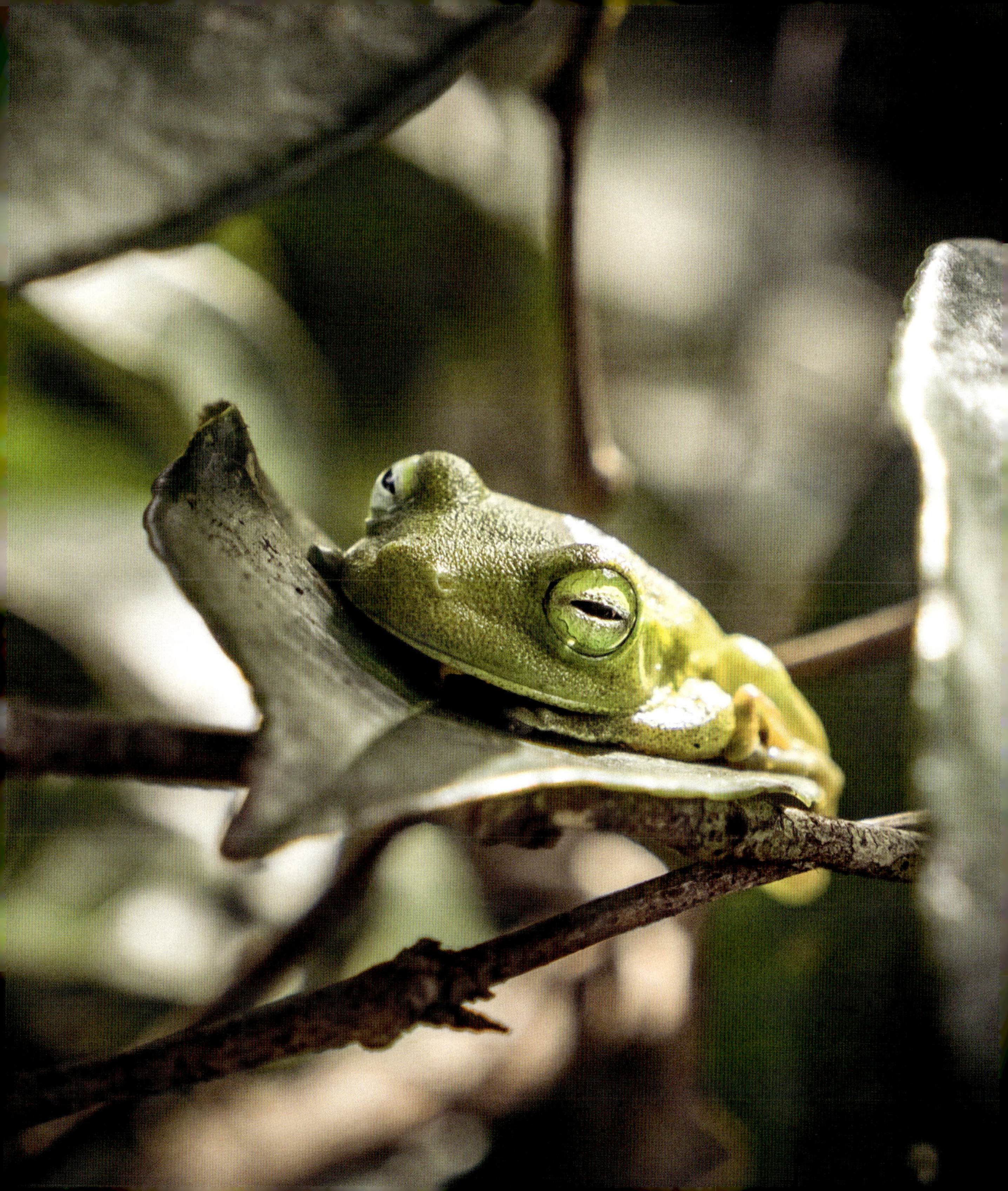

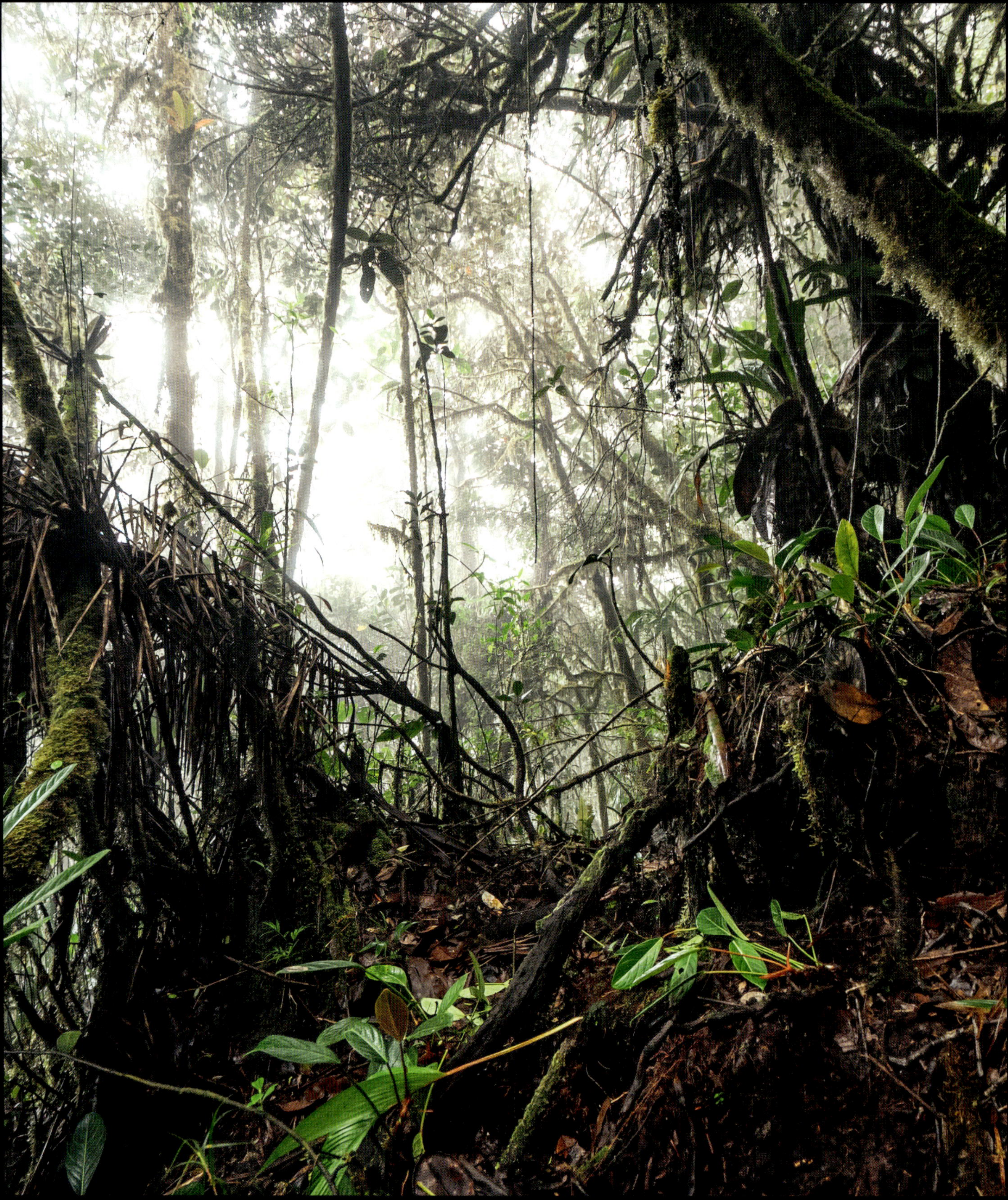

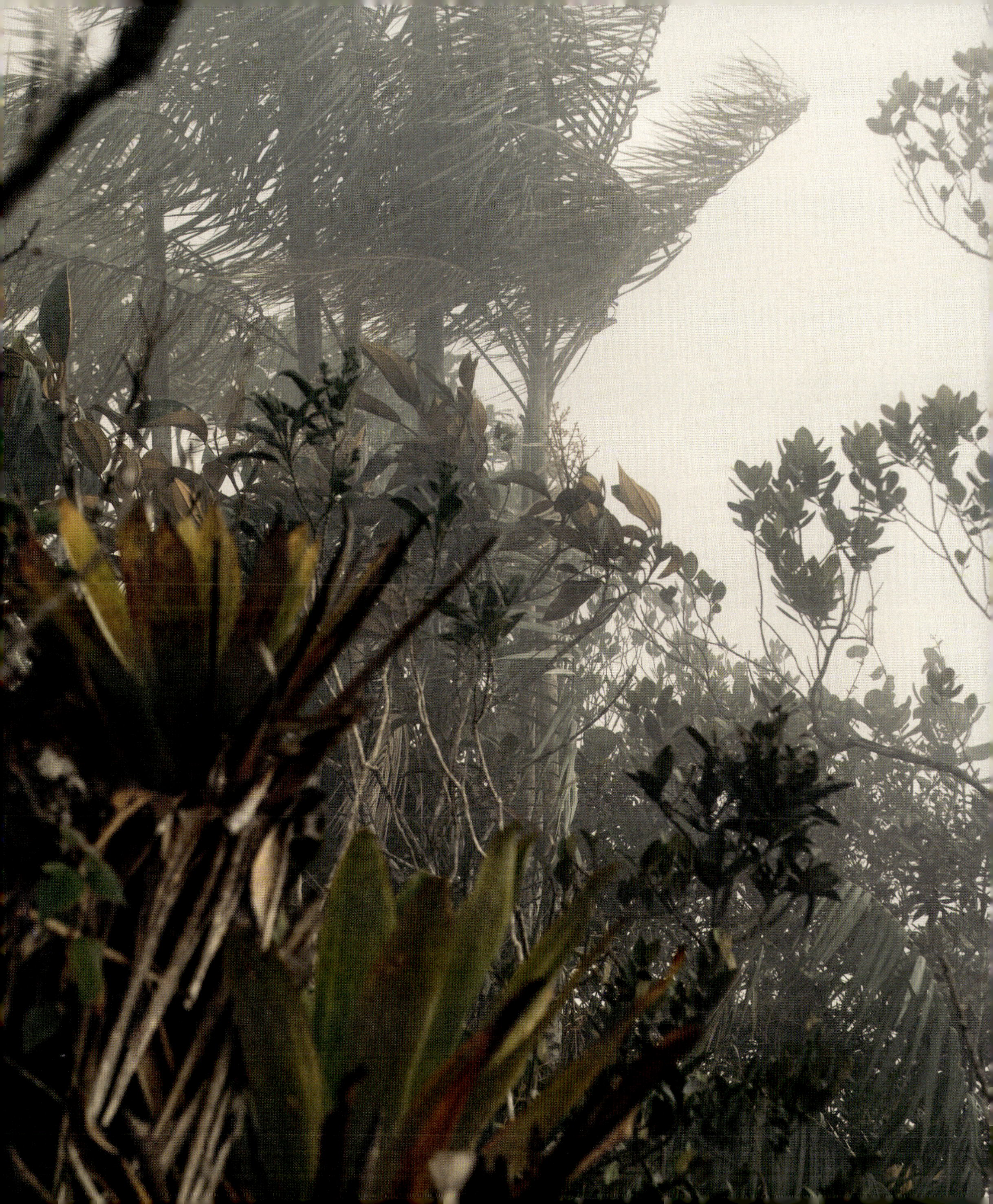

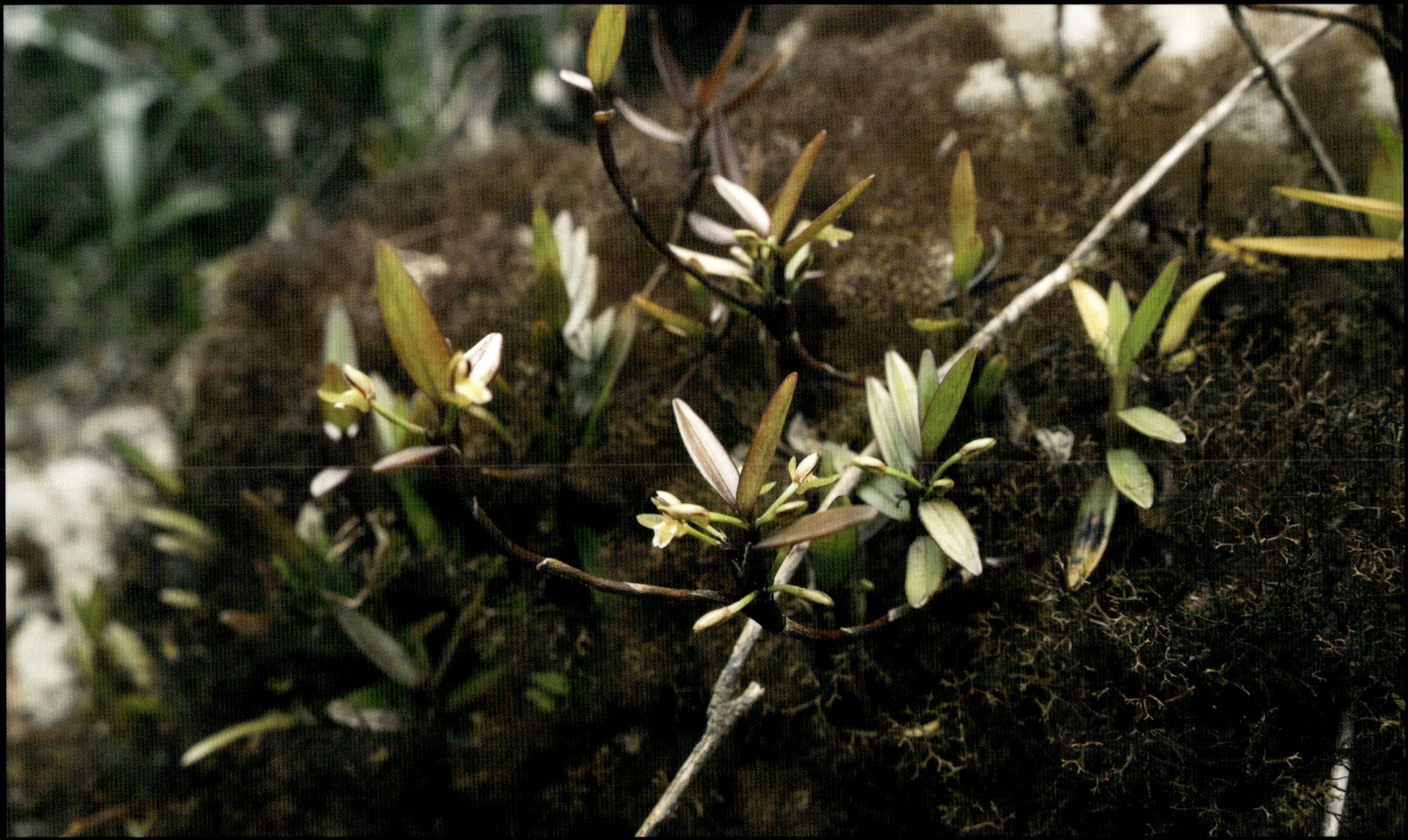

The higher I reach, the more the world around me slips out of my usual frames of perception. It feels almost as if I were entering into some warped and twisted version of reality, where each thing that feels somewhat familiar suddenly takes on a layer of strangeness that I cannot explain even to myself. I'm crossing a narrow ledge, being rained on by a trickle of cold water falling from somewhere above the treetops. On one side, I'm surrounded by exposed sandstone walls, from which protrude plumes of dark-green, sabre-shaped leaves, with bright yellow strands of roots falling down the wall. The roots are coated in some strange slime, growing ever thicker on the way down and dangling from the tips like shiny icicles. The slime covers everything around – the rocks, the trunks of the trees, and now also my clothes.

At the end of the ledge, I finally spot a clearing in the canopy. As I move past the last crests of palm leaves, I look up and see a gigantic rock wall with a jagged surface, stained a rusty hue. It shoots straight into the sky and disappears into the clouds somewhere far above. I have so many questions… and the answers appear to be waiting for me right up there.

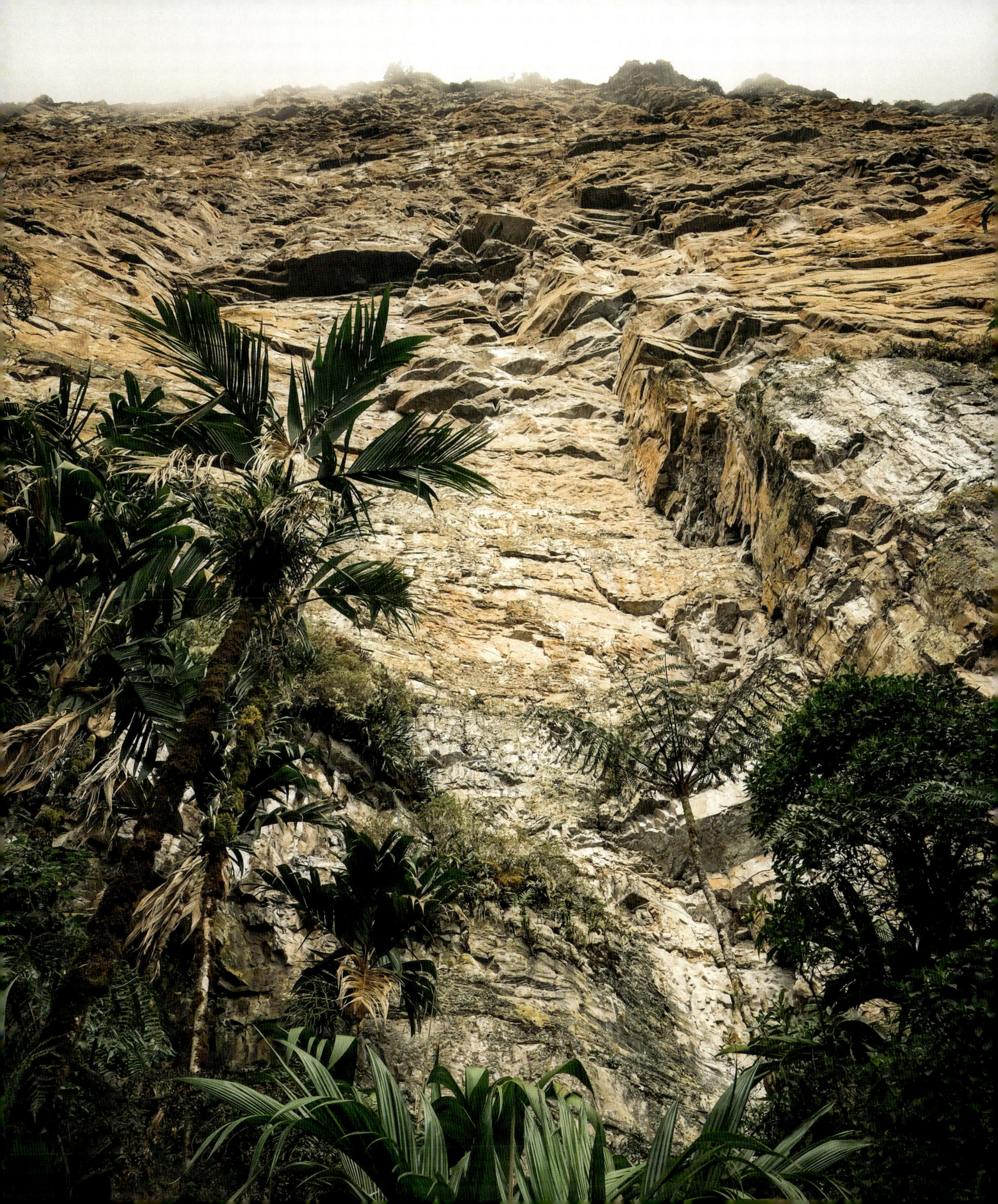

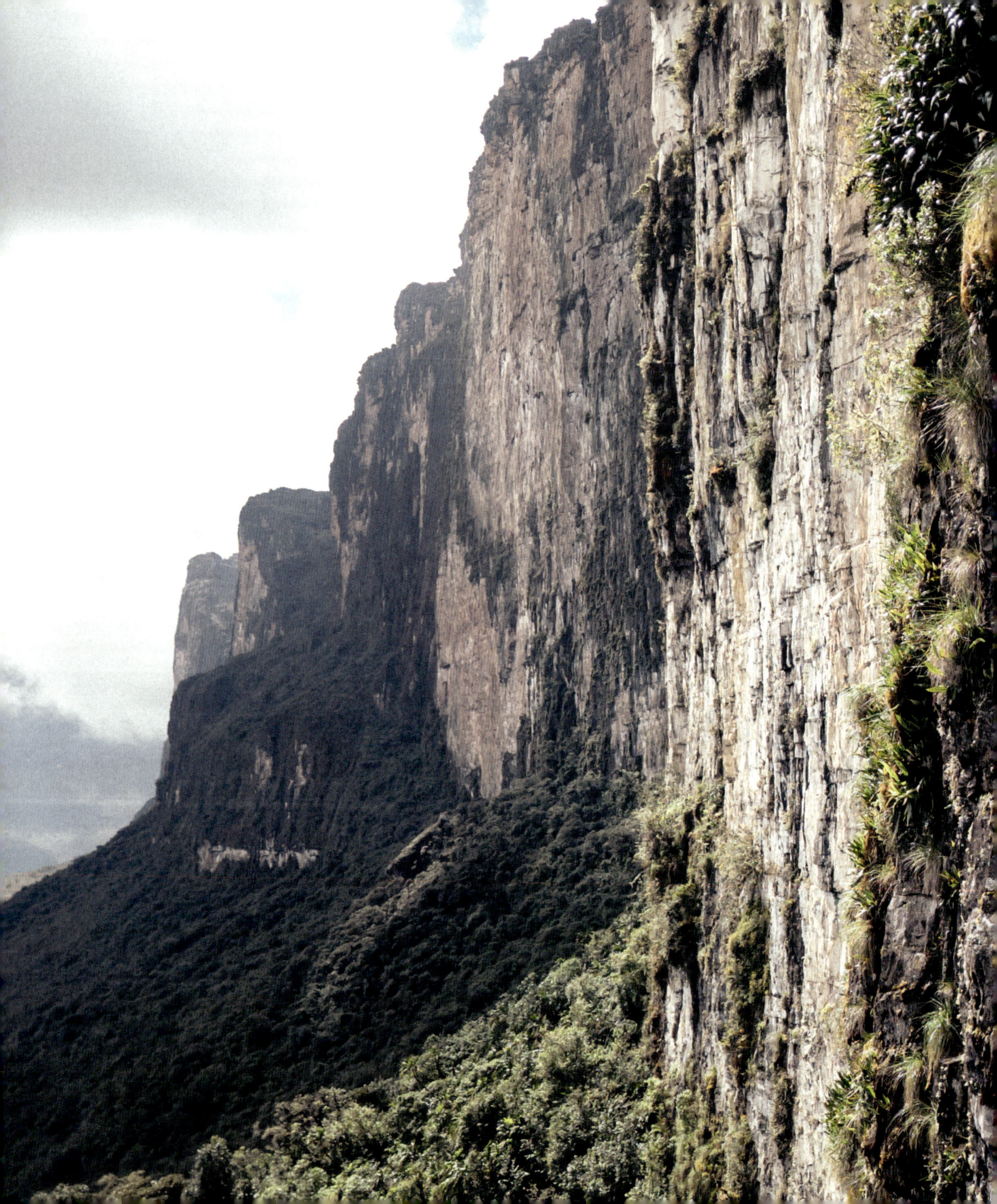

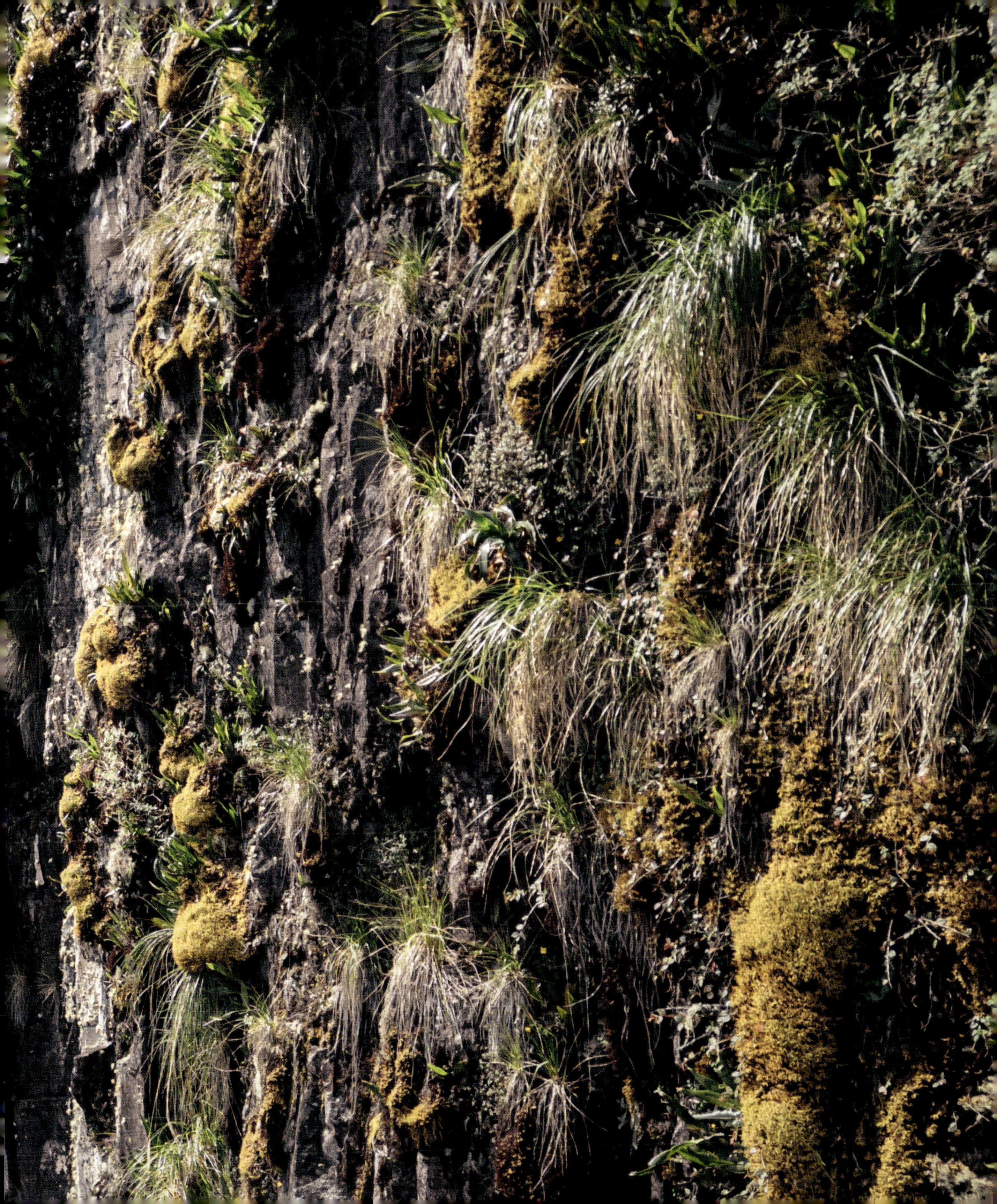

CHAPTER 5
Otherworlds

"Then the step was taken – and we saw surely as strange a sight, regarded simply as a product of nature, as may be seen in this world; nay, it would probably not be rash to assert that very few sights even as strange can be seen. The first impression was of inability mentally to grasp such surroundings; the next that one was entering on some strange country of nightmares for which an appropriate and wildly fantastic landscape had been formed, some dreadful and stormy day, when, in their mid career, the broken and chaotic clouds had been stiffened in a single instant into stone."

Everard im Thurn – *The Ascent of Mount Roraima*, 1885

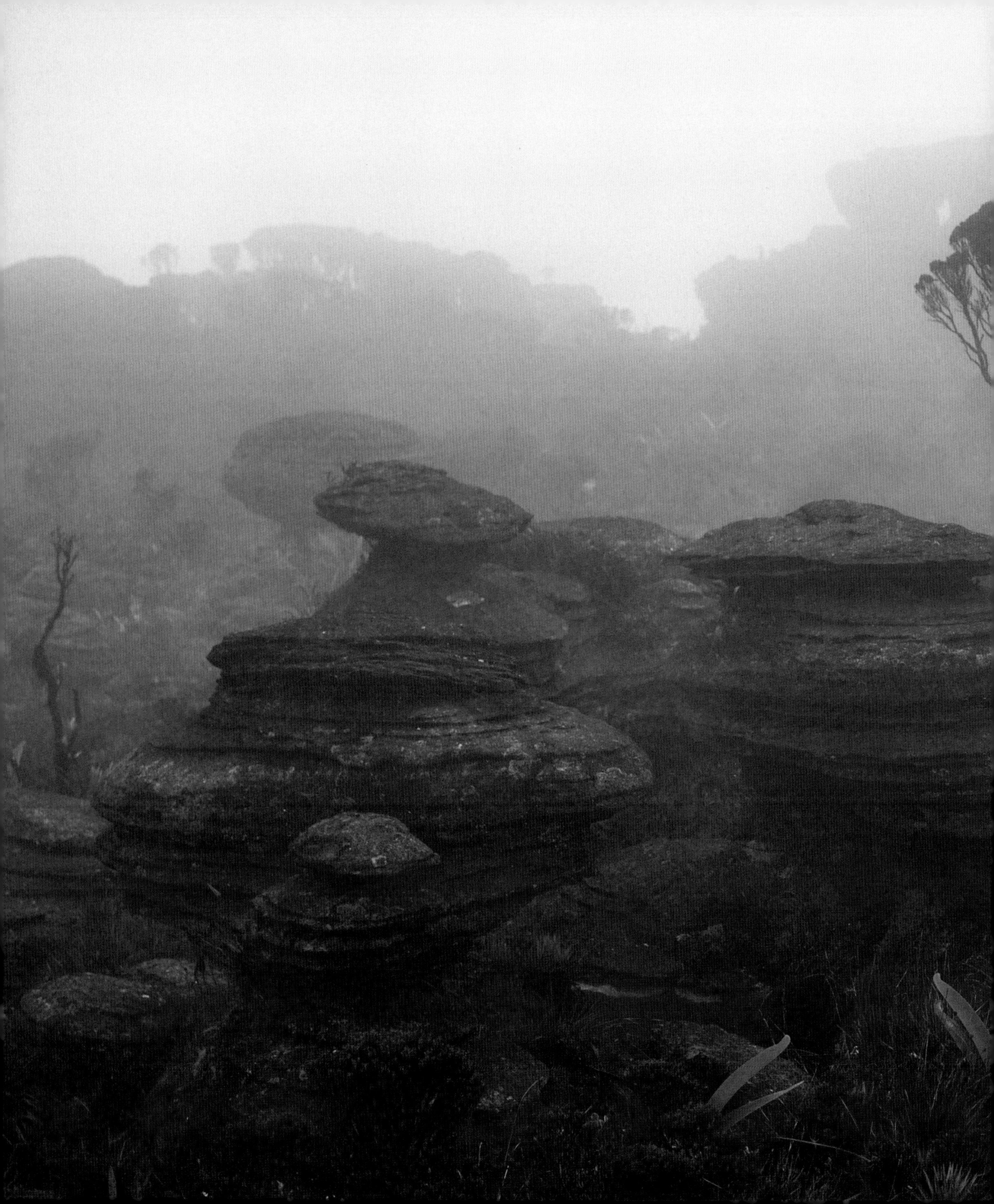

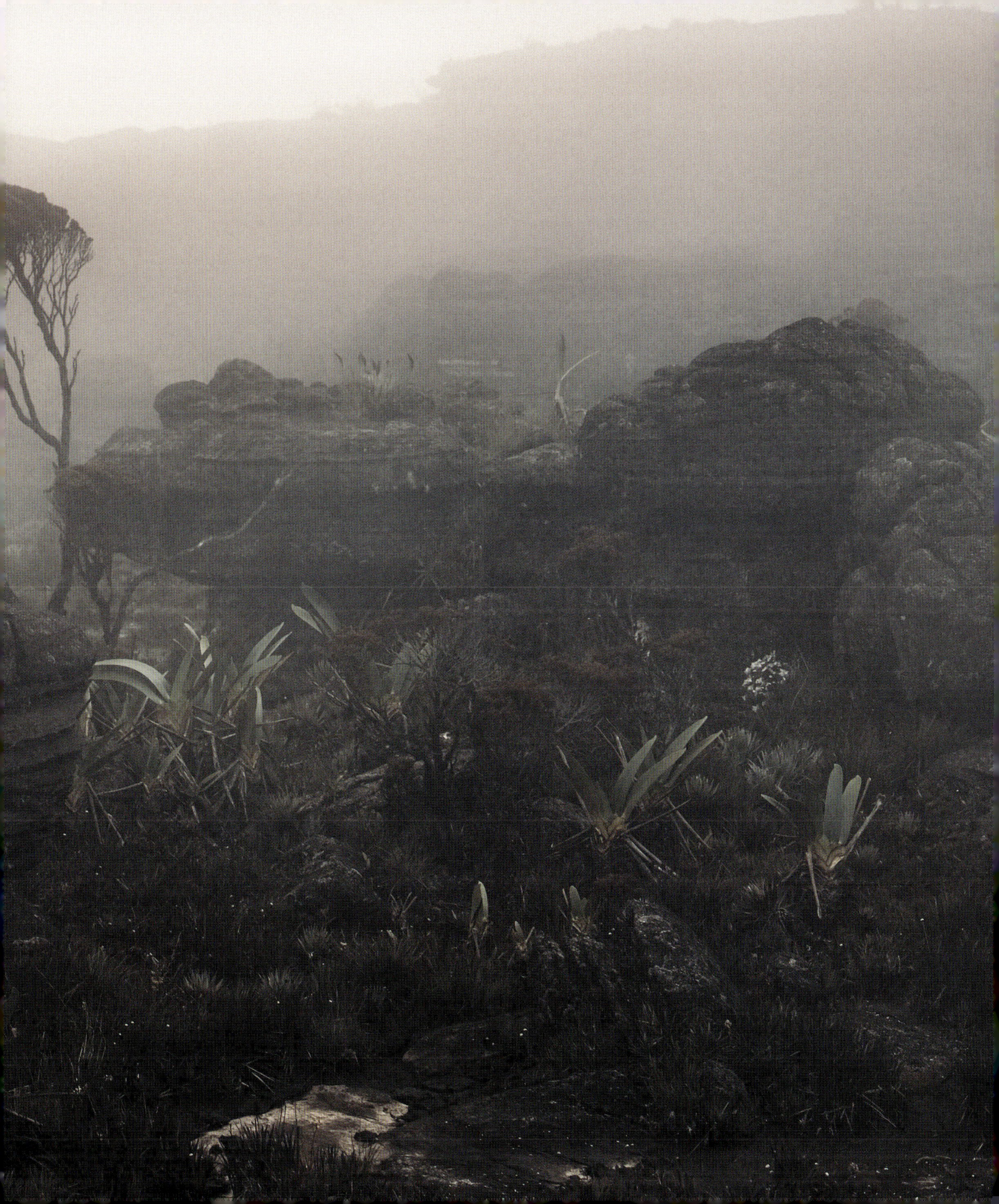

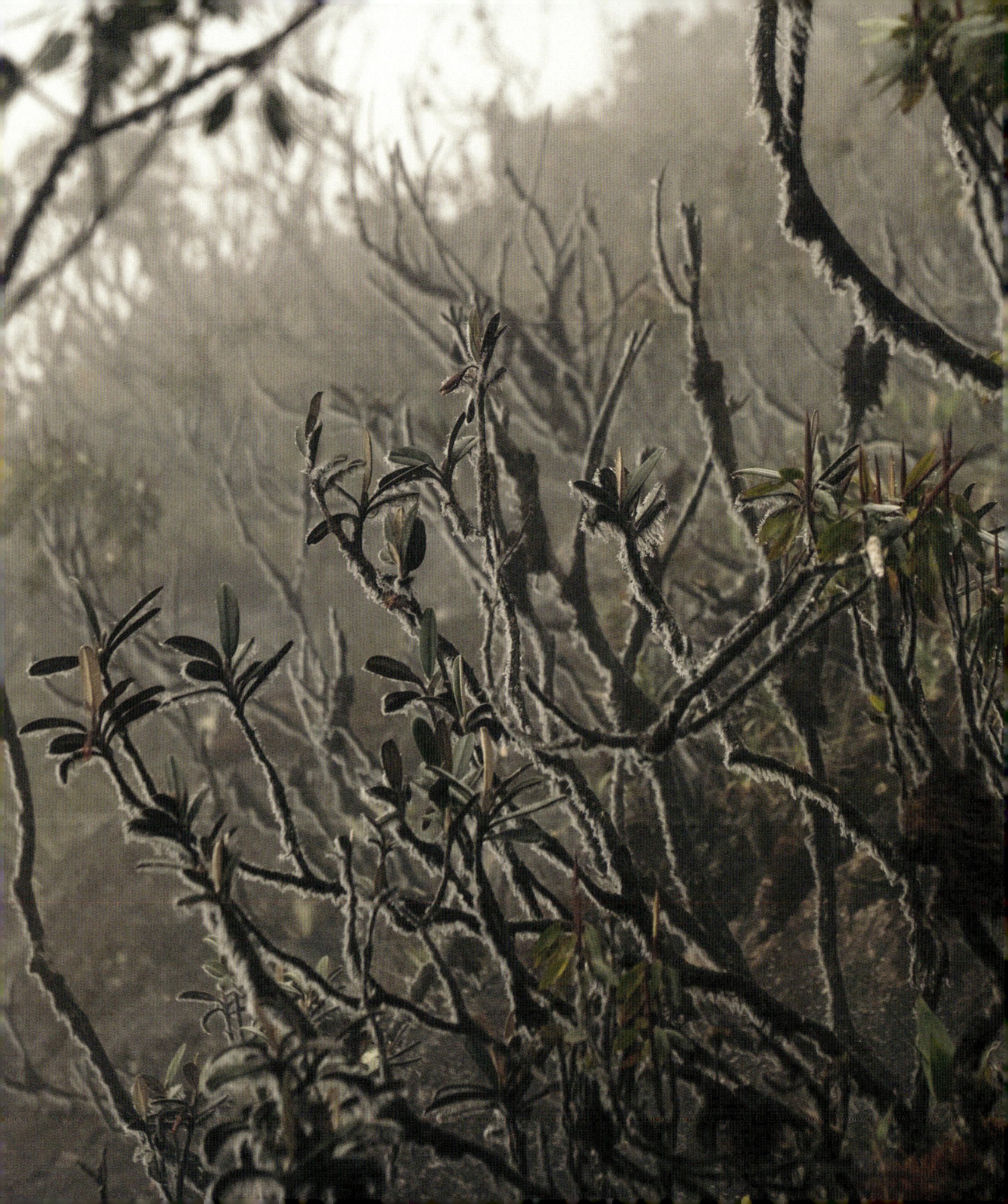

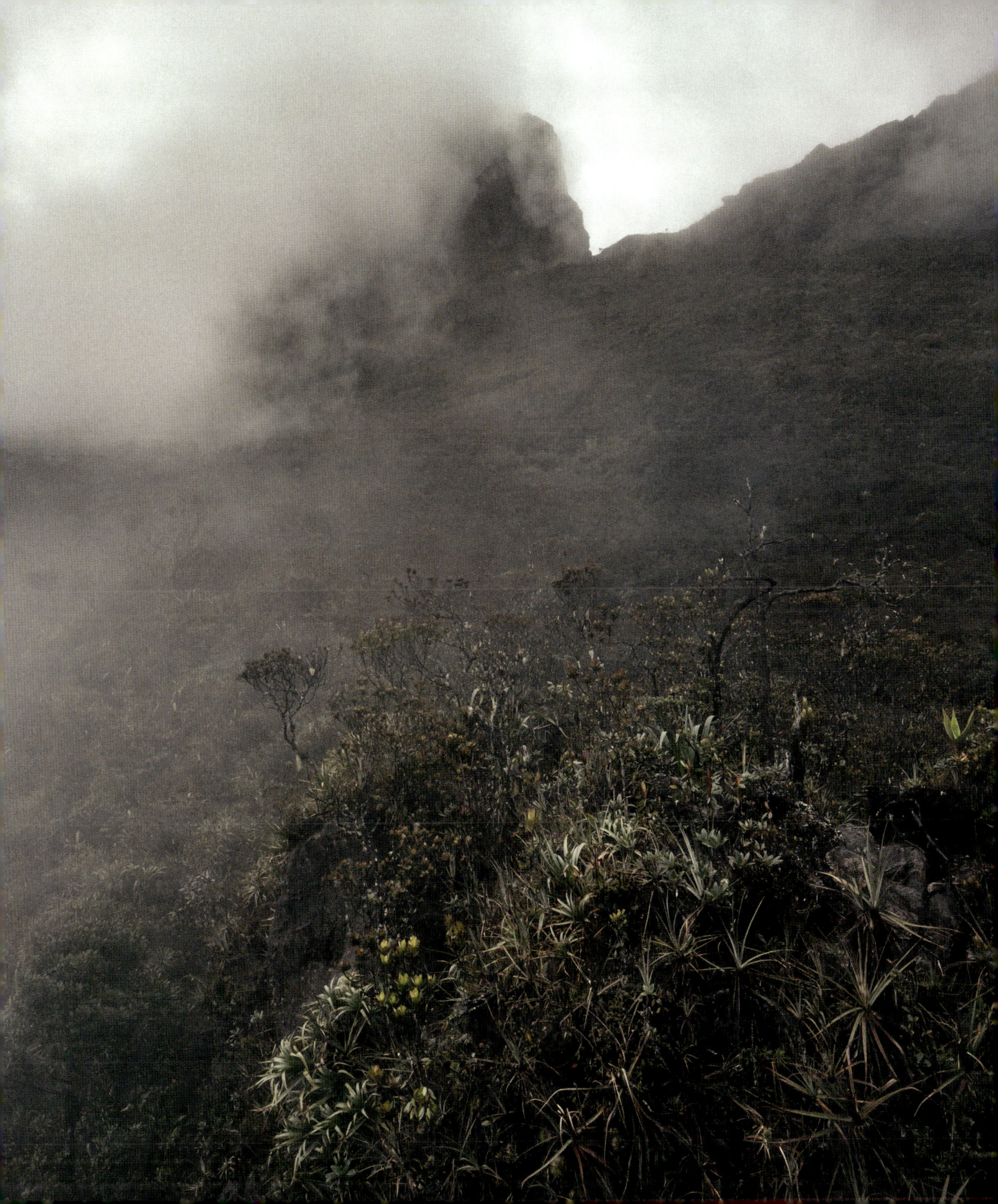

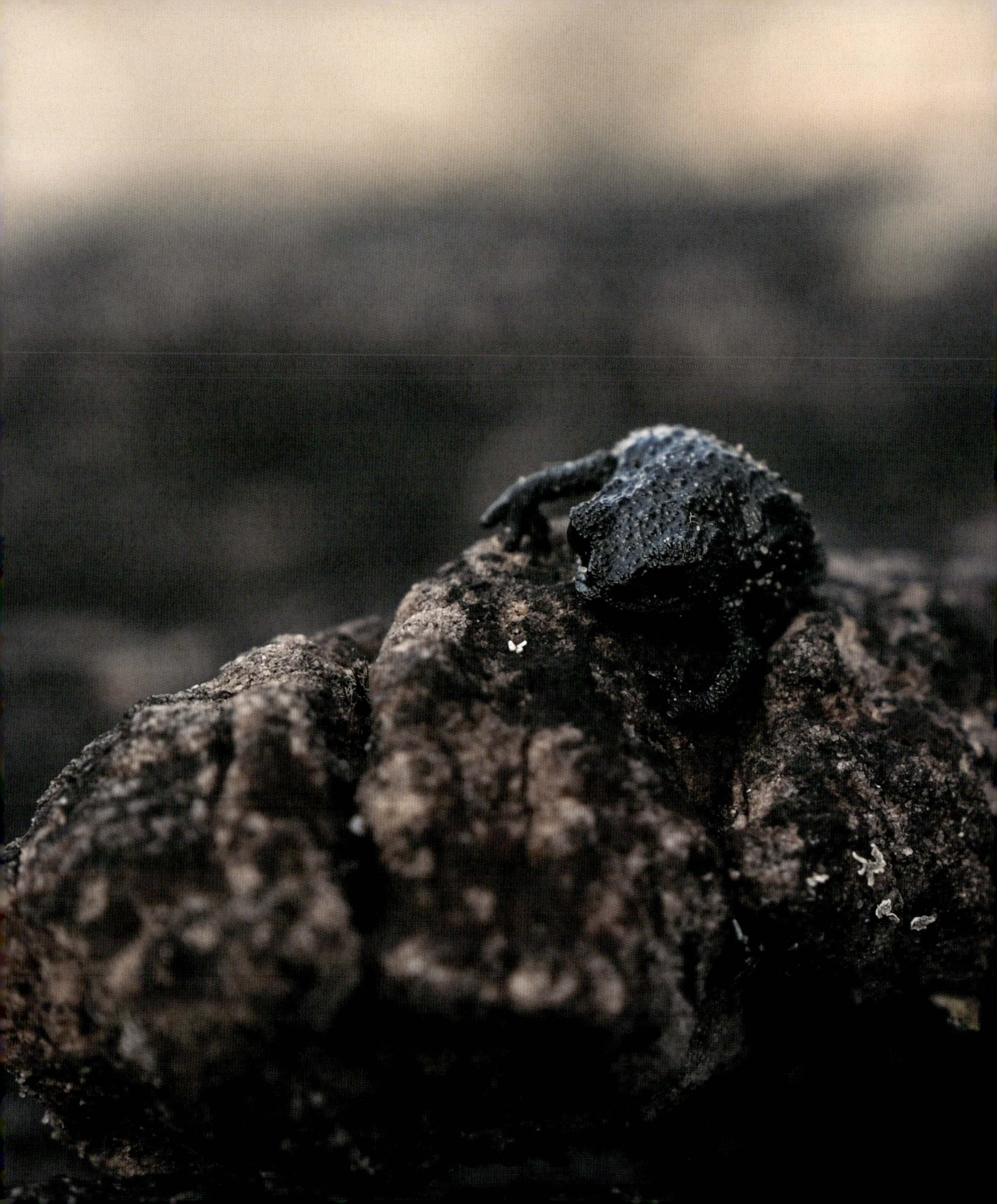

I move past the final stretch of the slime forest and enter an exposed shelf covered in short, twisted shrubs. With every step I take, I hear a crunch of quartz pebbles grinding against the coarse surface of wet sandstone. The trail is becoming more and more narrow, until it finally disappears behind a bend that curves around a large boulder. I decide to take a break to catch my breath, sheltering from the drizzle under a rock overhang covered in... something. I think they are ferns. Although, with their strange, spoon-like shape, they remind me more of some alien organism that doesn't really belong in this world. My body starts to tremble, but it doesn't bother me – my thoughts are consumed by what awaits me at the top of the cliff. It must be nearby, though I can't see it, being engulfed in the never-ending fog.

Finally, I get to my feet, walk around the boulder and the trail flattens out. Then... in an instant, everything around me becomes saturated with absolute silence. The slightest of sounds fade away, the gusts of cool wind disappear, raindrops seem to fall onto the leaves and rocks without making even a hint of noise. Even the birds have gone completely silent. I can hear nothing but my own frantic breathing and the beating of my heart.

I notice a small clearing in the fog ahead. As I walk closer to it, I realise that I'm standing on the edge of a gigantic precipice. Below me, stretching in the far distance, lies an ocean of golden hills, marked in places by streaks of low-hanging rain clouds and rainbows. I feel as though I'm peering through a portal into another world. I don't know how much time passes, but the window finally closes, enveloping me once again in the embrace of the cold mists. Tears begin to fall from my eyes as my mind goes into a frenzy, unable to grasp what really is happening. In this overload of confusing feelings, there is only one thing that somehow feels natural and obvious. I was supposed to come here. Something... or someone... made me come here.

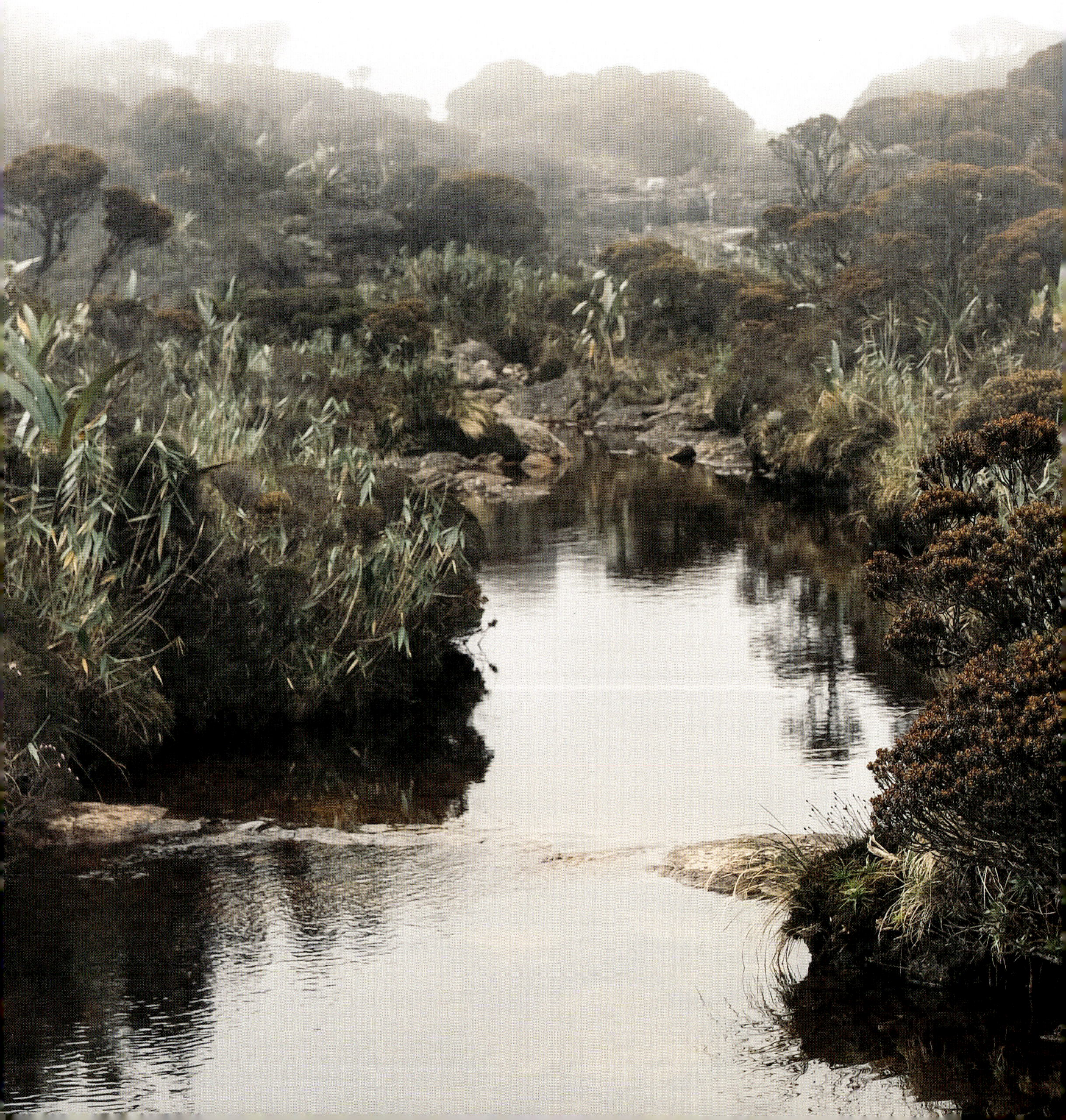

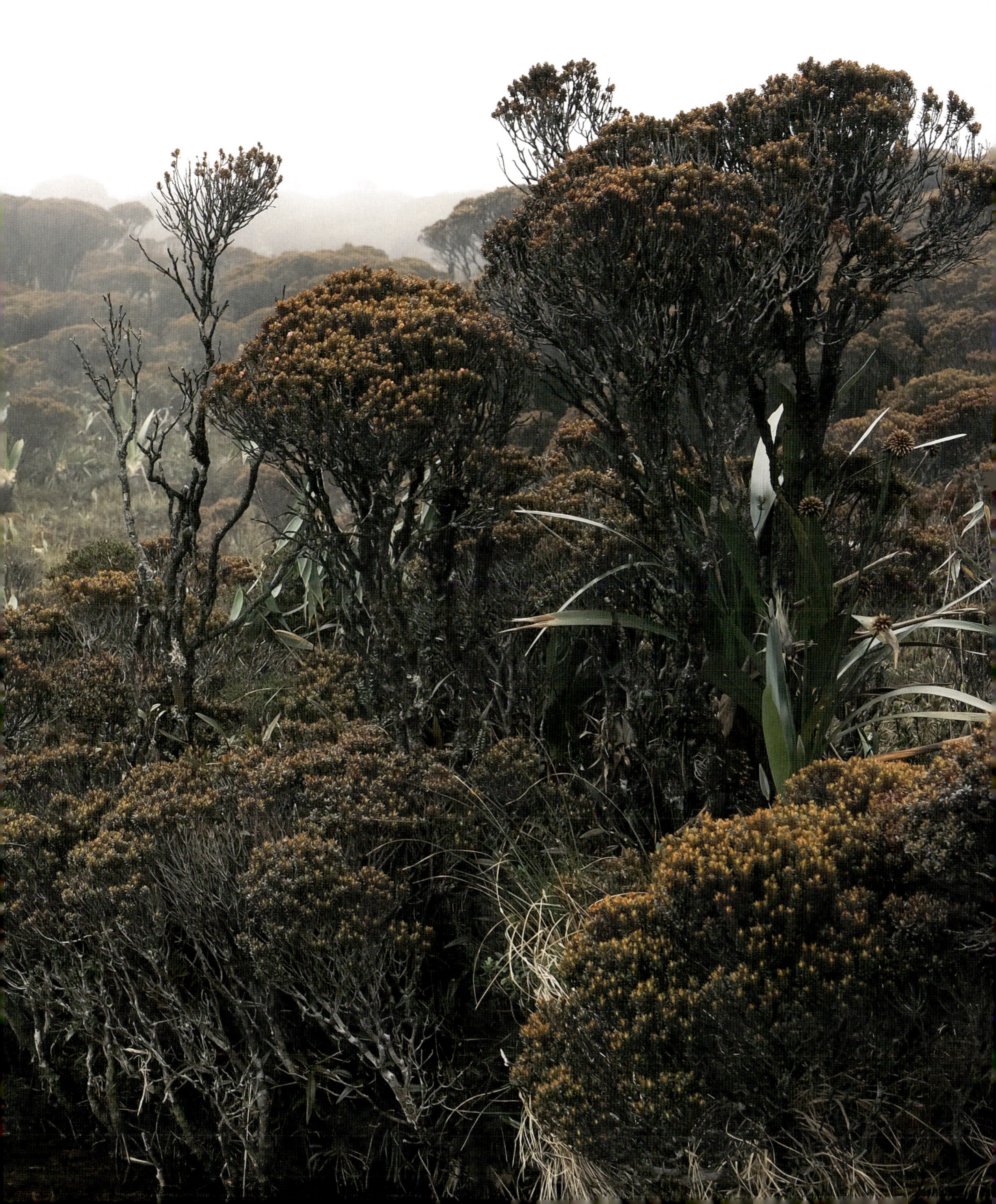

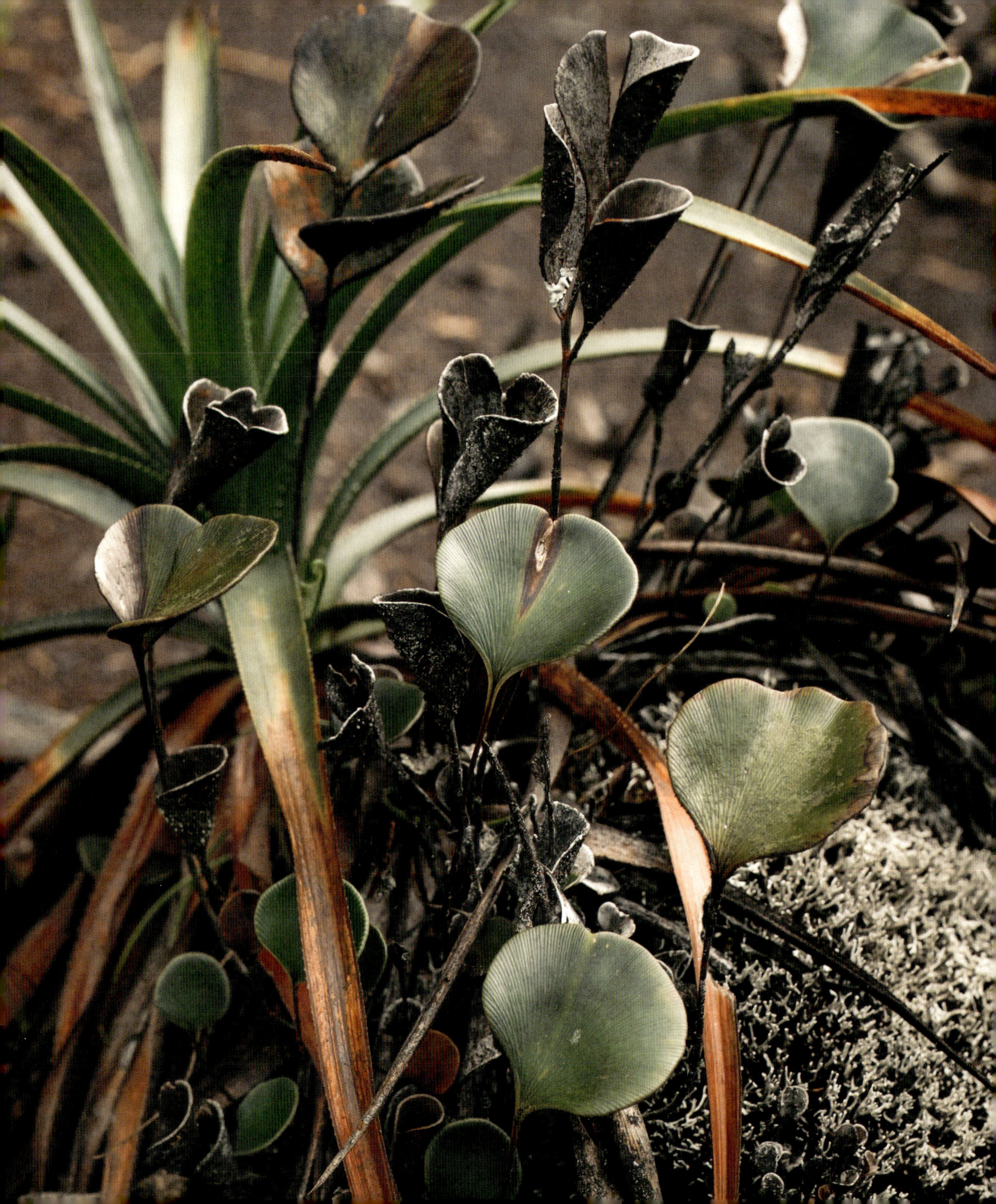

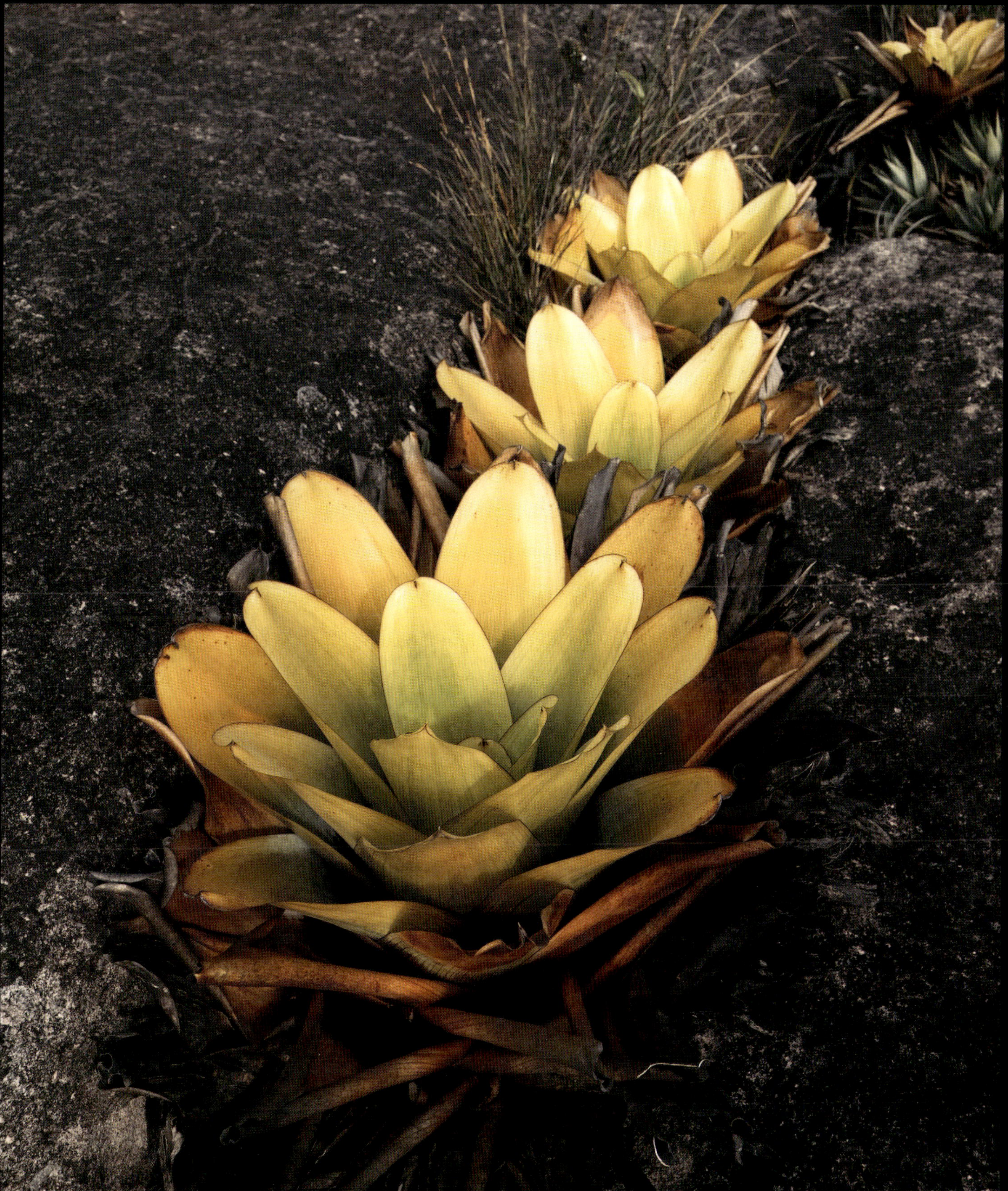

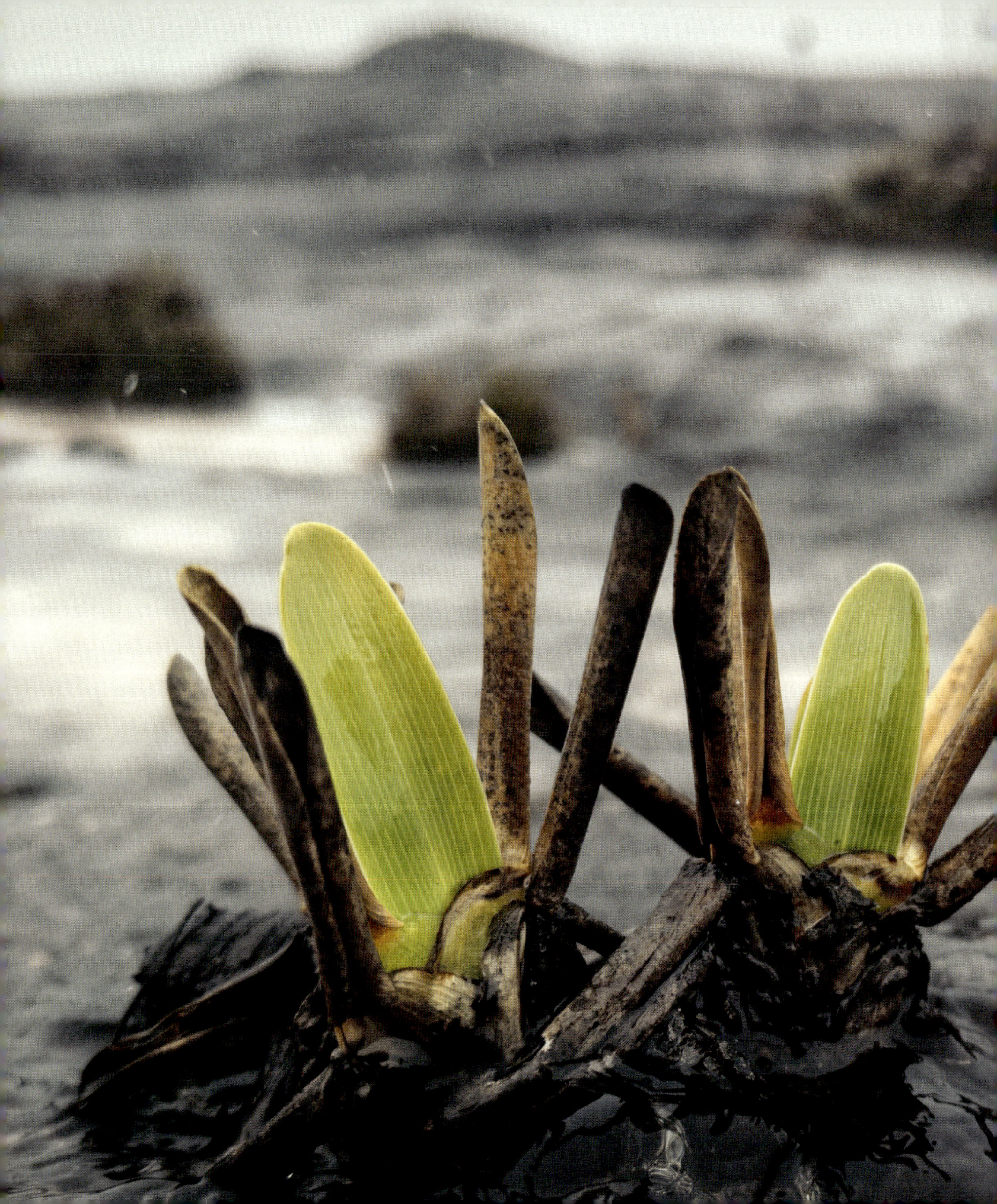

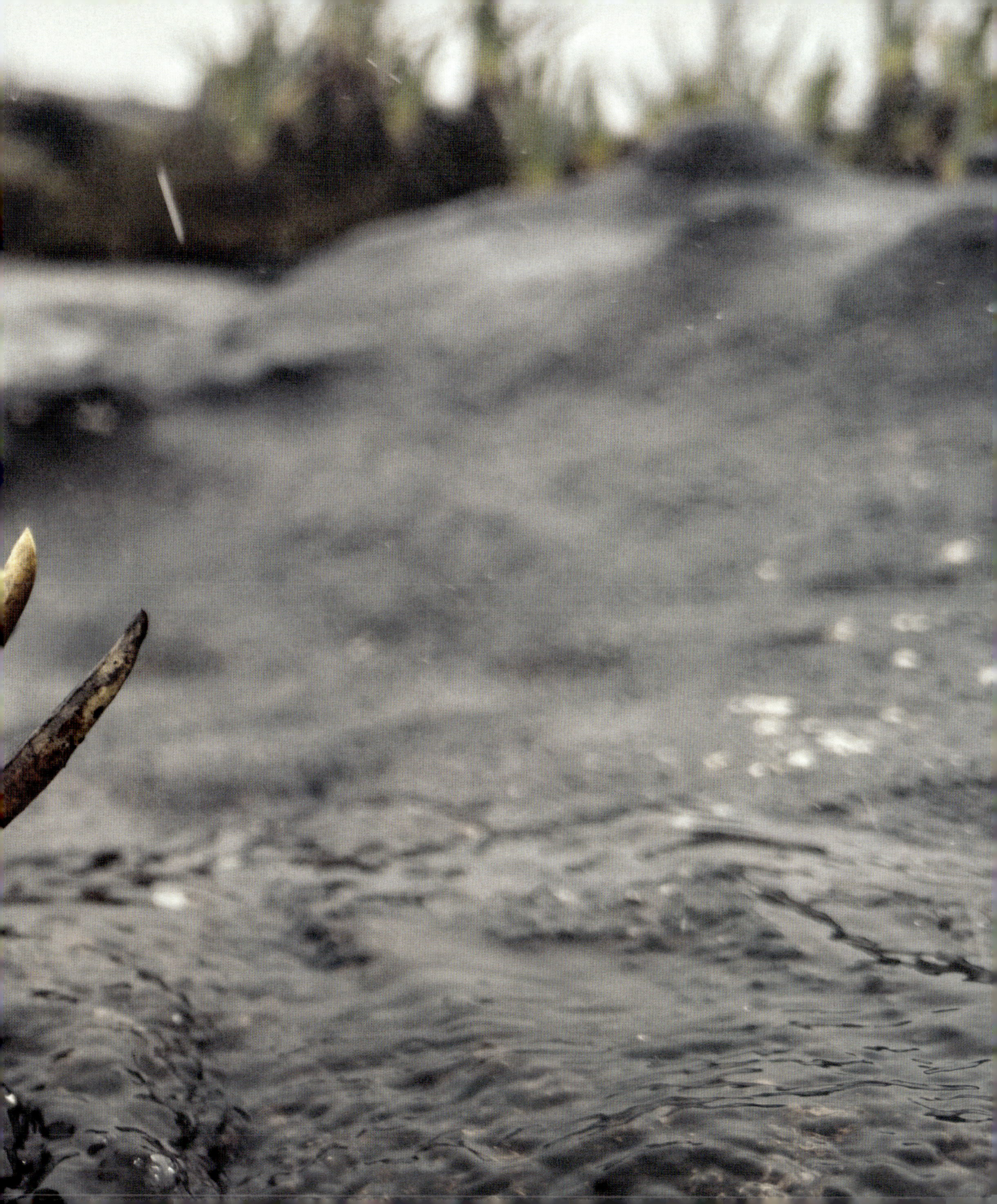

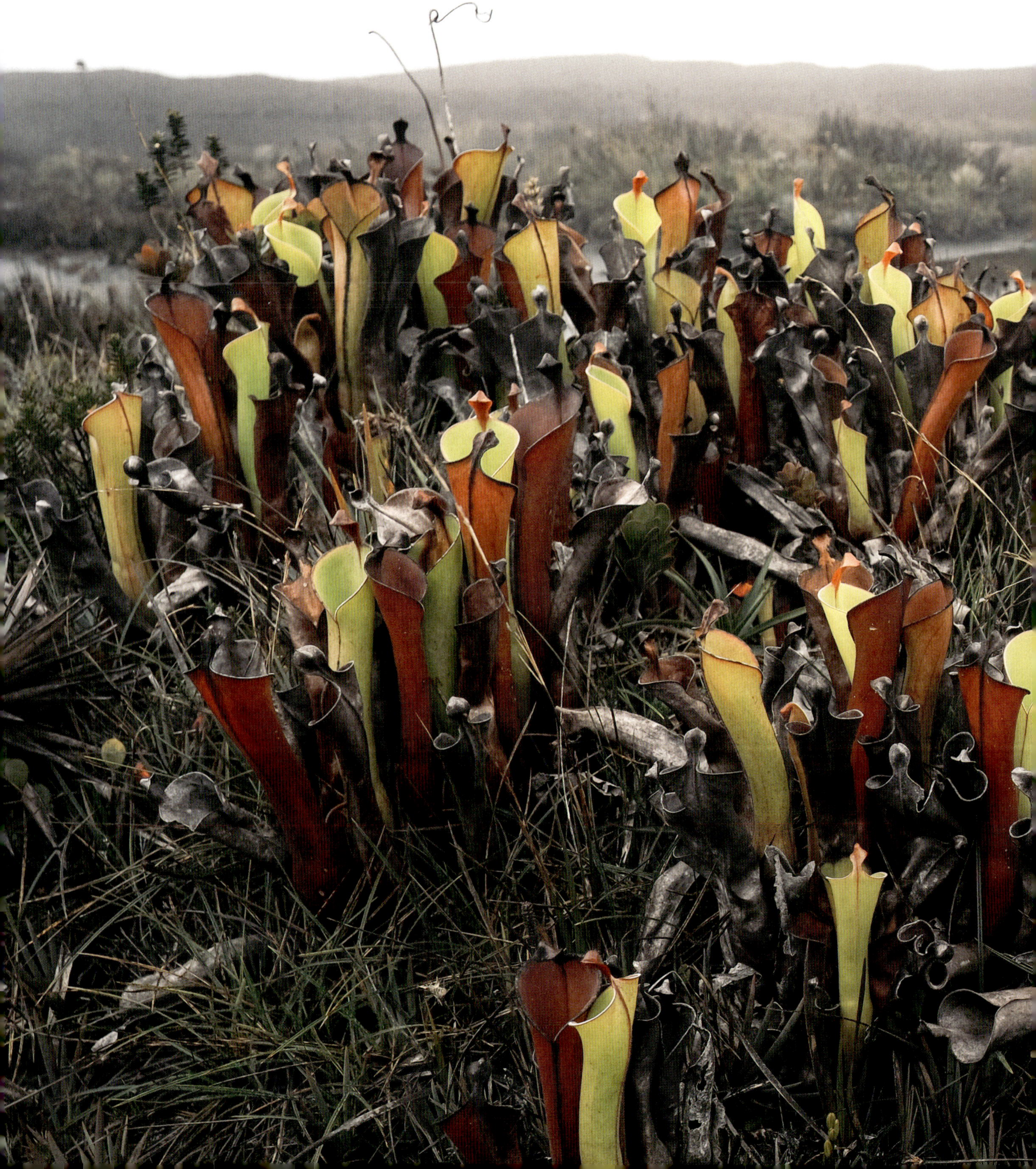

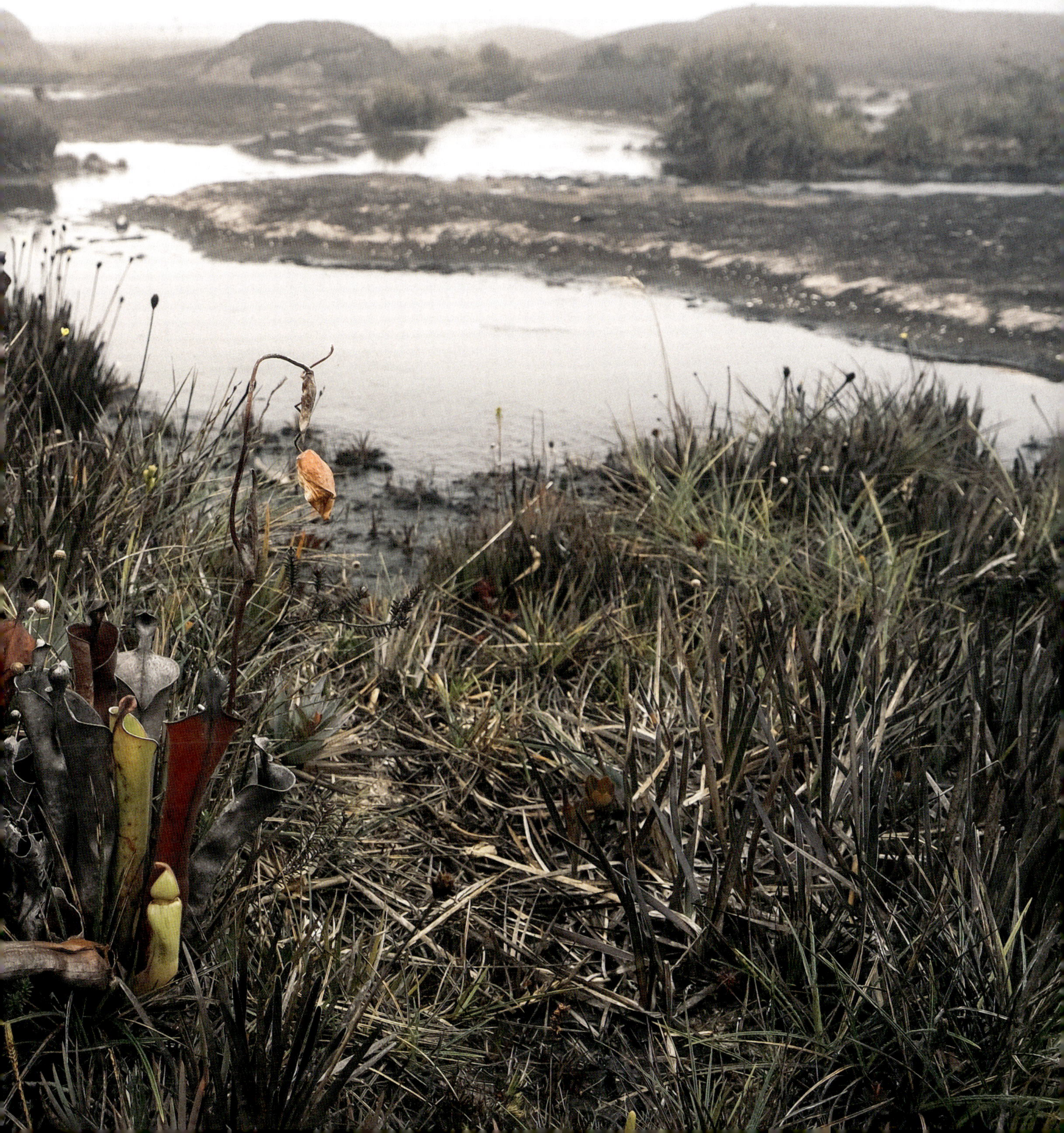

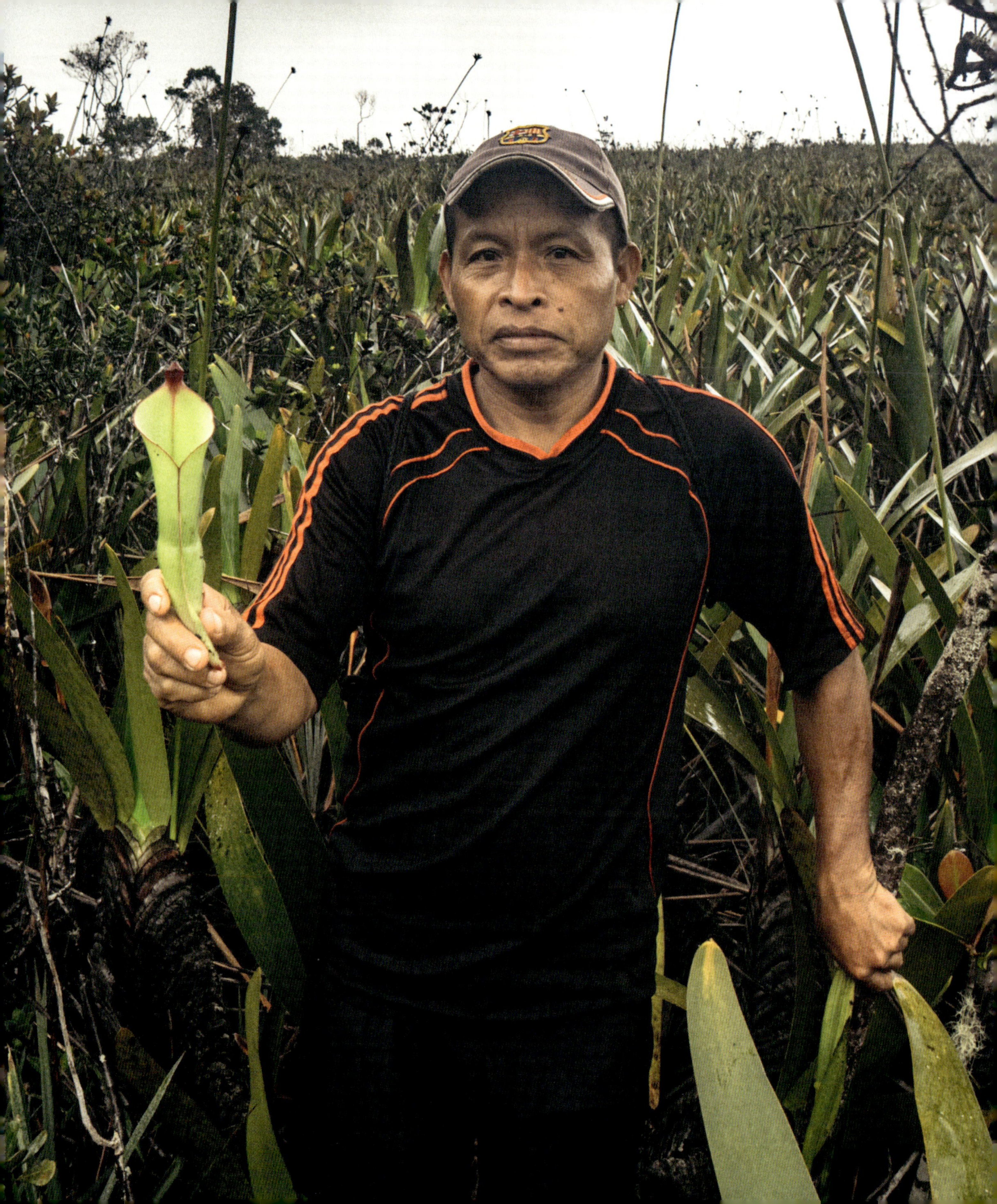

I'm wandering through something that feels more like a hallucination than a real place. My mind struggles to process the overflow of contradictory feelings, keeping me in a state of dissociation, faced with a reality so far outside of anything I'd ever known that no previous experience can give me any anchor to make sense of what unfolds before my eyes.

The plateau is a labyrinth of rocks sculpted into fantastic shapes tinted a grim grey and a dark, rusty red. Through its surface run veins of fine, perfectly white sand, forming a network of narrow pathways, allowing me to navigate through the murky limbo. There appears to be no such thing as pleasant conditions here. It is bone-chilling cold in the impenetrable mists and in the occasional, passing drizzles. But when the sun comes out from behind the layer of clouds, it immediately sends down violent blows of scorching heat. None of this really matters to me though, as the sole fact of being in this strange realm is the most infatuating thing I've ever felt.

Words lose any meaning when I try to describe what surrounds me. Life finds a way in this seemingly barren land. Everything looks ancient; every single living thing, and even the rock itself, appears to possess some kind of primeval sentience and wisdom which elevates it to a higher form of existence. I continue on the path, walking past the succulent blood-red fronds of dwarf ferns, patches of meadows filled with neon-green pitcher plants, and twisted shrub branches entangled in eerie strings of fine fungal webs. Clouds roll over the landscape, continuously revealing another wonder to behold.

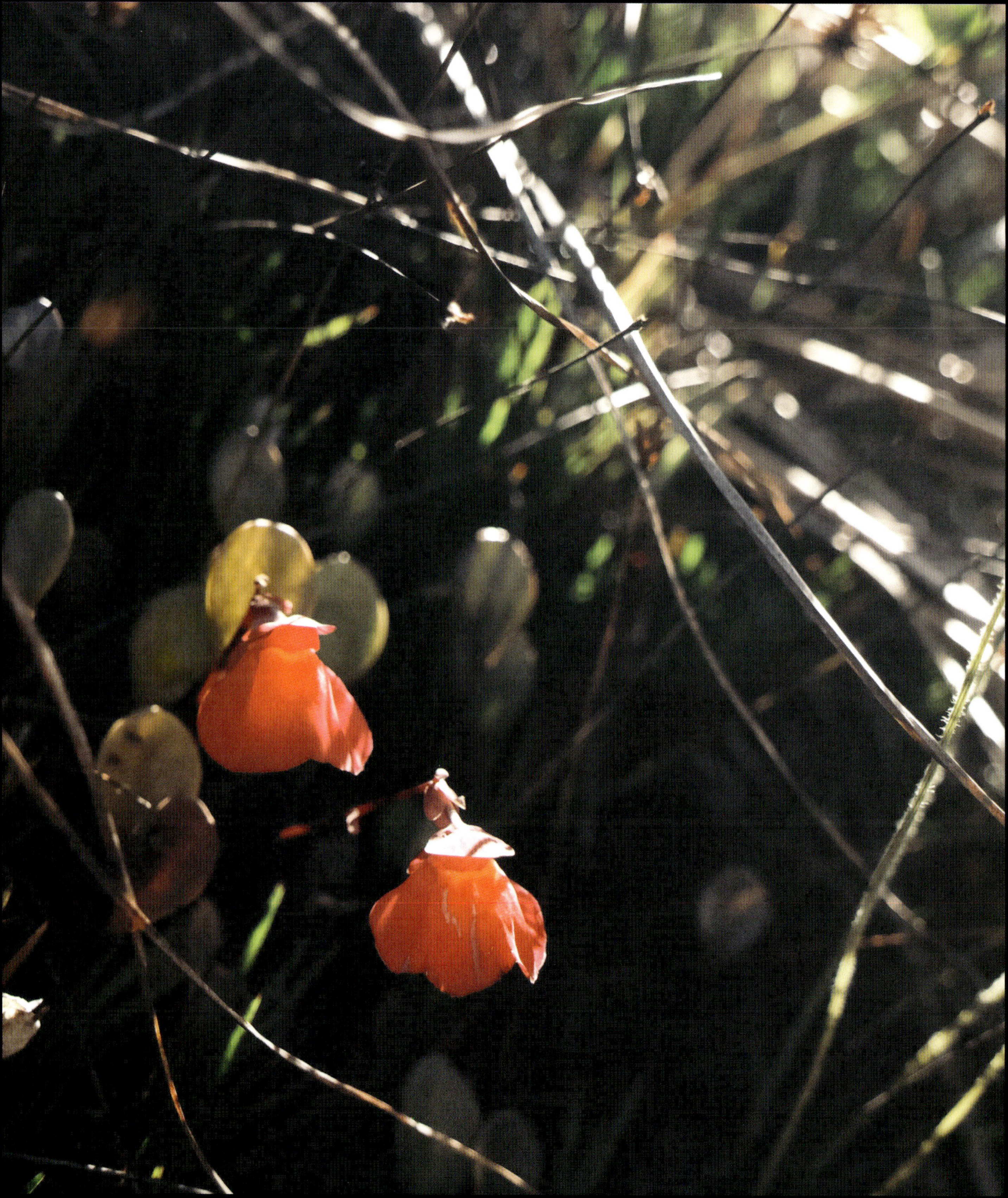

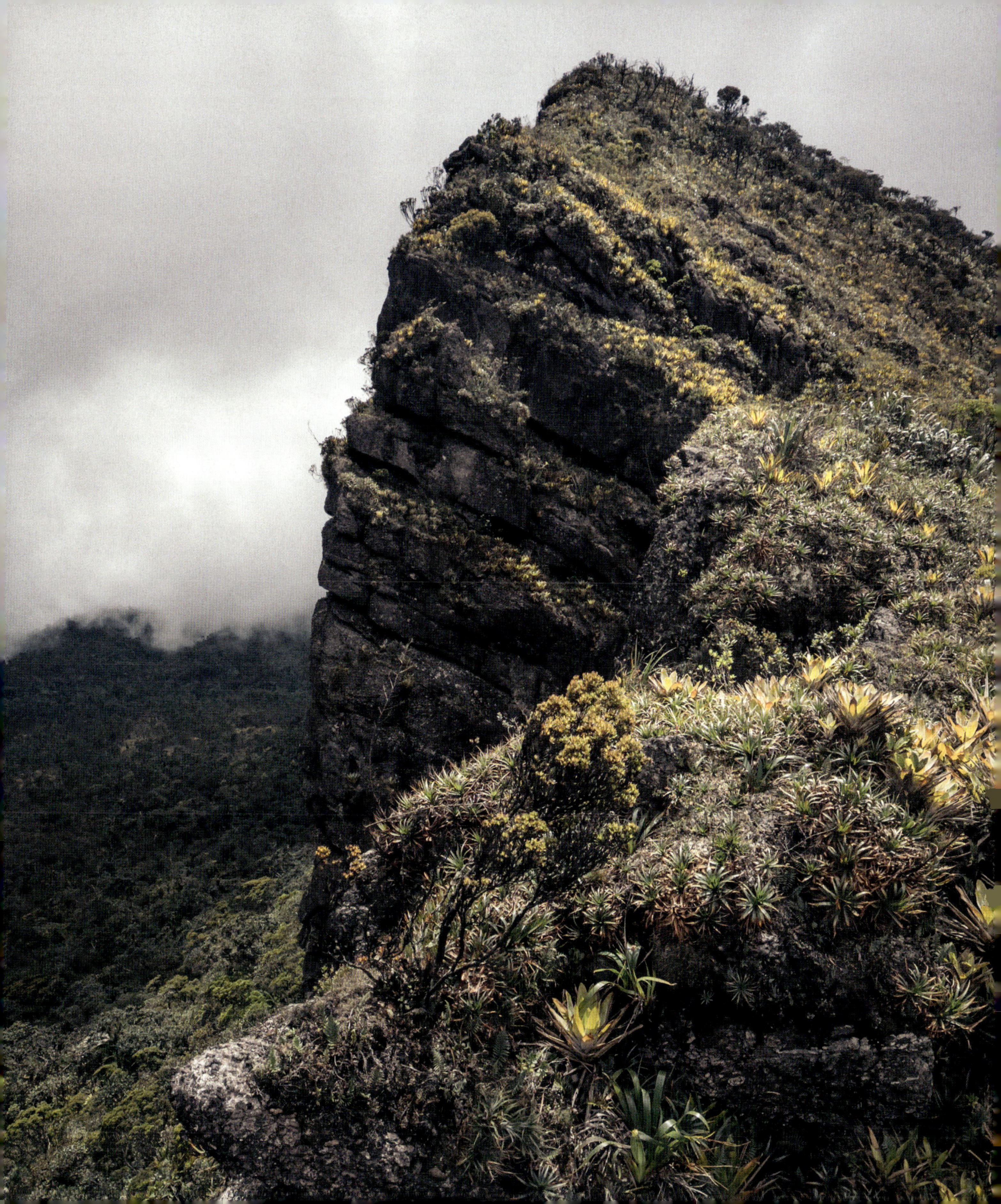

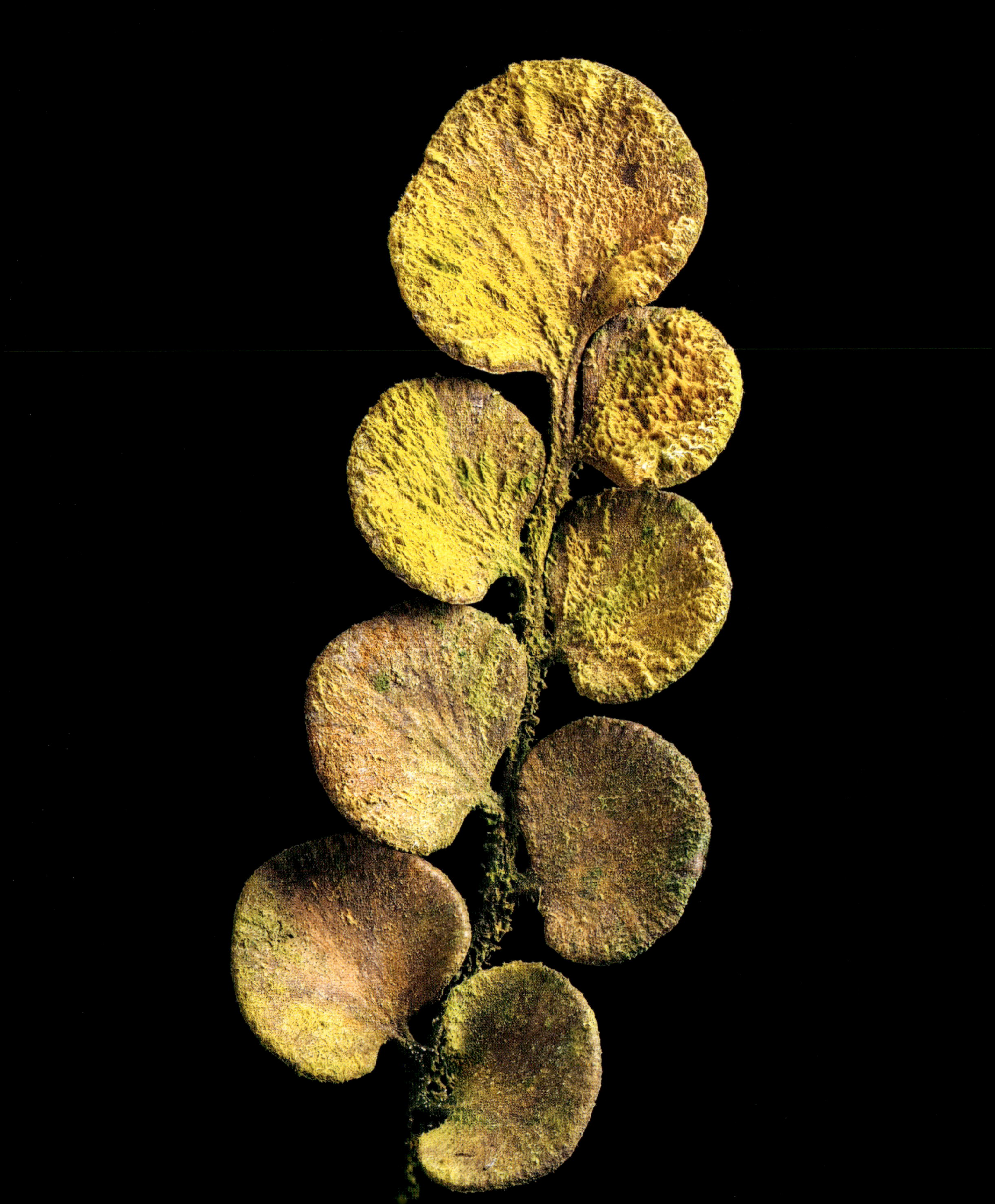

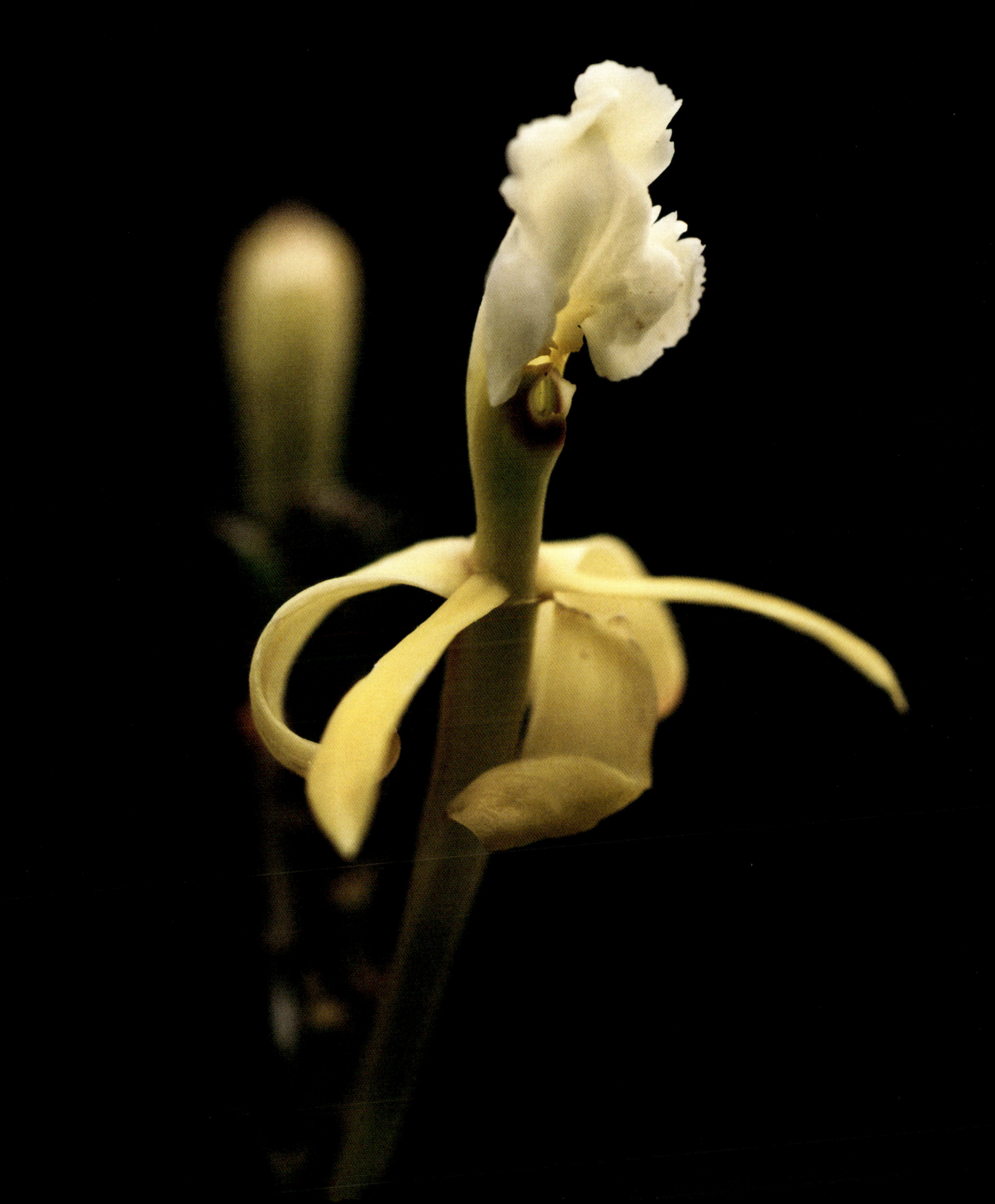

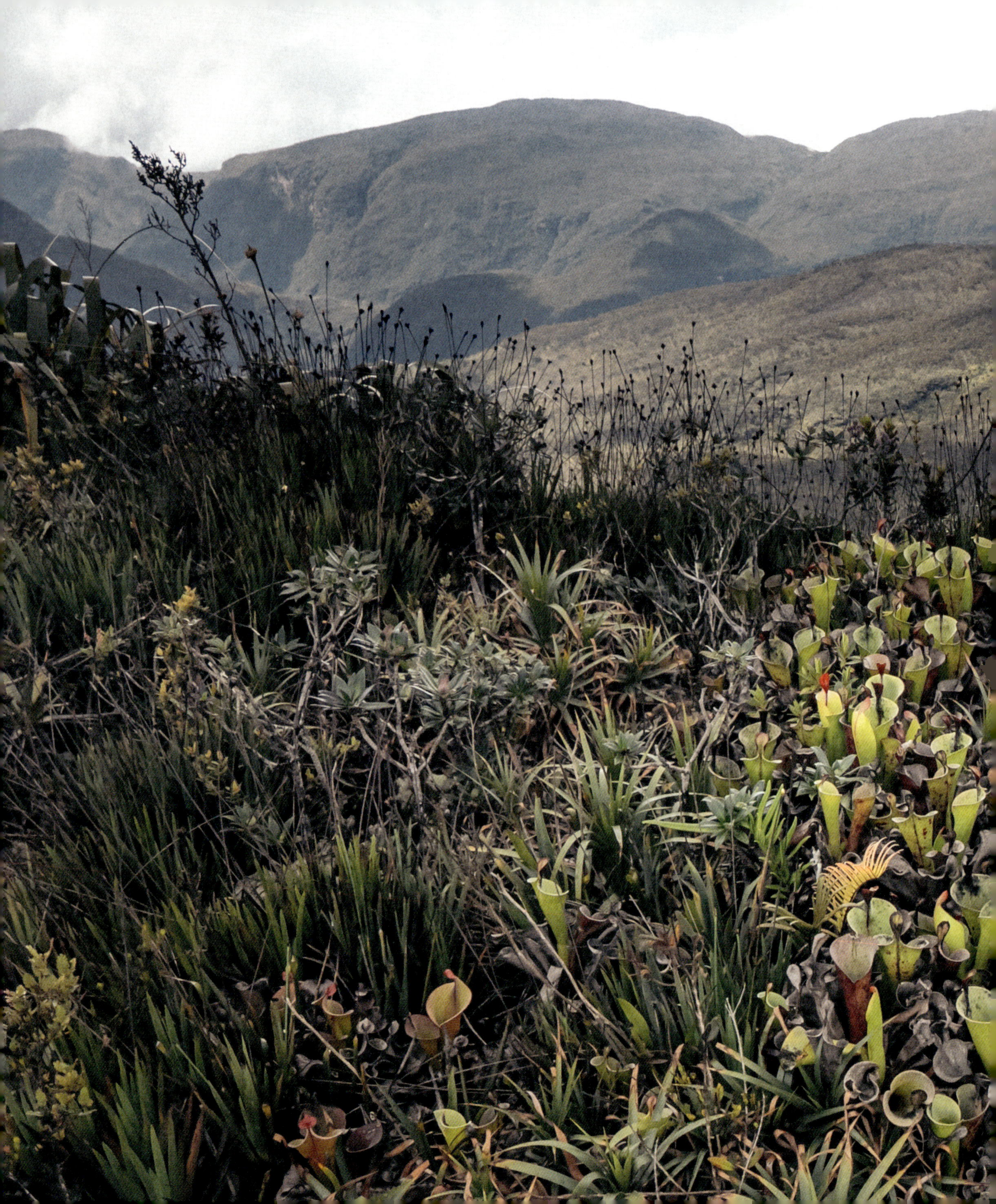

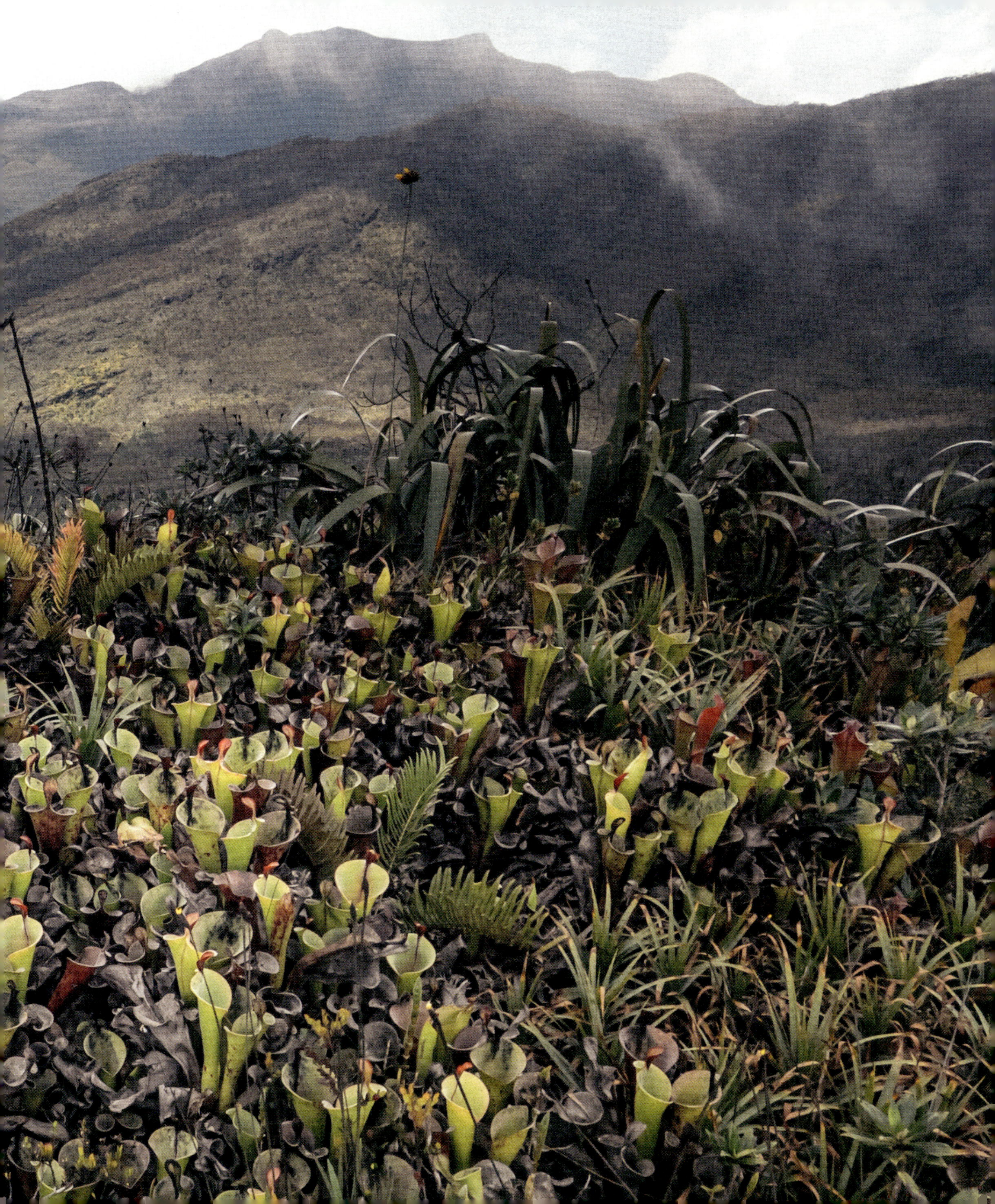

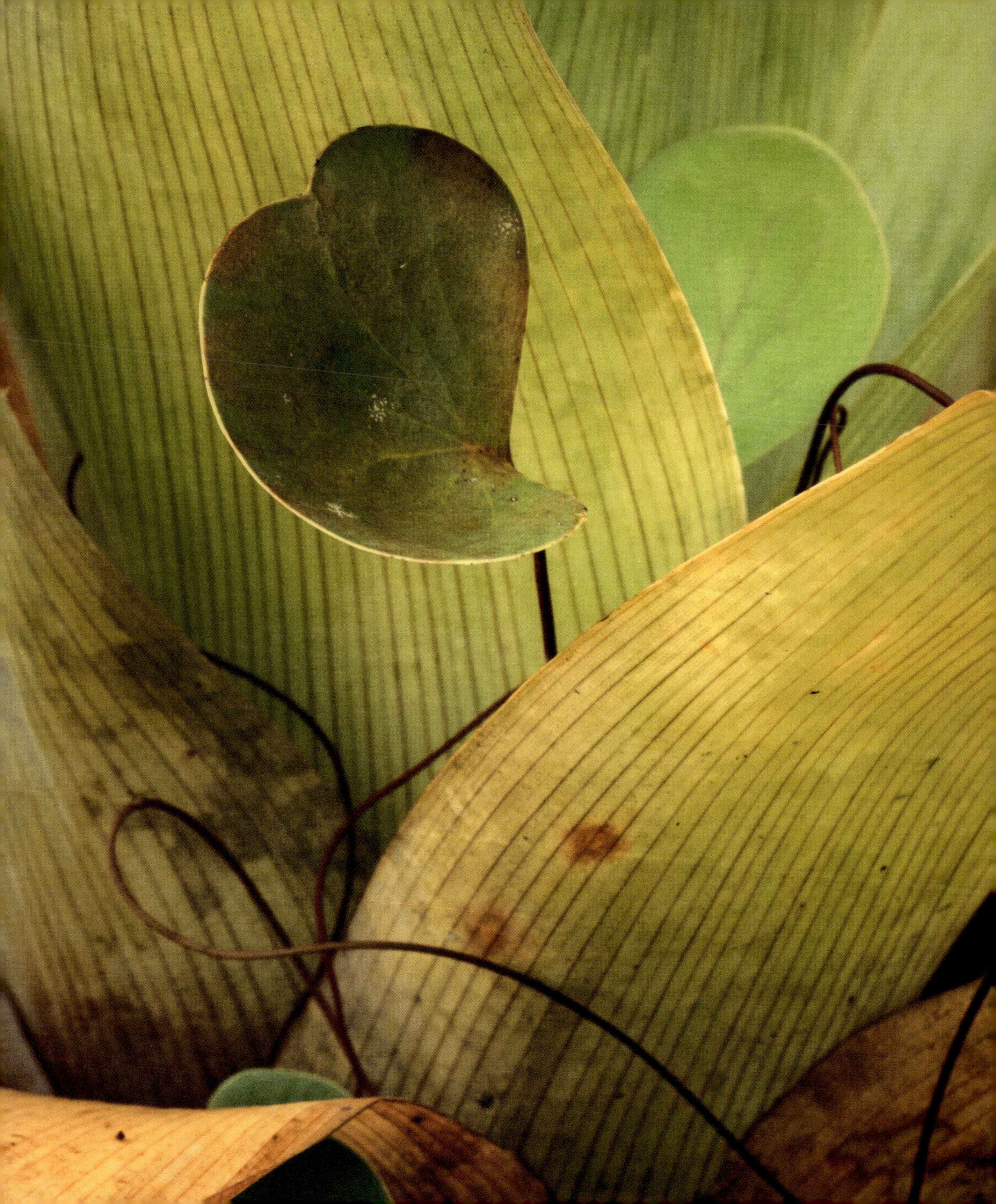

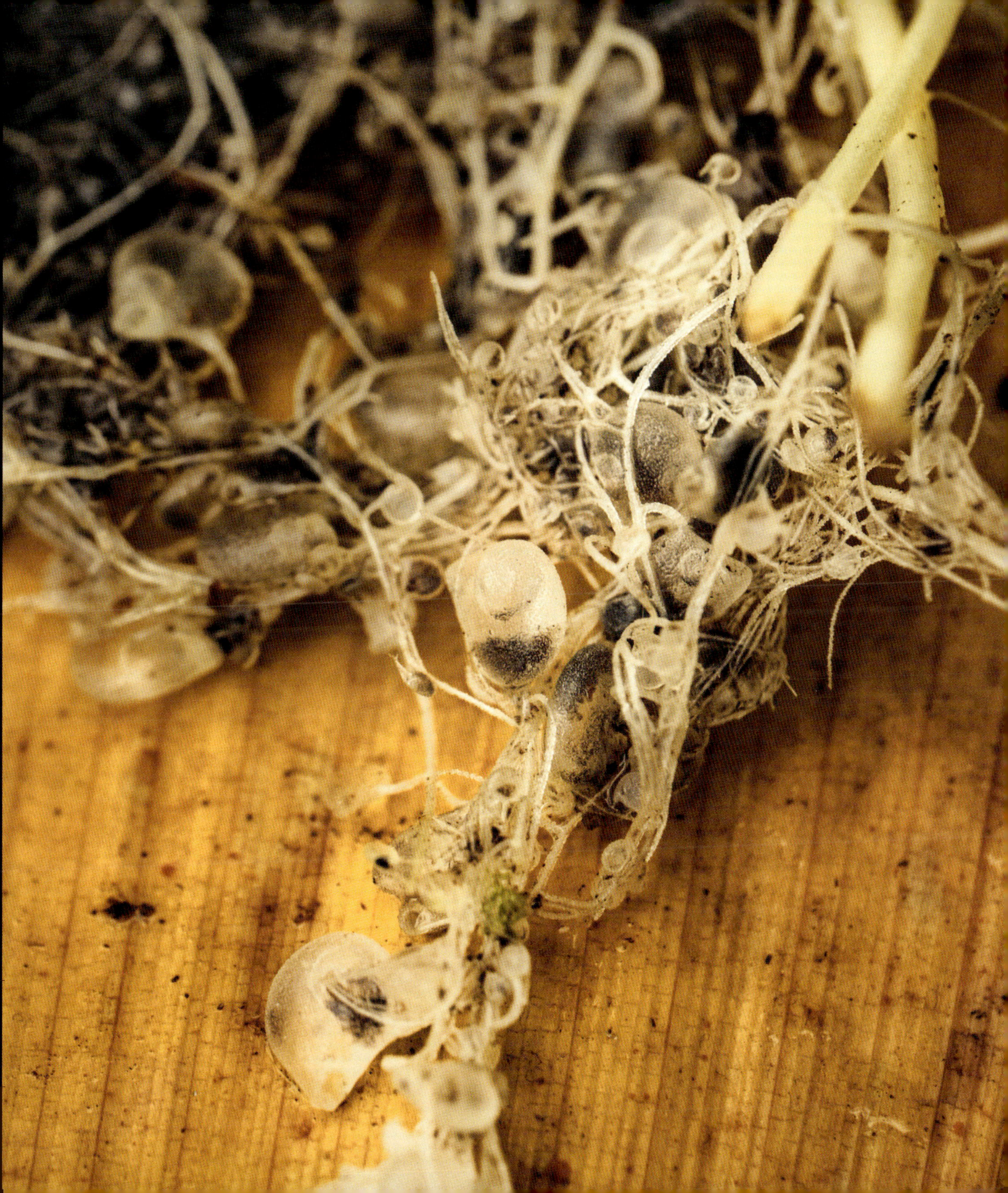

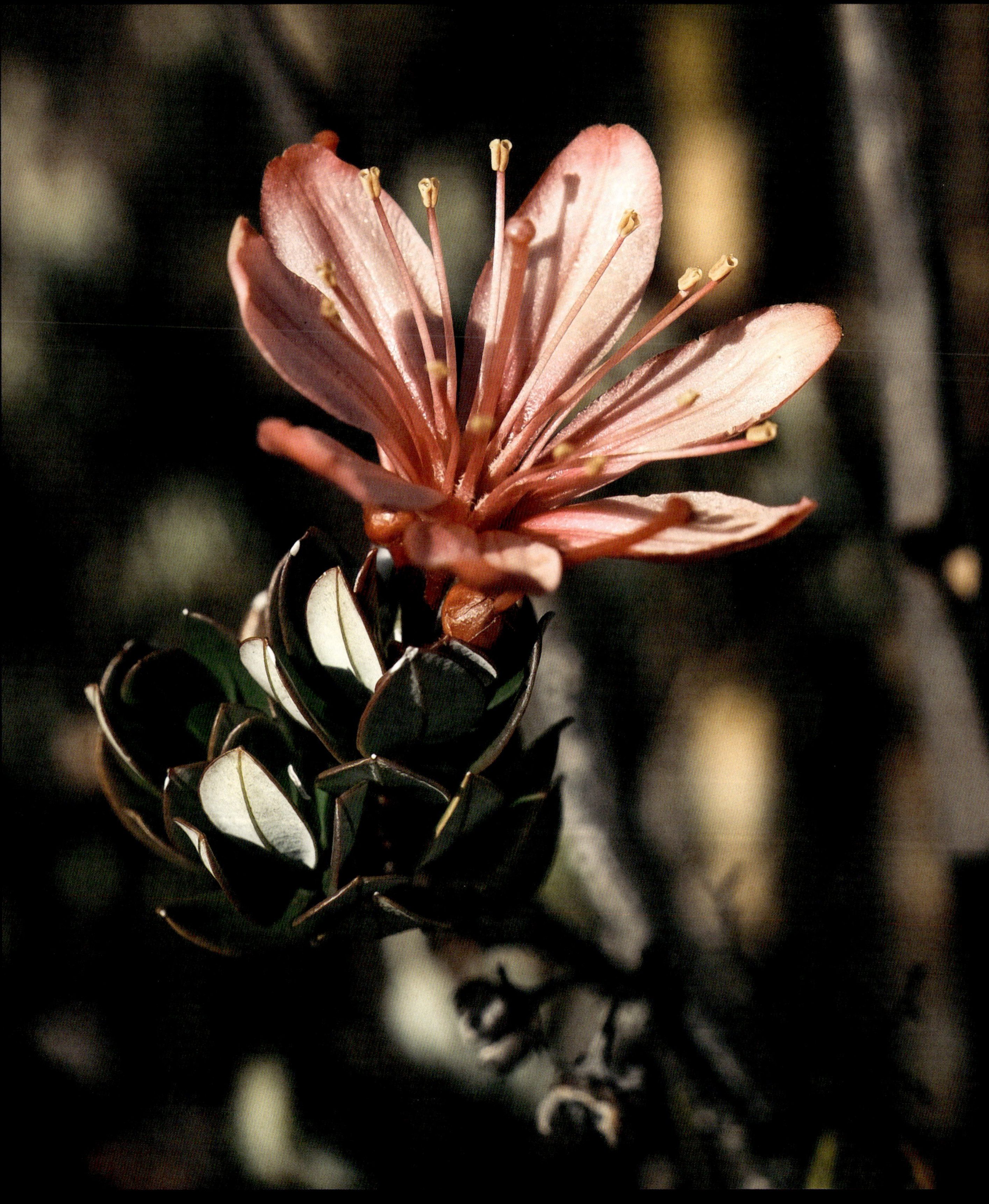

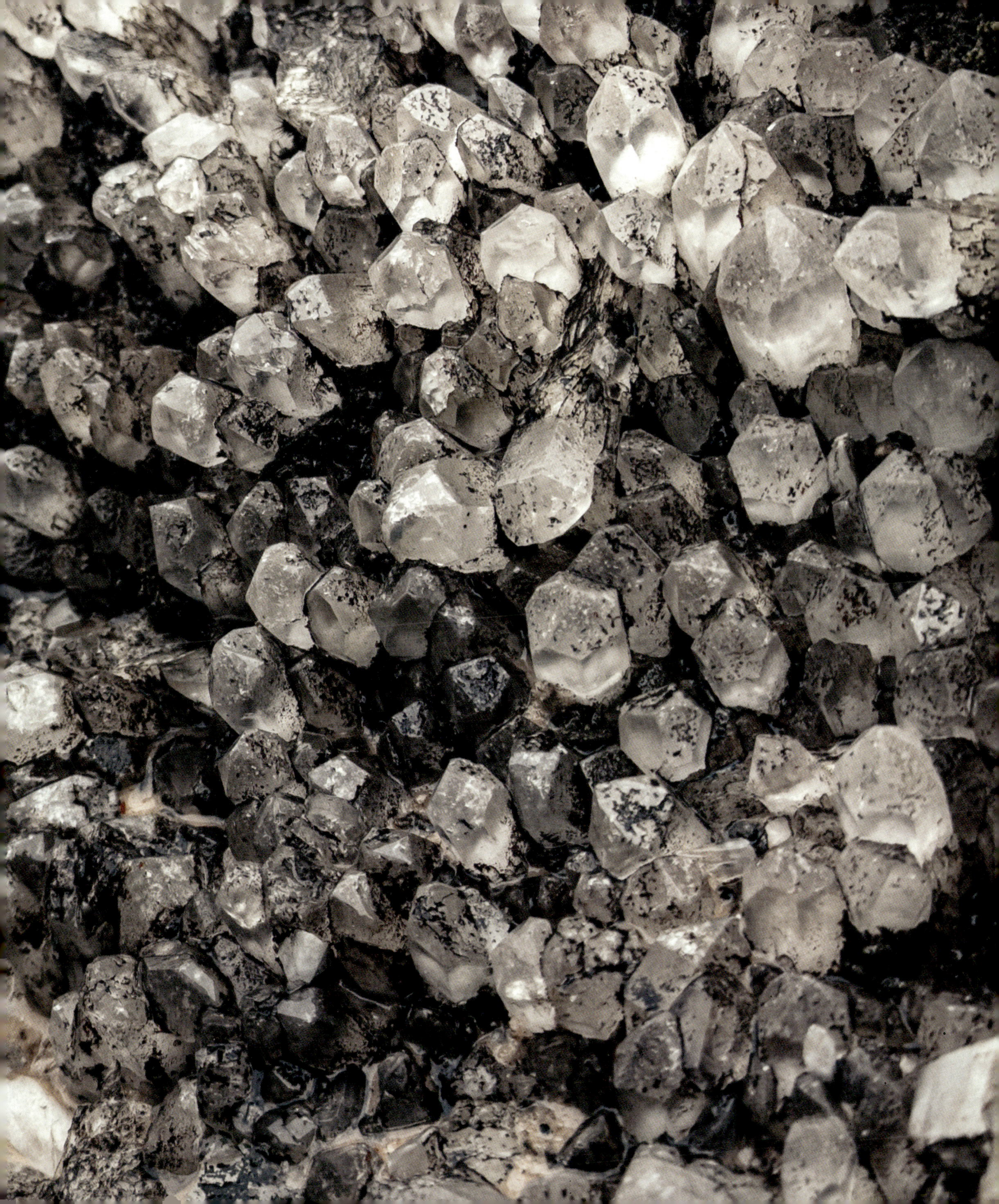

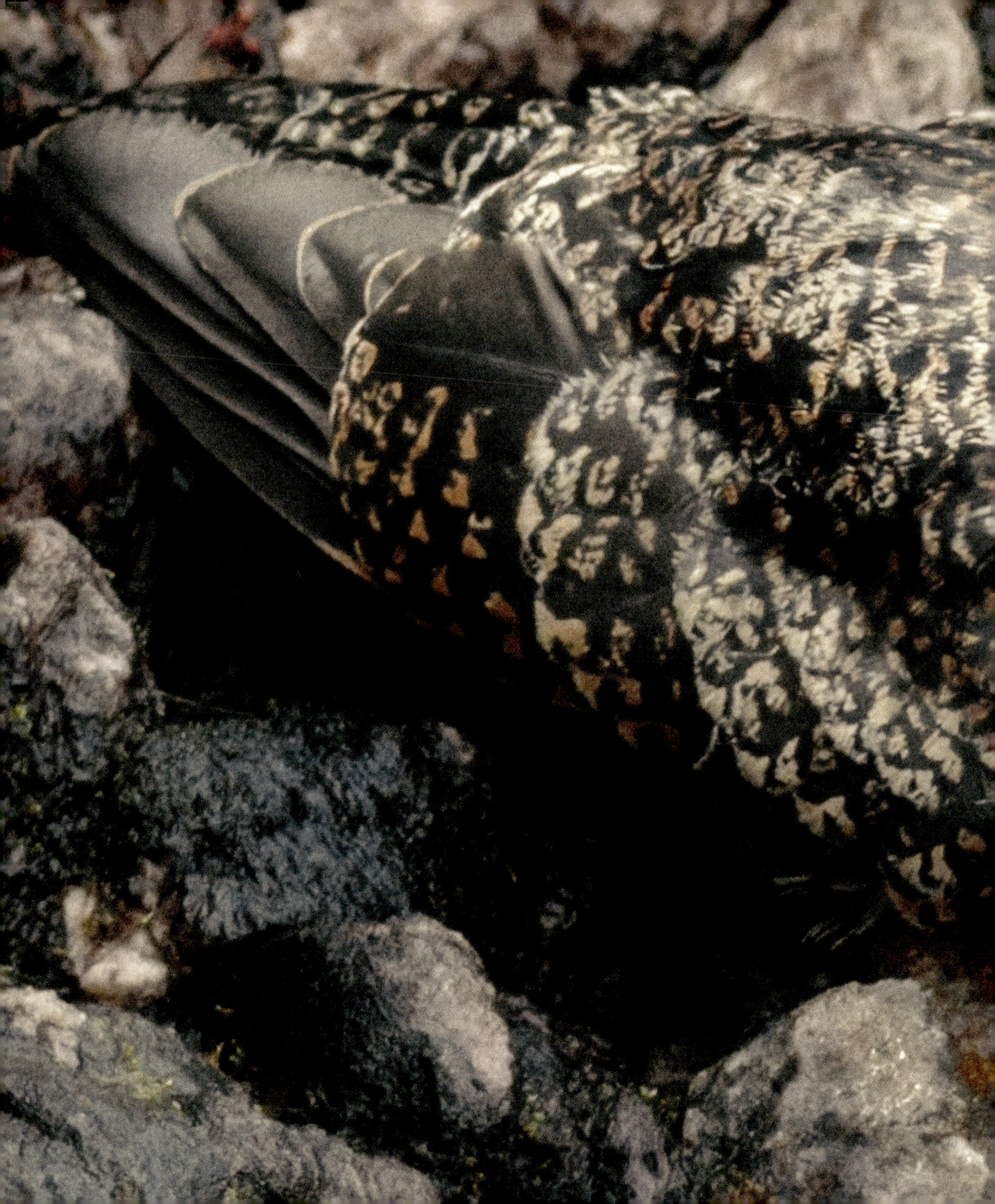

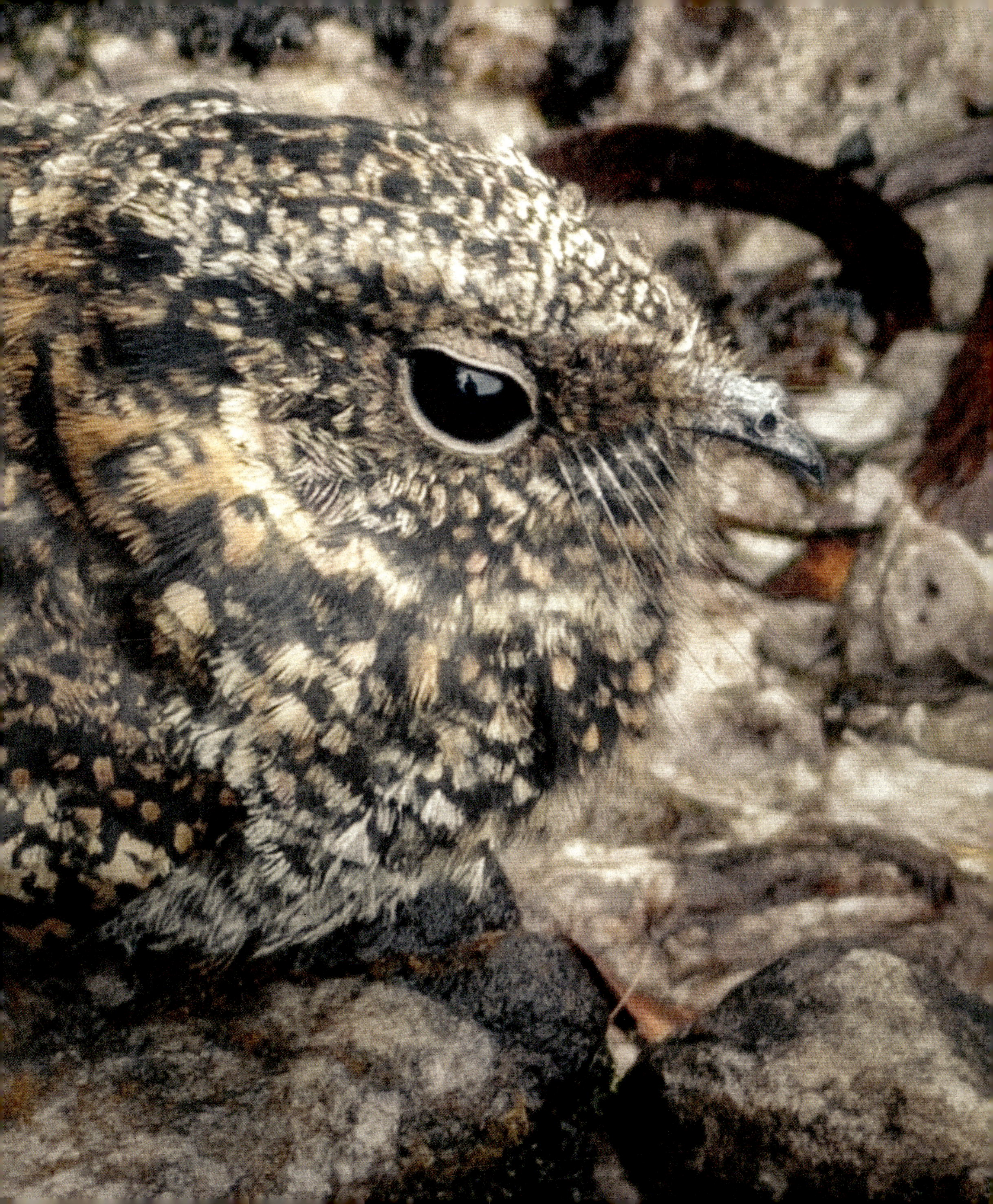

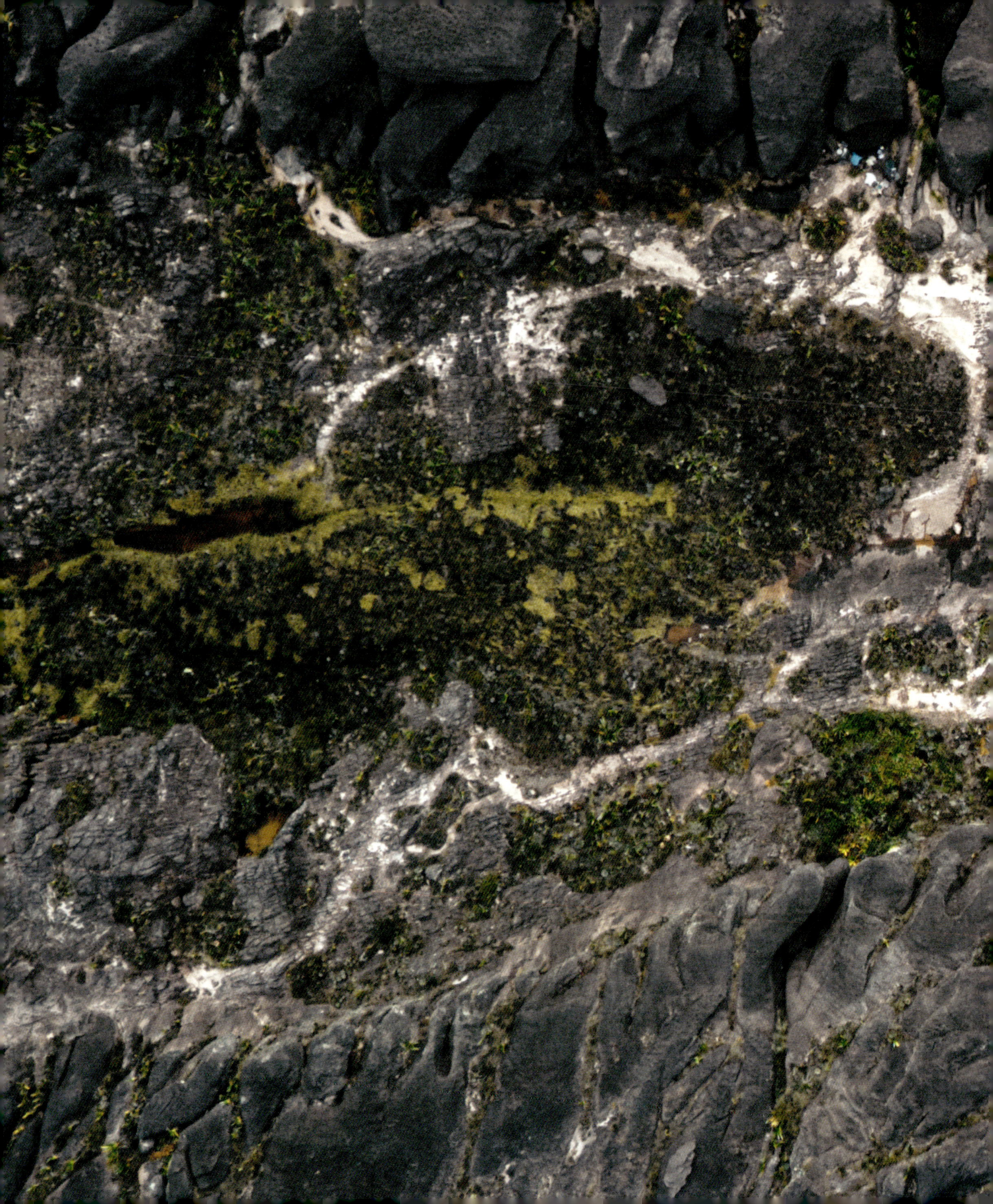

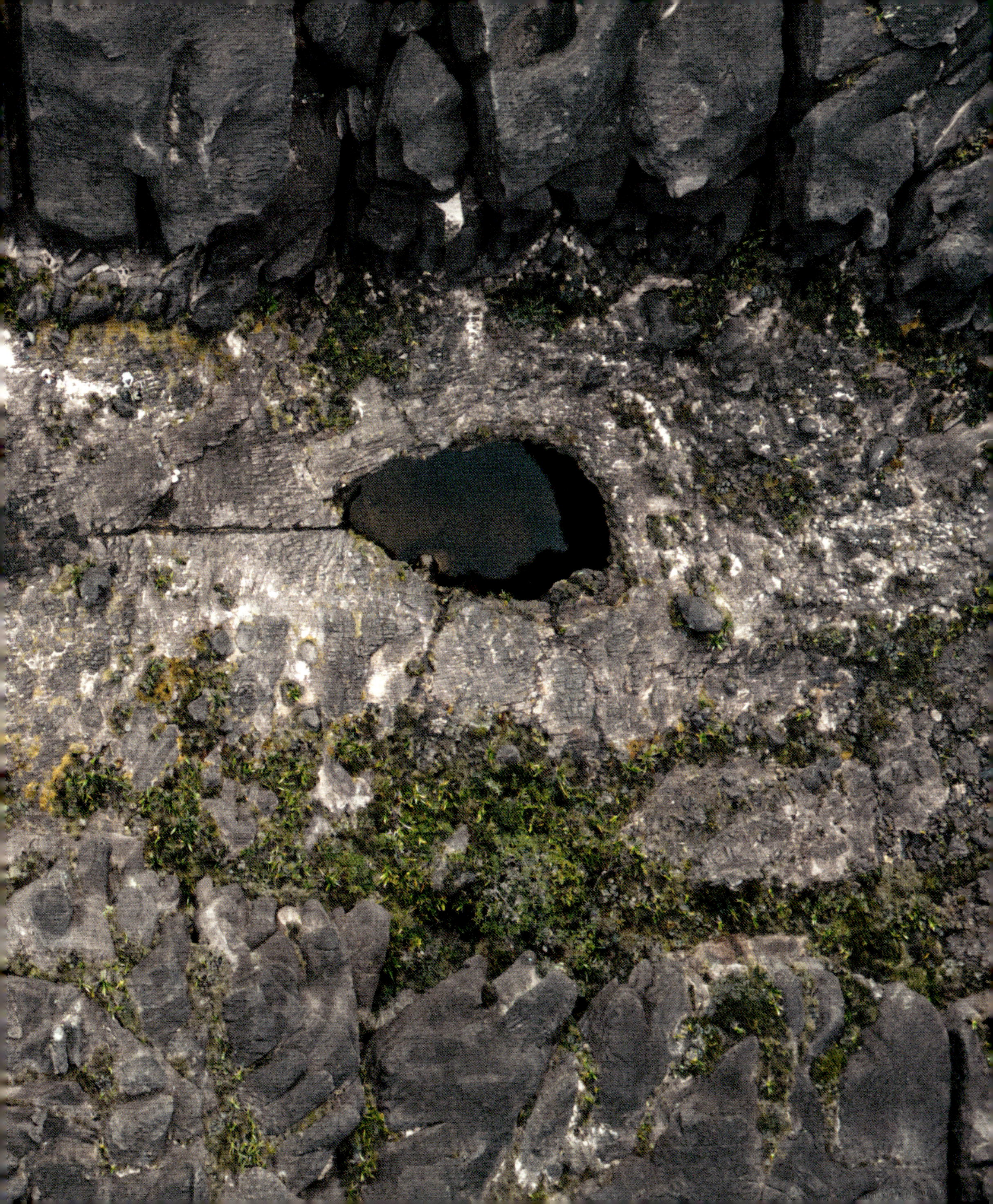

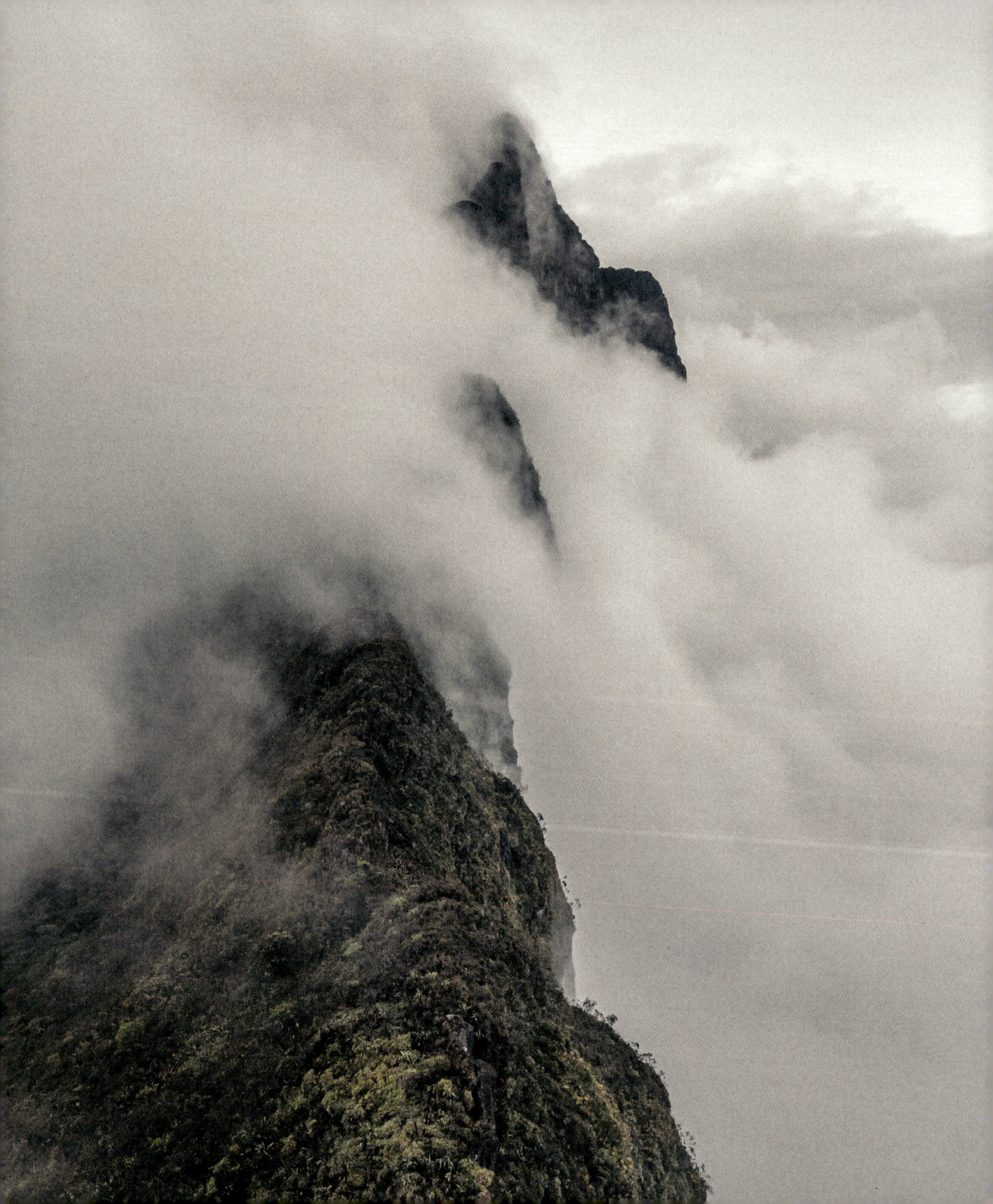

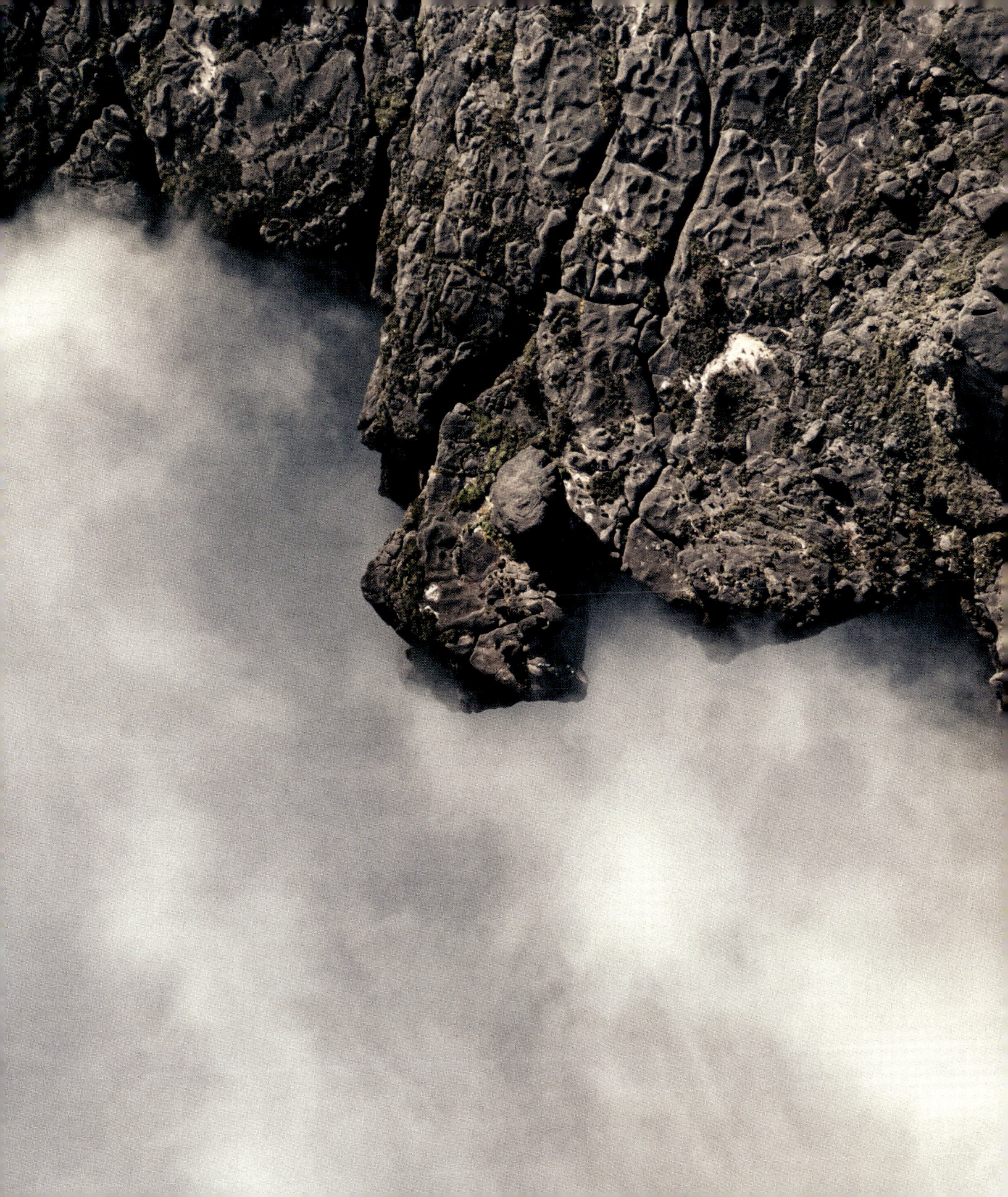

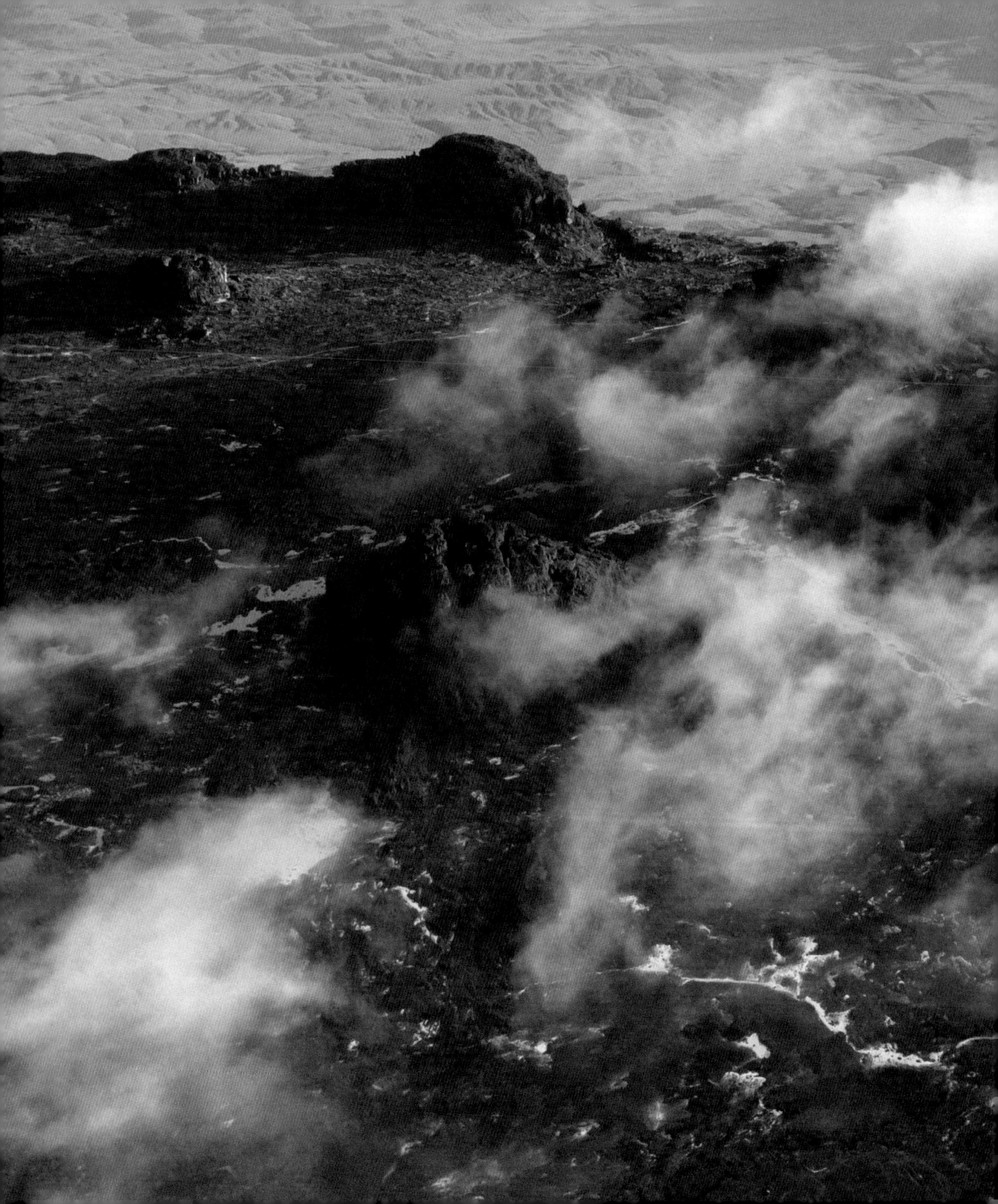

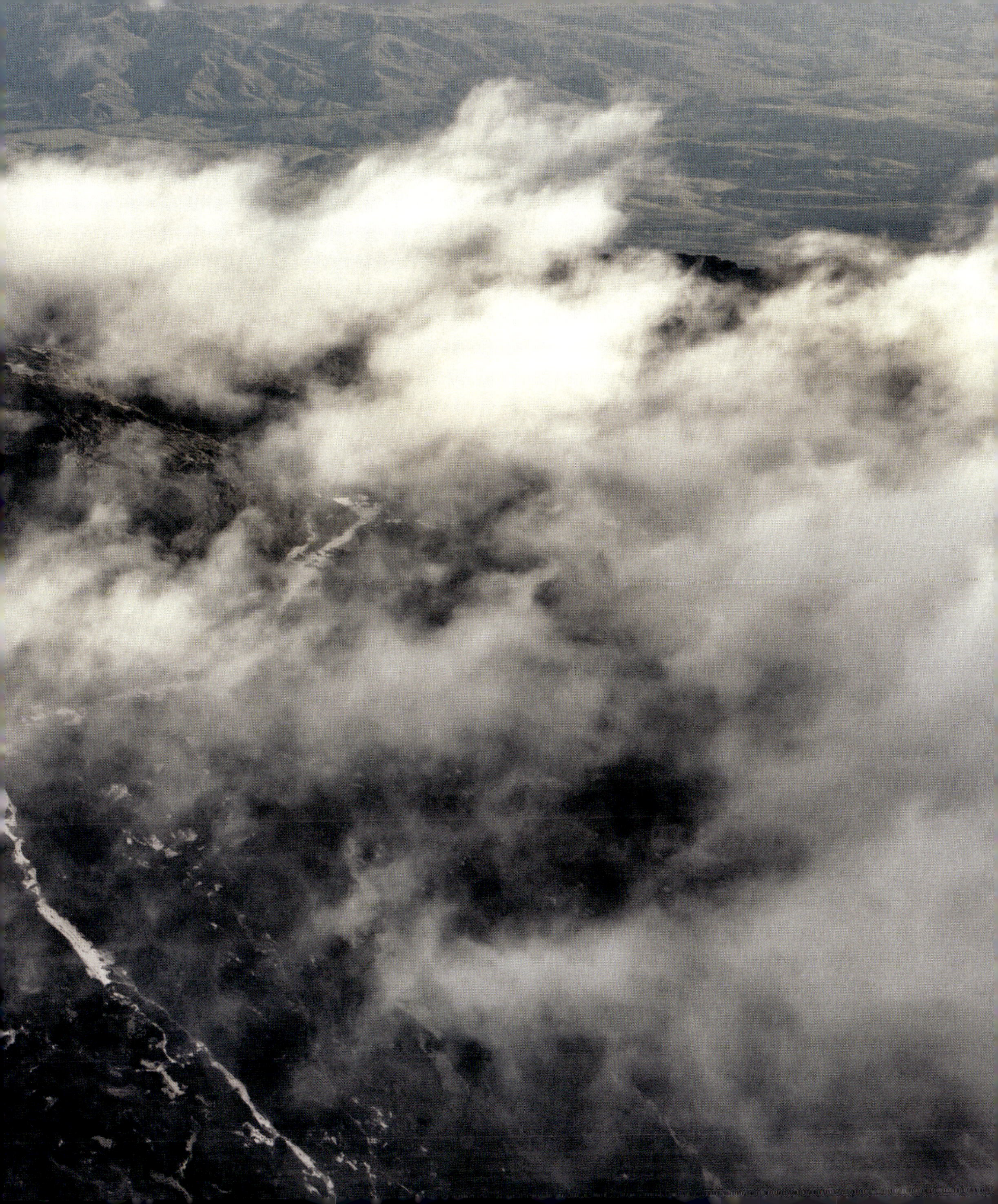

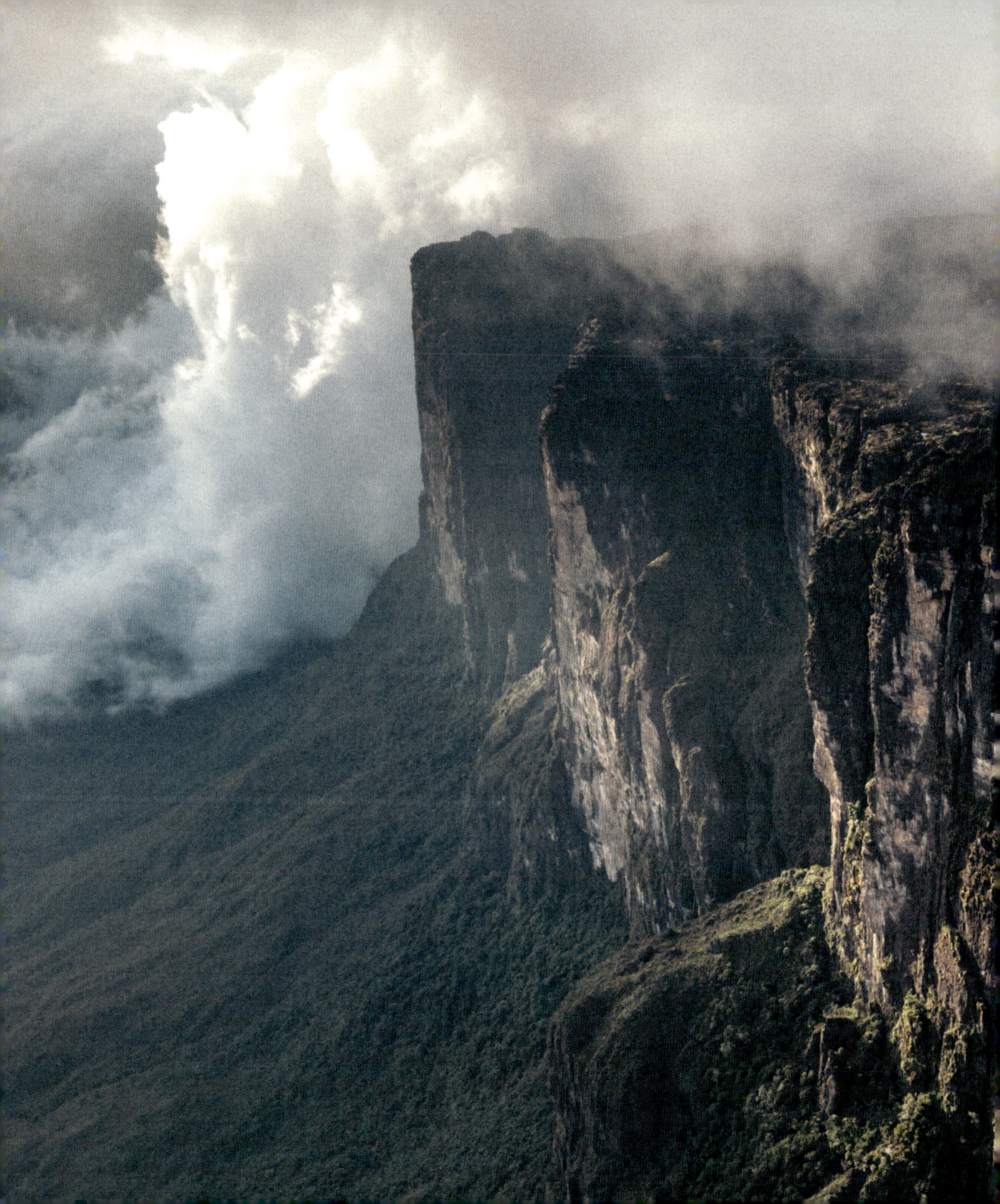

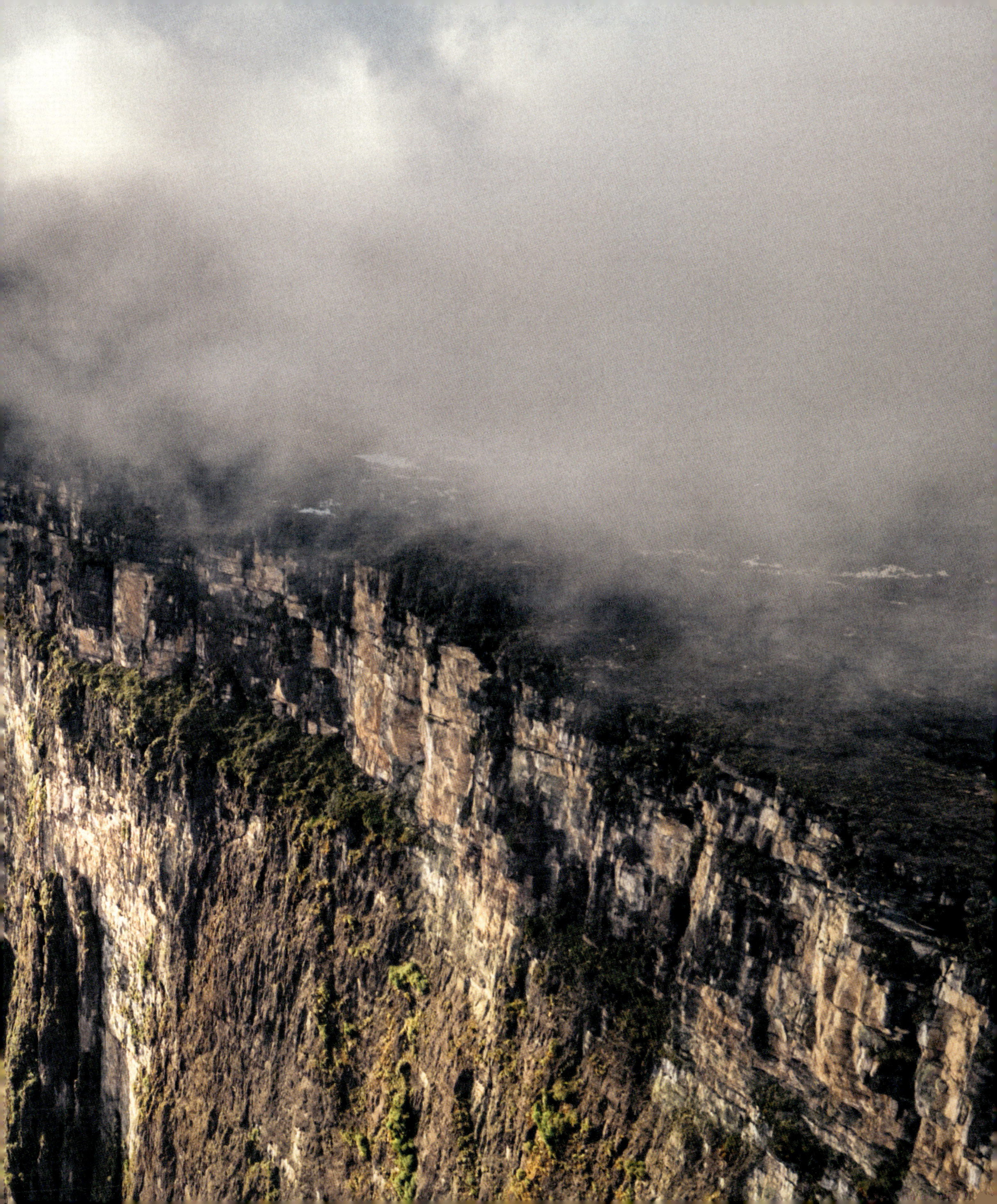

It is so quiet here that my own senses begin to play tricks on me. Every time the wind blows through the crevices and narrow rock passages, I could swear I hear someone whispering. I feel delighted and terrified at once. I am smitten with awe, confusion and fear, all blended into one. And I don't want to leave. Something within me keeps urging me to go deeper into the unknown.

Even my sense of self appears to retreat – it dissolves, blending with something which transcends this place; some intangible presence I can sense all around me. It feels as though my very consciousness is being connected with something far outside my usual field of perception. Words and sentences simply appear in my thoughts, as though they were not really the products of my own mind's work. And it all feels strangely natural. For reasons I cannot understand, it seems to me that everything that happened in my life – every painful moment, every decision, every loss and every gain, everyone I loved and everything I despised – converged only to bring me here. I feel I'm exactly where I'm supposed to be. In the most alien place imaginable.

I stand alone by a shallow pond carved into the rock bed, surrounded by flocks of glistening sundew leaves and gnarled shrubs stunted by decades of haunting alpine winds. At the bottom of the pond, I notice a layer of perfectly clear crystals, looking like diamonds scattered carelessly, as though they were part of an intentionally designed, fantastic scenography. The water is ice-cold, but I decide to undress and take a plunge. The moment the water touches my skin, I feel as though I am being stung by a million needles. Confusion finally subsides, and when I walk out of the water, a sense of perfect clarity befalls me. I'm shivering, my wet body exposed to the frigid mountain air. I look around and see nothing but strange silhouettes obscured by the all-encompassing mist. I might not really belong here, but I feel at home. Alive.

The very thought of returning to the world I left behind days ago fills me with a sense of unease. Is that even my world anymore?

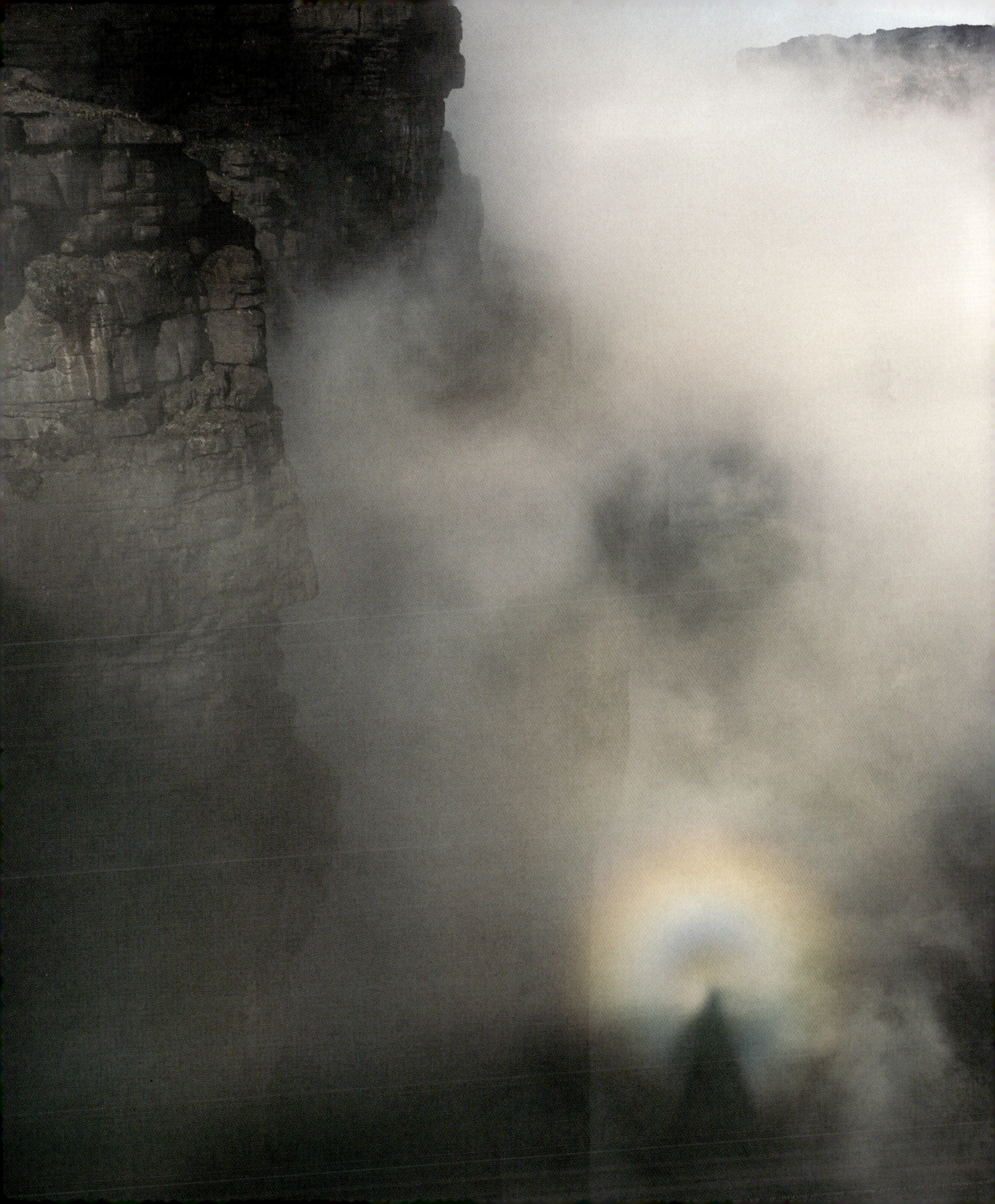

PHOTO INDEX

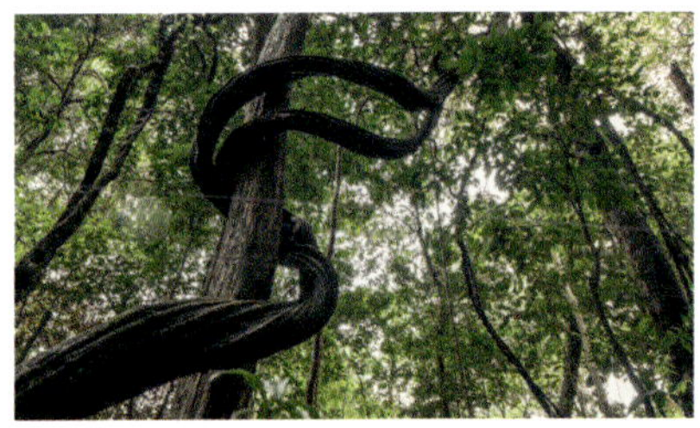

A vine, *Schnella* aff. *guianensis*, in the lowland forest on the slopes of Shiriri Mountain, South Rupununi, 2018.

A juvenile plant of *Marcgravia* sp. climbing on a tree bark in the lowland rainforest. Trail to Irokae camp, Pico da Neblina National Park, 2025.

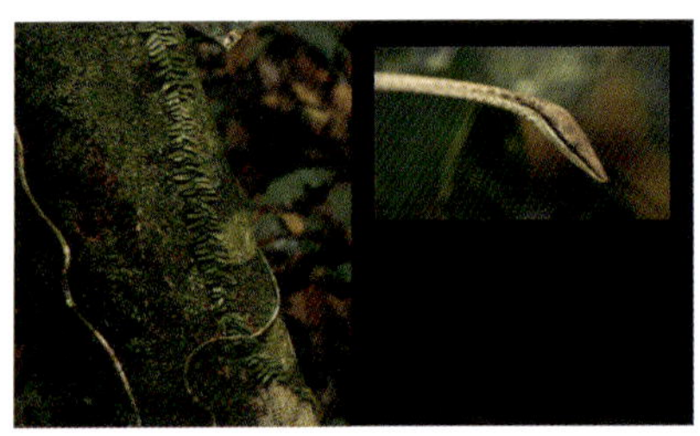

Vine snake (*Oxybelis aeneus*). Lowland forest of Pico da Neblina National Park, 2025.

A swarm of juvenile spiders, photographed near the boat landing site – “Boca do Tucano”, Pico da Neblina National Park, 2025.

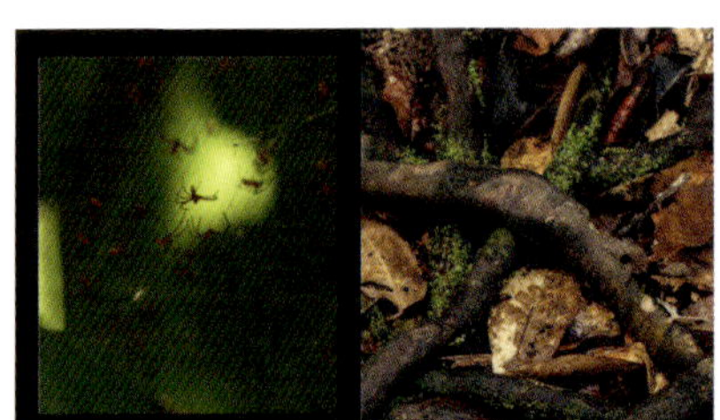

Exposed tree roots in the lowland rainforest. Pico da Neblina National Park, 2025.

Opilionid (harvestman) – likely an undescribed species. Found in the lowland forest of Pico da Neblina National Park, 2025.

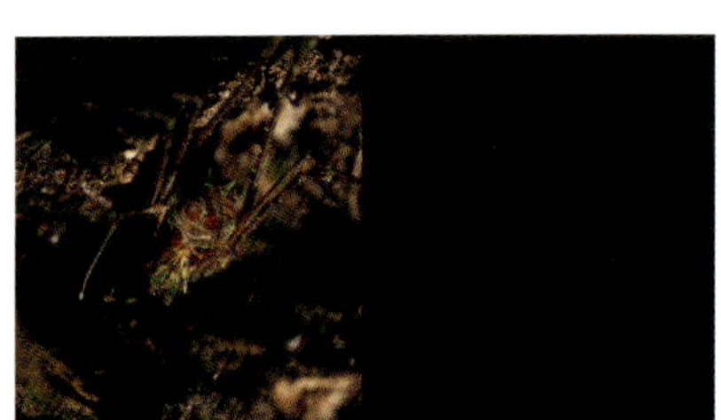

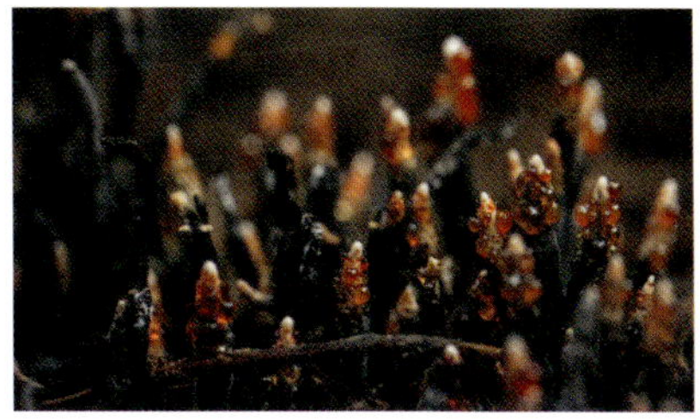

Guttation on the stromata of *Xylaria* sp. fungus. Trail to Irokae camp, Pico da Neblina National Park, 2025.

Exposed stilt roots of the so-called "walking palm", likely *Iriartea deltoidea*. Trail to Irokae camp, Pico da Neblina National Park, 2025.

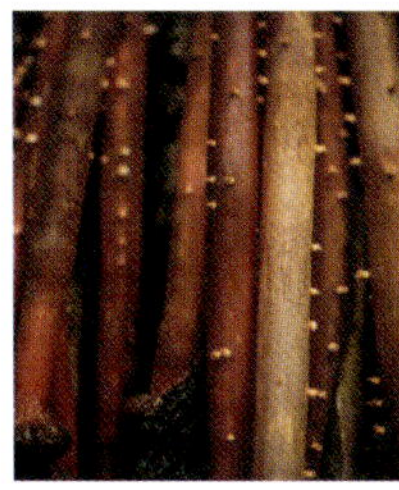

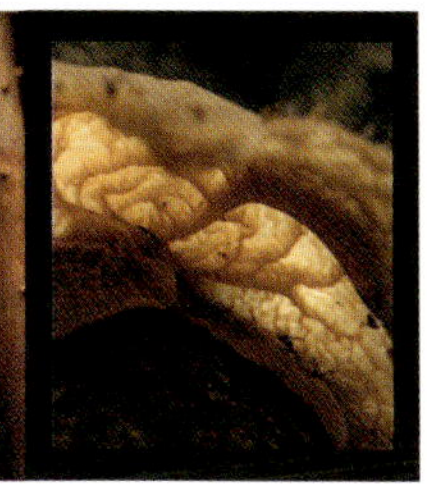

Fruiting body of *Auricularia* sp., the so-called "wood ear" fungus. Lowland forest of Pico da Neblina National Park, 2025.

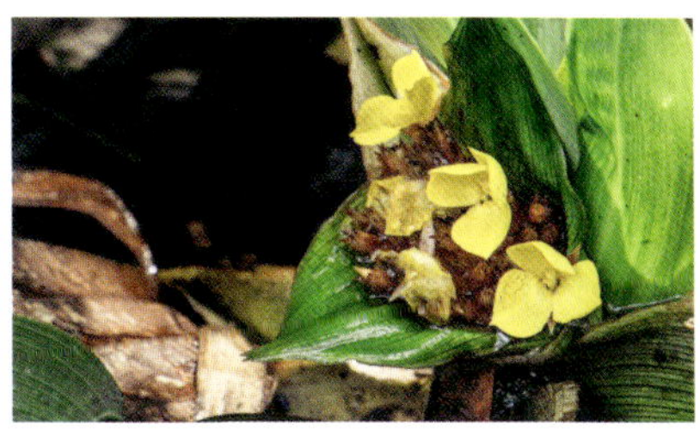

Rapatea steyermarkii, a member of Rapateaceae, a family of plants centered in the Guiana Shield. Rainforests north of Roraima-tepui, around the upper Waruma River, Cuyuni-Mazaruni, 2019.

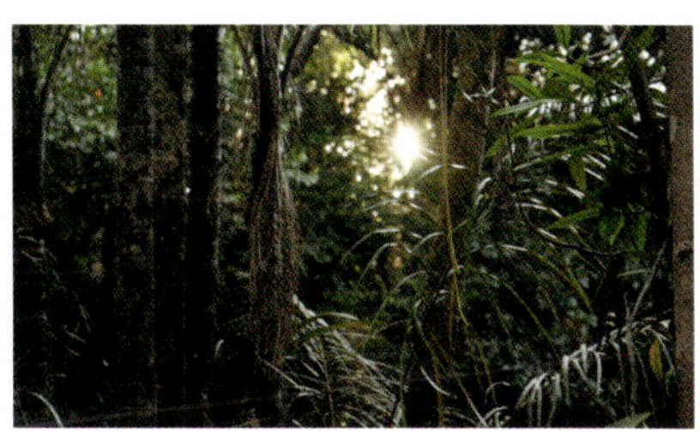

Lowland rainforest of the upper Rio Negro. Vicinities of São Gabriel da Cachoeira, 2025.

Ficus sp. growing in the forest on the slopes of Shiriri Mountain, South Rupununi, 2018.

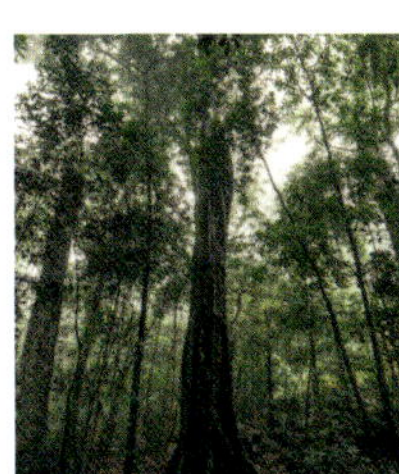

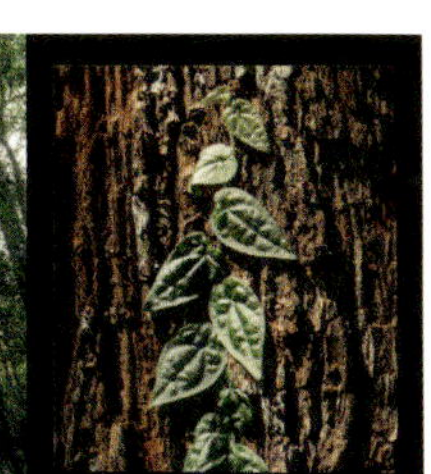

Juvenile plant of *Piper* sp. growing in the vicinity of Bebedouro Novo camp, Pico da Neblina National Park, 2025.

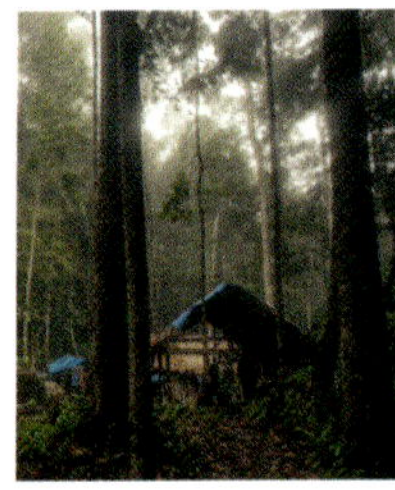

Approaching the Bebedouro Novo camp.
Pico da Neblina National Park, 2025.

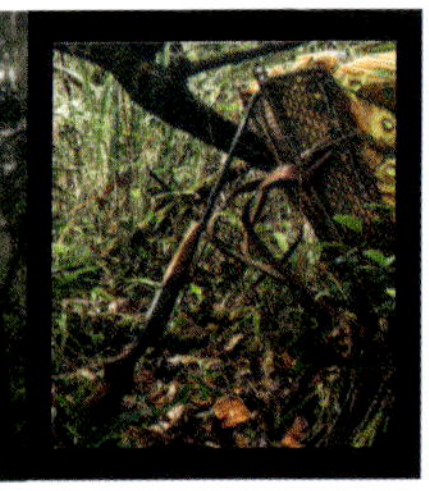

Hunting shotgun with a traditional *warishi* basket, popular among the Indigenous communities in the Guiana Highlands. Rainforests north of Roraima-tepui, around the upper Waruma River, Cuyuni-Mazaruni, 2019.

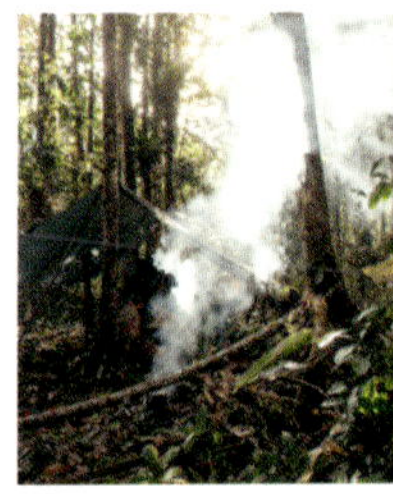

Campsite in the forests north of Roraima-tepui, by the upper Waruma River, Cuyuni-Mazaruni, 2019.

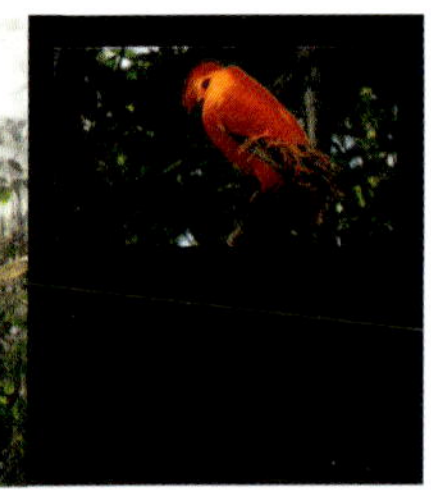

Guianan cock-of-the-rock (*Rupicola rupicola*).
Kaieteur National Park, 2026.

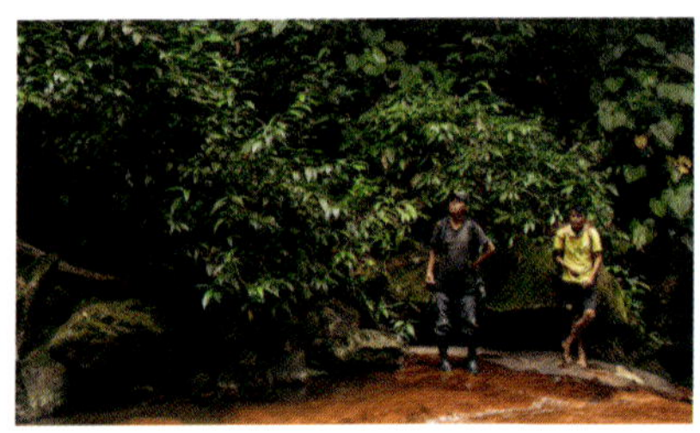

Juan and Robert from the community of Purpurken, on the trail to Cueva Del Fantasma on the foothills of Aprada-tepui. Canaima National Park, 2017.

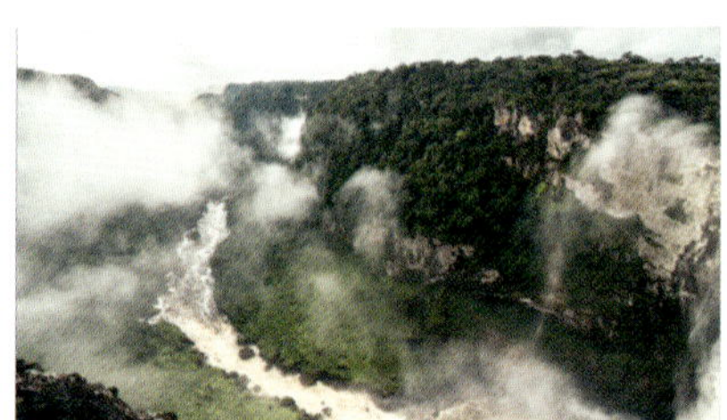

Potaro River gorge,
right next to Kaieteur Falls.
Kaieteur National Park, 2018.

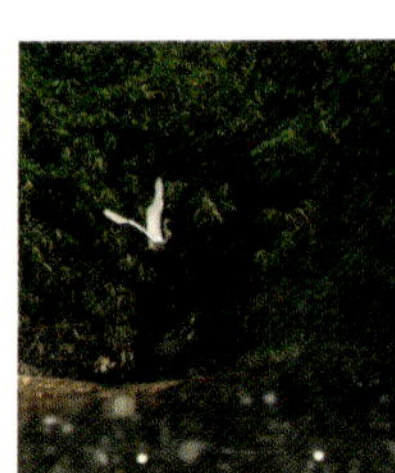

Great egret (*Ardea alba*). Rio Maturacá,
Pico da Neblina National Park, 2025.

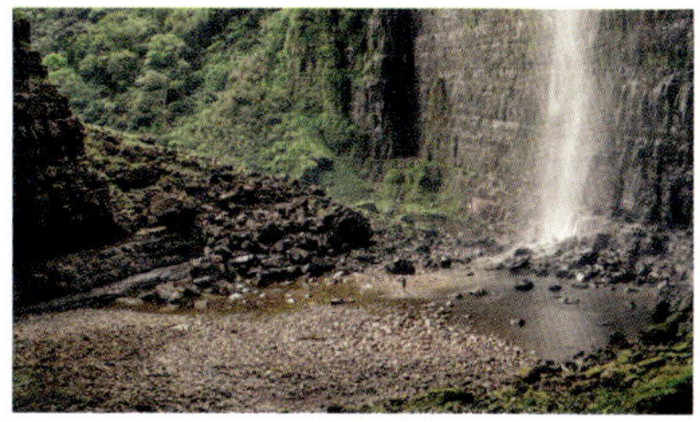

Cueva del Fantasma, located on the foothills of Aprada-tepui, Canaima National Park, 2017.

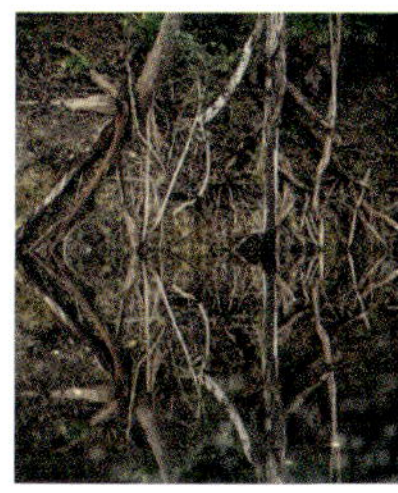

Water reflections. Rio Negro tributaries northwest of Manaus, 2017.

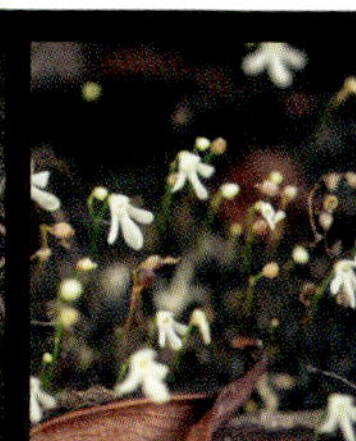

Utricularia oliveriana growing in a stream. Vicinities of Purpurken, Canaima National Park, 2017.

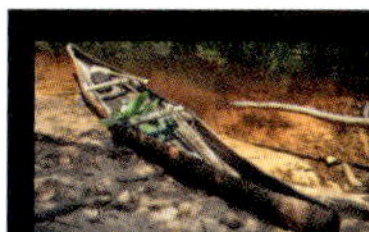

Traditional "woodskin" canoe, usually made with the bark of *Copaifera* sp. trees. Upper Kiara (or Cara) Creek, Cuyuni-Mazaruni, 2019.

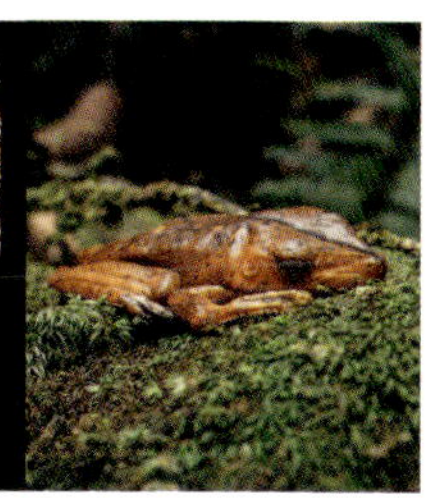

Boana boans in the forest on the trail to Cueva del Fantasma, Aprada-tepui foothills. Canaima National Park, 2017.

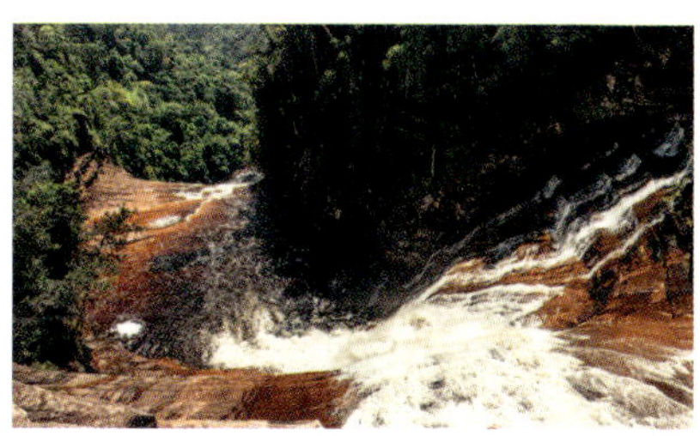

Oruwandad Falls on the upper Kiara (or Cara) Creek, Cuyuni-Mazaruni, 2019.

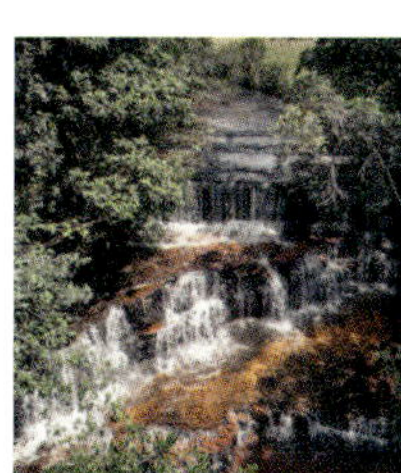

Kako Parú (Quebrada de Jaspe, or Jasper Creek). Canaima National Park, 2023.

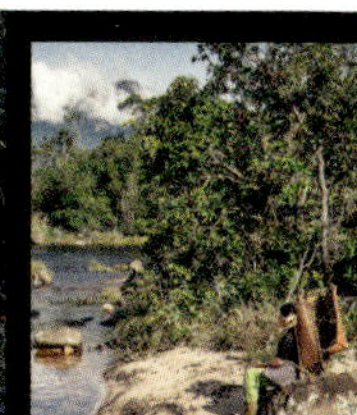

Gregoria, from the community of Yunék, waiting by the bank of Rio Karuay with the cliffs of Acopán-tepui in the background. Yunék, Canaima National Park, 2017.

Frank, Hondel and Kelly in a dugout, travelling down the Kako River, Cuyuni-Mazaruni, 2019.

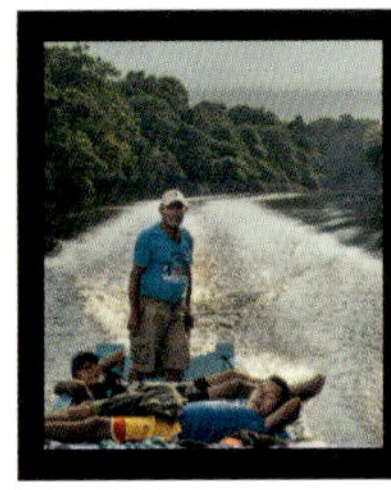

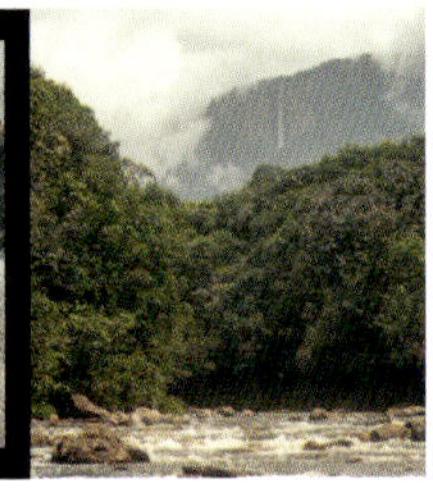

Cliffs of Kukenán-tepui seen from the banks of upper Waruma River, Cuyuni-Mazaruni, 2019.

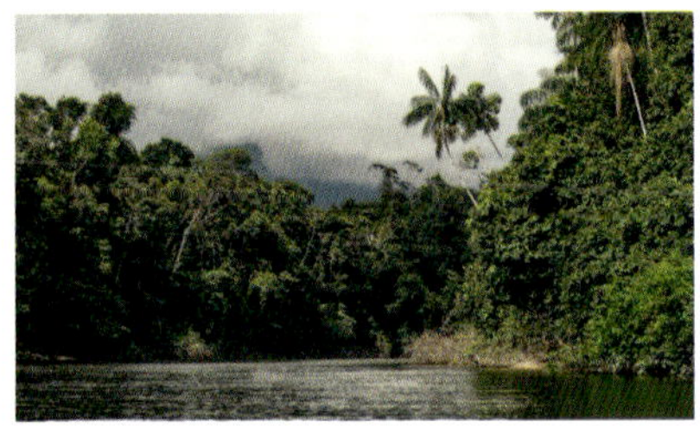

Rainforest with cliffs of Serra Imeri in the background. Pico da Neblina National Park, 2025.

Opota Mountain seen from the village of Maturacá. Pico da Neblina National Park, 2025.

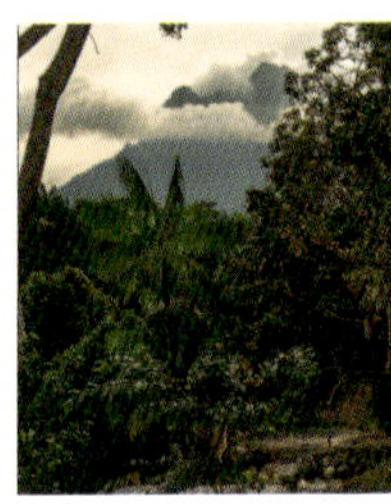

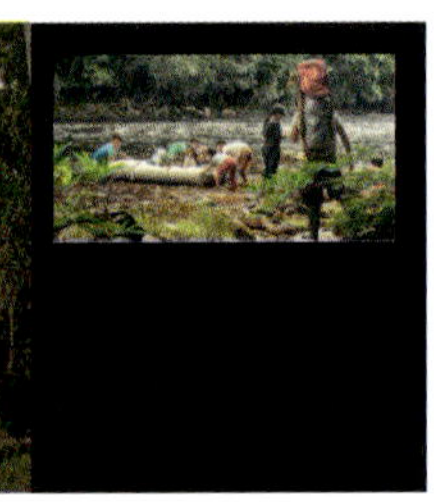

Family preparing to travel down the Kamarang River using an inflatable mattress. Vicinities of Uchii Falls, Cuyuni-Mazaruni, 2019.

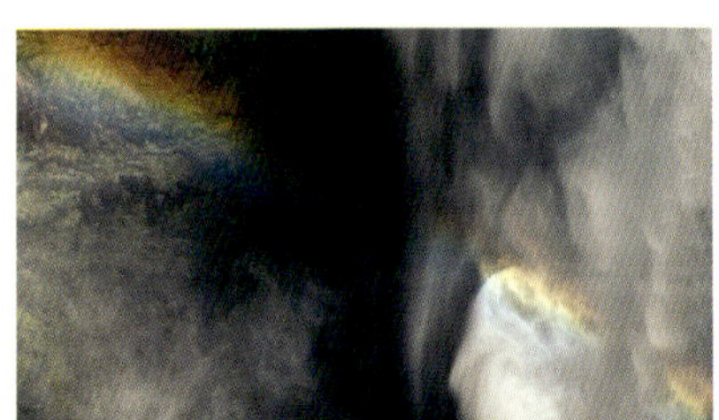

Mist forming at the bottom of Kaieteur Falls. Kaieteur National Park, 2026.

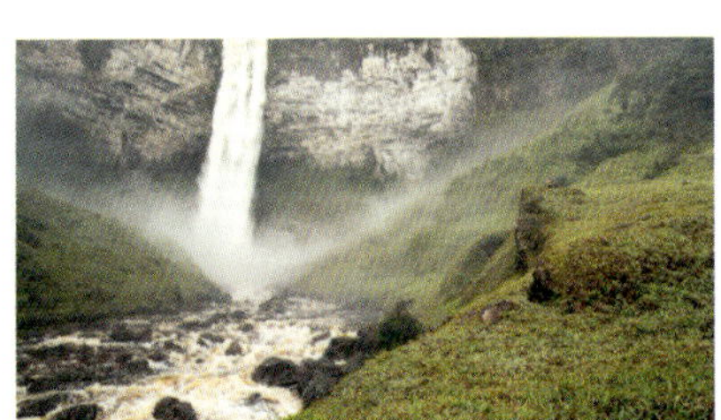

Uchii Falls. Cuyuni-Mazaruni, 2019.

Dillon under a rock overhang, behind a curtain of water. Kumerau Falls on the Kurupung River, Cuyuni-Mazaruni, 2026.

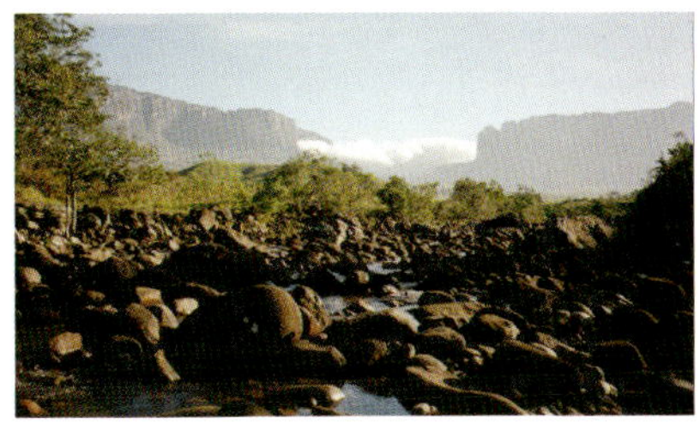

Kukenán-tepui (left) and Roraima-tepui (right) seen from Rio Kukenán camp. Canaima National Park, 2023.

Acopán-tepui towering above the village of Yunék in the Gran Sabana. Canaima National Park, 2017.

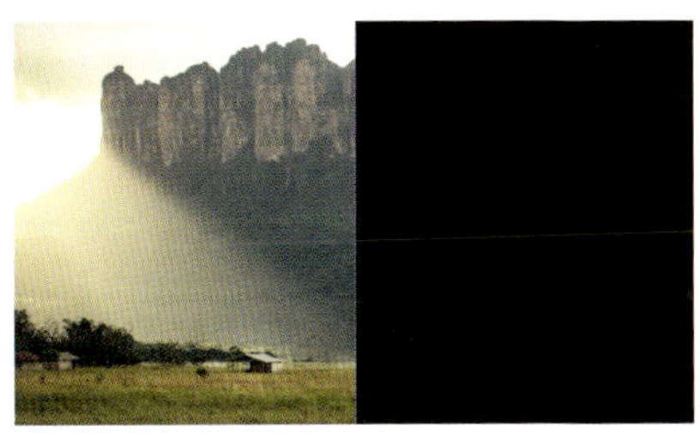

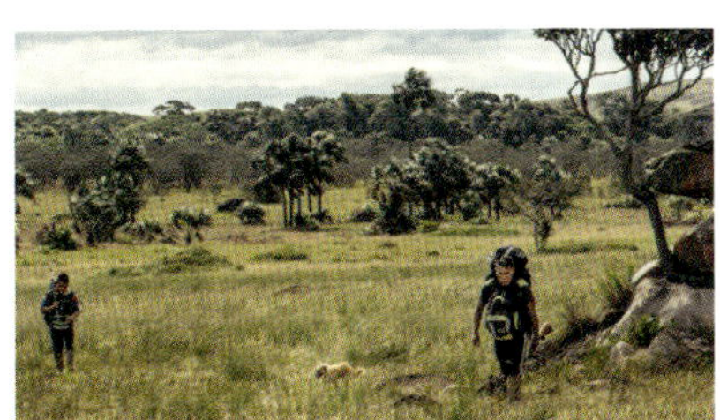

Hunters from the community of Yunék on a trail leading to the forested talus slopes of Acopán-tepui, with moriche palms (*Mauritia flexuosa*) in the background. Canaima National Park, 2017.

Leafcutter ants (*Atta laevigata*) in the Gran Sabana. Canaima National Park, 2017.

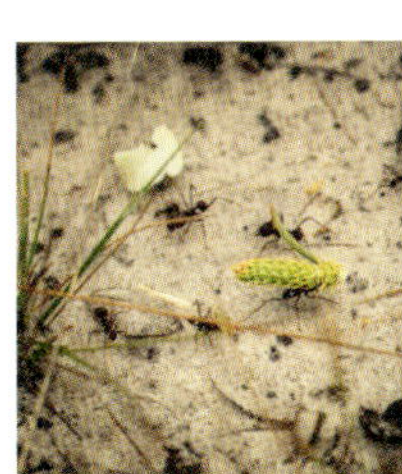

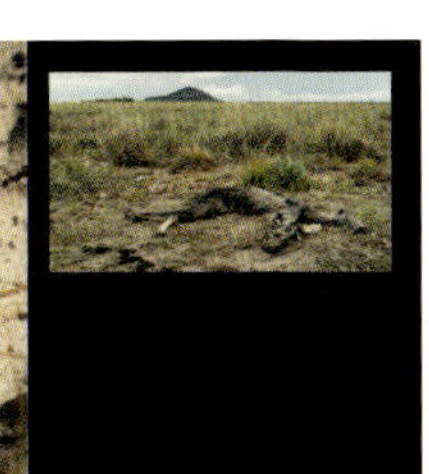

Carcass of a giant anteater (*Myrmecophaga tridactyla*) found in the Rupununi savanna, 2018.

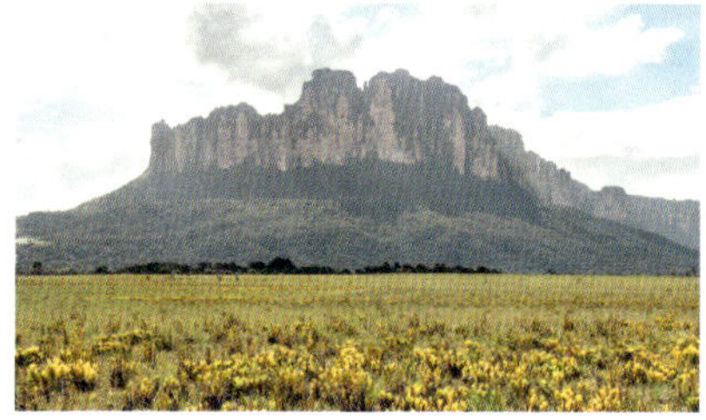

Acopán-tepui towering above a field of *Brocchinia reducta* and *Brocchinia hechtioides*. Near the village of Yunék, Canaima National Park, 2017.

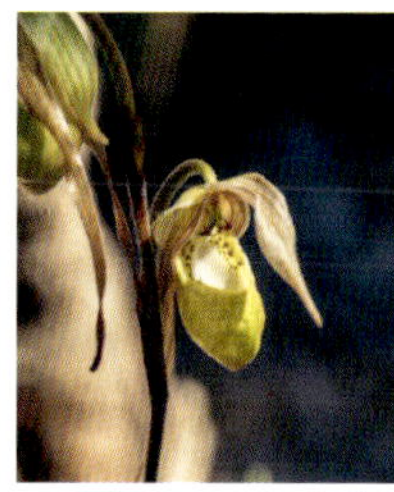

Phragmipedium klotzschianum found in the Gran Sabana. Canaima National Park, 2017.

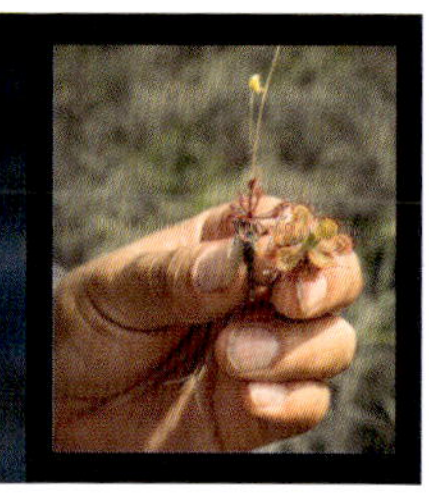

Sergio holding specimens of *Drosera communis* (left), *Utricularia* sp. (top) and *Drosera sessilifolia* (right). Savannas near Rio Orinoco, Vichada, 2018.

Ancient pictograms on a rock face near Upuigma-tepui. Valley of Rio Arauák, Canaima National Park, 2017.

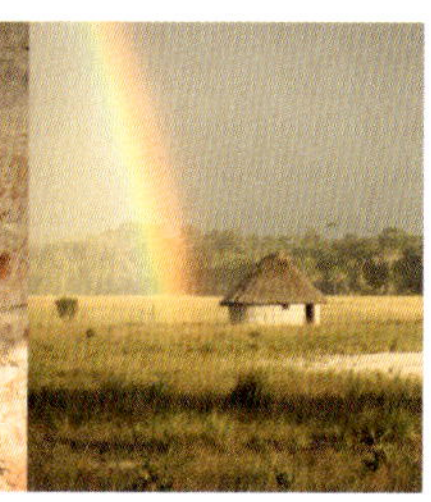

Churuata – a traditional, clay-walled house, in the village of Yunék. Canaima National Park, 2017.

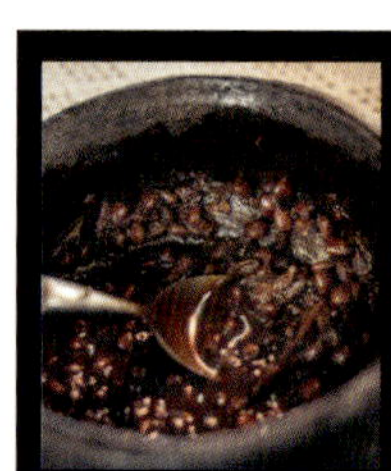

Traditional hot salsa made of spicy peppers and termites. Village of Liwo Riwo near Salto Aponguao. Canaima National Park, 2023.

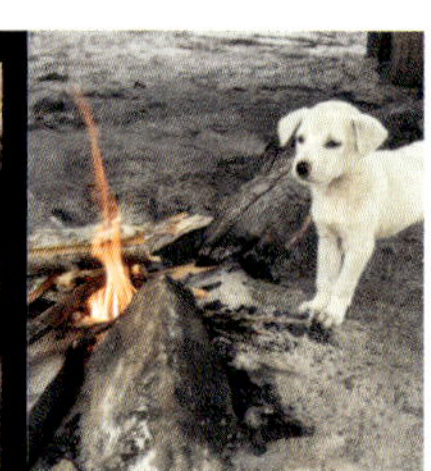

Chilly morning in a settlement near Uchii Falls, on the Uchii River, Cuyuni-Mazaruni, 2019.

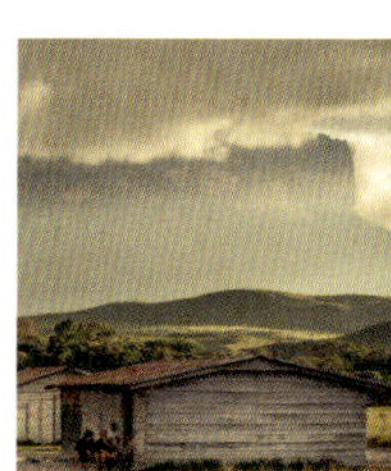

Cliffs of Upuigma-tepui seen from the village of Yunék. Canaima National Park, 2017.

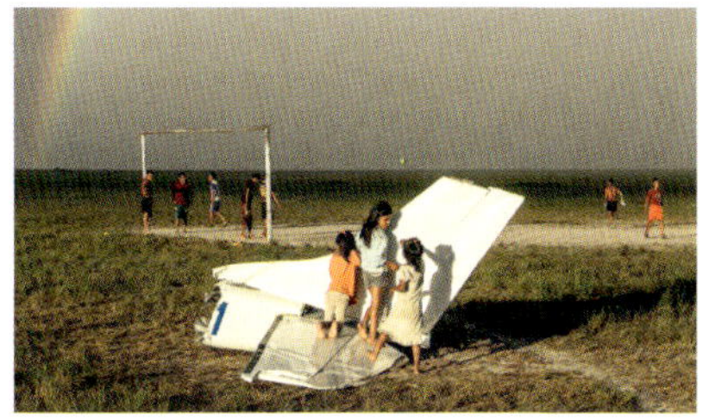

Children playing, awaiting an evening storm. Yunék, Canaima National Park, 2017.

Trail in the Gran Sabana leading to the base of Roraima-tepui. Canaima National Park, 2023.

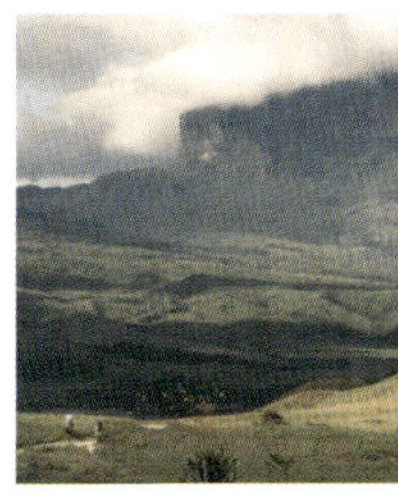

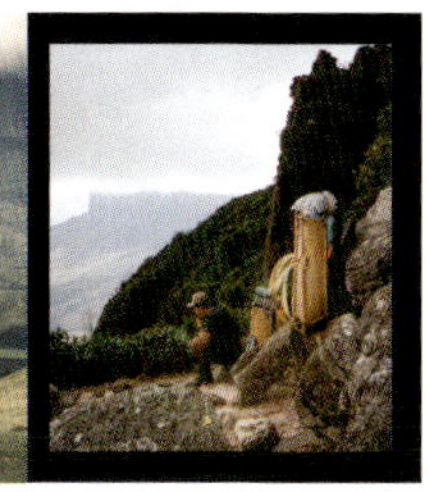

Yonatan during a short break on “La Rampa” – a natural “ramp” serving as an access path to the summit of Roraima-tepui. Next to him are the *guayare* – traditional baskets, used to carry heavy loads. Canaima National Park, 2023.

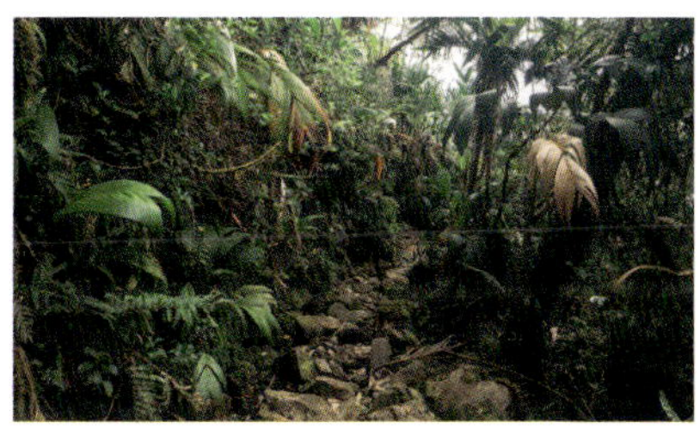

Highland cloud forest on the slopes of Roraima-tepui. Canaima National Park, 2023.

Trail to Cueva del Fantasma on the foothills of Aprada-tepui. Canaima National Park, 2017.

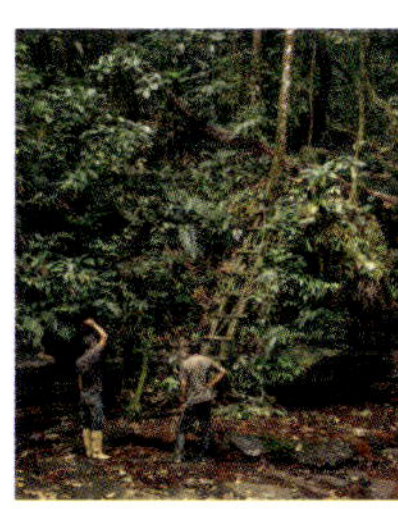

Cloud forest on the slopes of Serra Imeri, above Bebedouro Novo camp. Pico da Neblina National Park, 2025.

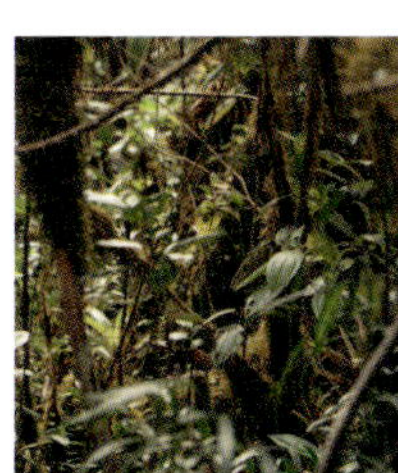

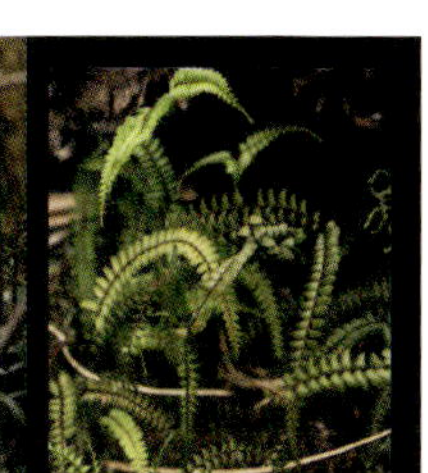

Lindsaea stricta growing in the cloud forest on the plateau under Pico da Neblina. Pico da Neblina National Park, 2025.

Unfurling fern frond, likely *Parablechnum* sp., in the cloud forest on the slopes of Serra Imeri. Pico da Neblina National Park, 2025.

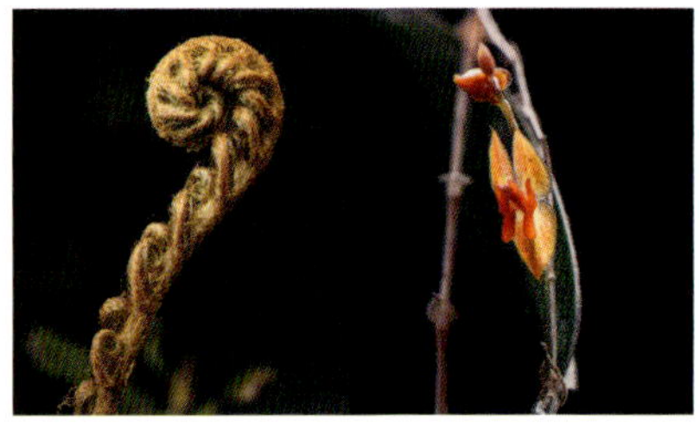

Lepanthes sp. in the montane cloud forest on Acopán-tepui. Canaima National Park, 2017.

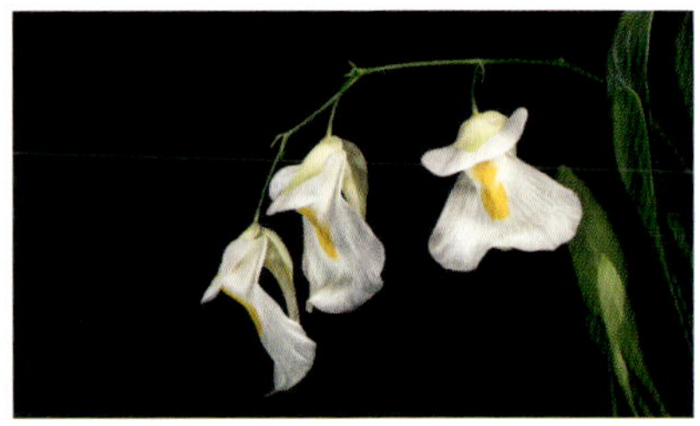

Utricularia alpina from Oruwandad Falls on the upper Kiara (or Cara) Creek, Cuyuni-Mazaruni, 2019.

Brocchinia uaipanensis and *Utricularia quelchii* from Auyán-tepui. Cultivated specimens, 2020.

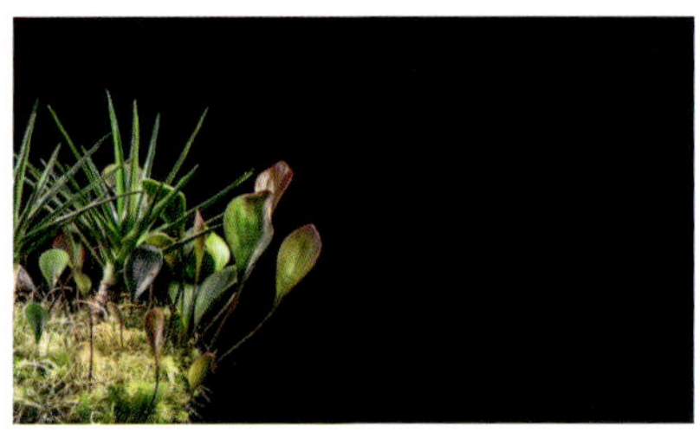

Unfurling tree fern frond, likely *Cyathea* sp., in the cloud forest on the slopes of Serra Imeri. Pico da Neblina National Park, 2025.

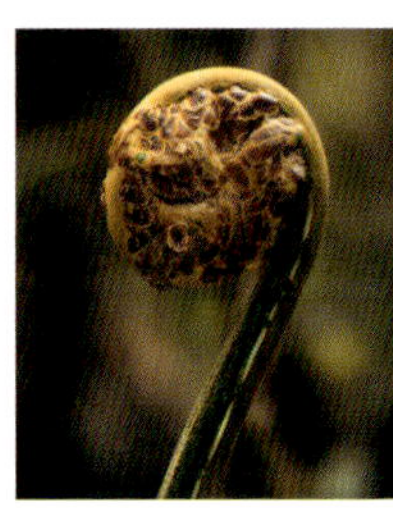

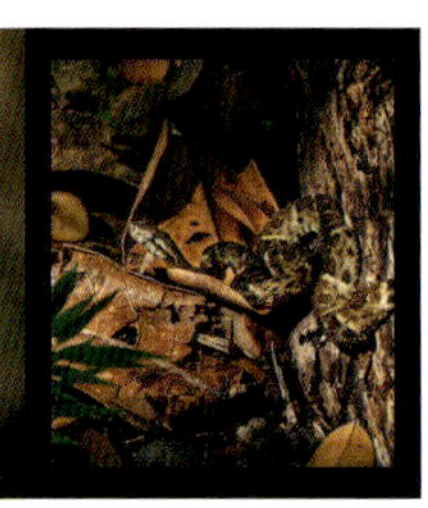

Bothrops atrox, known as "labaria" or "mapanare". Photographed in close vicinity of Oruwandad Falls on the upper Kiara (or Cara) Creek, Cuyuni-Mazaruni, 2019.

Orectanthe sceptrum – a characteristic plant endemic to the Guiana Highlands. Roraima-tepui, Monte Roraima National Park, 2023.

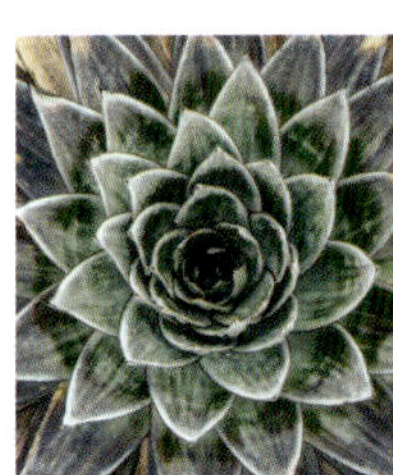

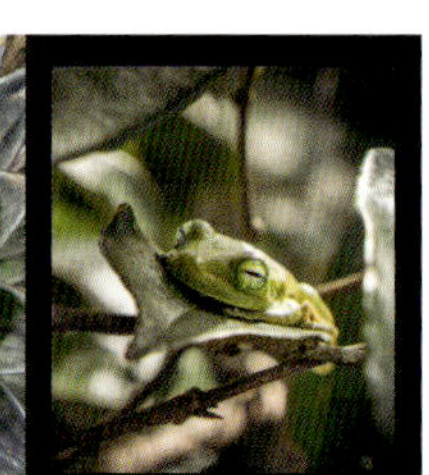

Boana xerophylla found on the trail to Cueva del Fantasma, Aprada-tepui foothills. Canaima National Park, 2017.

Montane cloud forest on the summit of Waukauyengtipu, Cuyuni-Mazaruni, 2019.

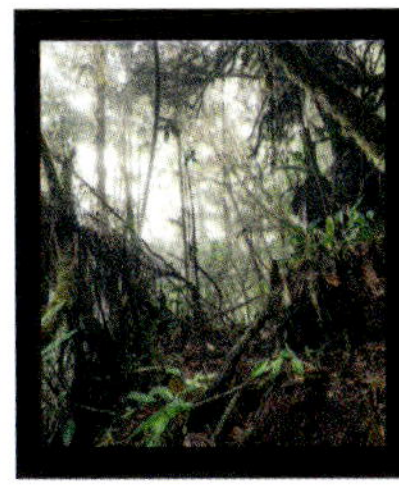

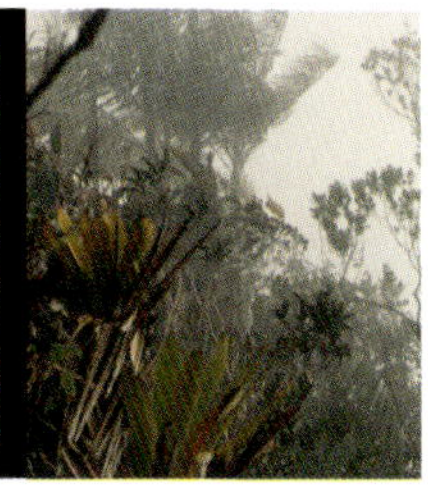

Montane cloud forest on the plateau under Pico da Neblina, with *Brocchinia tatei* in the front and *Euterpe* aff. *catinga* palm trees in the back. Pico da Neblina National Park, 2025.

Maxillaria aff. *alpestris* in the cloud forest on the southwestern slopes of Roraima-tepui. Canaima National Park, 2023.

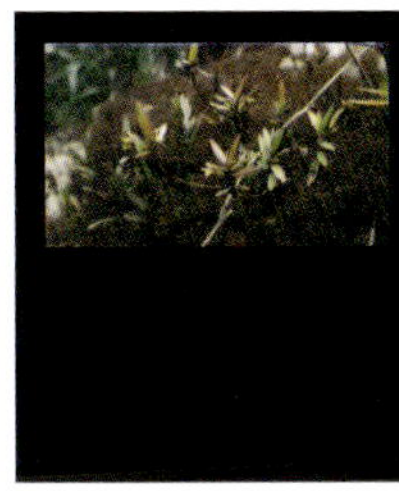

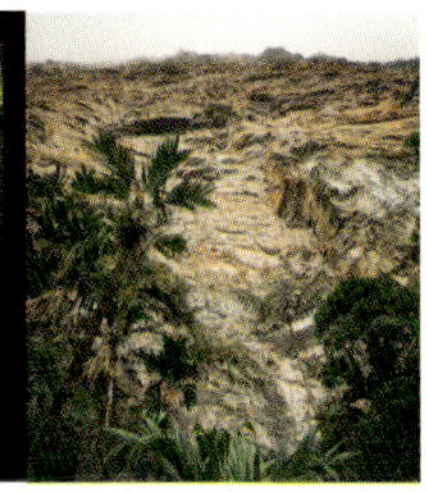

Looking up the wall of Roraima-tepui, at the beginning of “La Rampa” leading to the summit of the tepui. Canaima National Park, 2023.

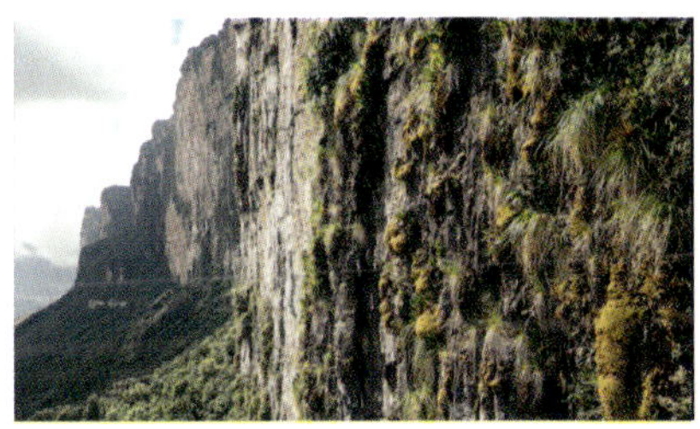

Southwestern wall of Roraima-tepui. Canaima National Park, 2023.

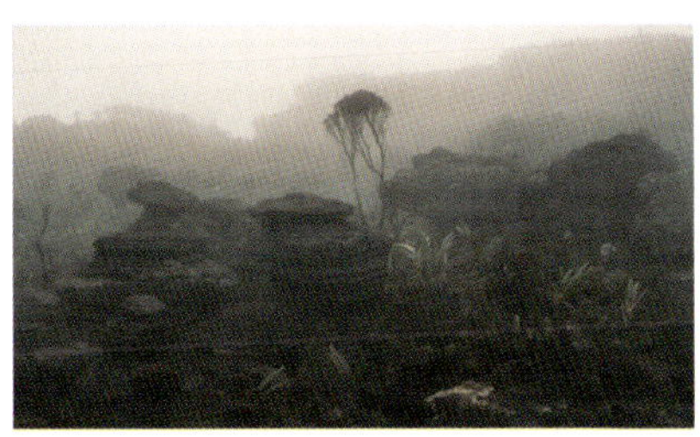

Summit of Roraima-tepui. Canaima National Park, 2023.

Vegetation of the upper Pantepui zone (over 2,000 m above sea level) leading up to Pico da Neblina (Yaripo). Pico da Neblina National Park, 2025.

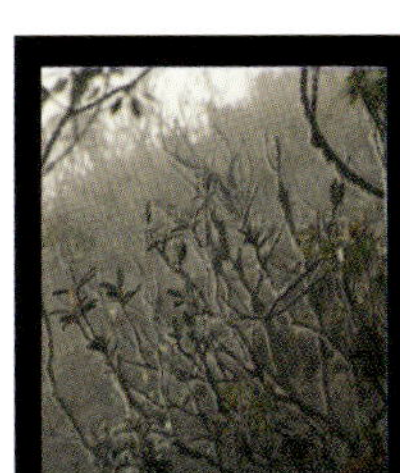

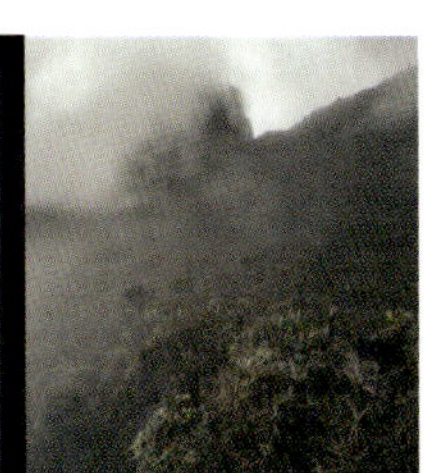

Vegetation of the upper Pantepui zone (over 2,000 m above sea level) with the summit of Pico da Neblina (Yaripo) – covered in clouds in the background. Pico da Neblina National Park, 2025.

Oreophrynella quelchii, commonly known as the Roraima bush toad or Roraima black frog, resting on a pebble on the summit of Roraima-tepui, near Coati camp. Monte Roraima National Park, 2023.

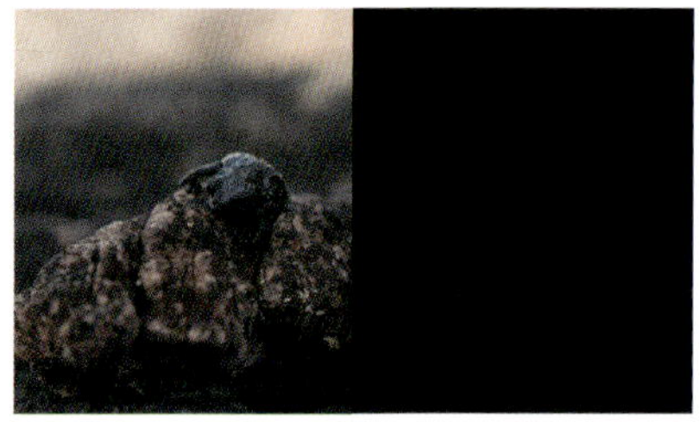

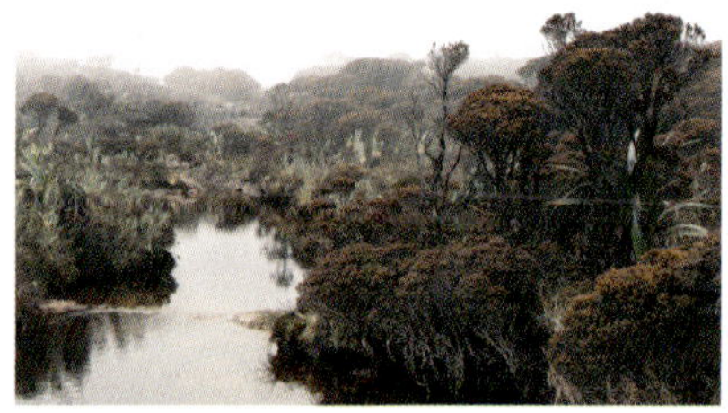

Forest of *Bonnetia roraimae* at the headwaters of Rio Cotingo, on the summit of Roraima-tepui, 2023.

Pterozonium maguirei, a fern known only from the upper slopes of Sierra de la Neblina / Serra Imeri. Pico da Neblina National Park, 2025.

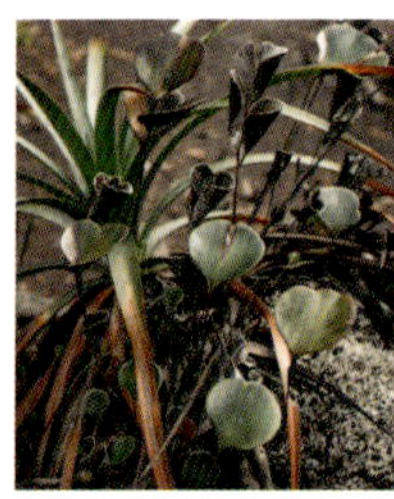

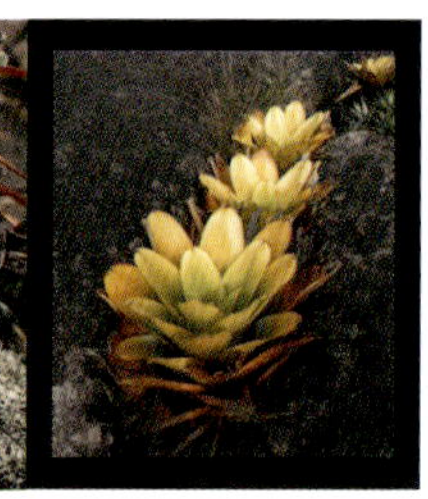

Brocchinia tatei on the summit of Roraima-tepui. Canaima National Park, 2023.

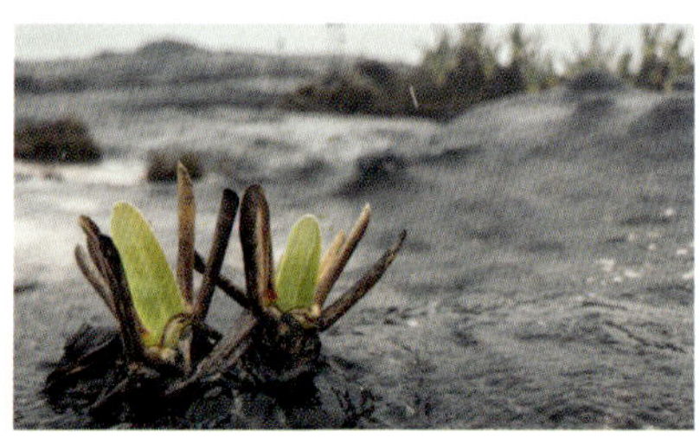

Young *Stegolepis guianensis* plants on the summit of Roraima-tepui, growing on exposed sandstone. Canaima National Park, 2023.

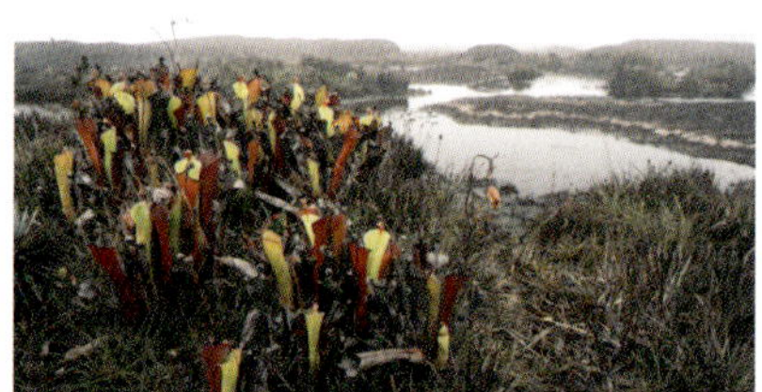

Heliamphora glabra on the summit of Roraima-tepui, near Lake Gladys, 2023.

Calio holding a leaf of *Heliamphora heterodoxa*. Summit of Waukauyengtipu, Cuyuni-Mazaruni, 2019.

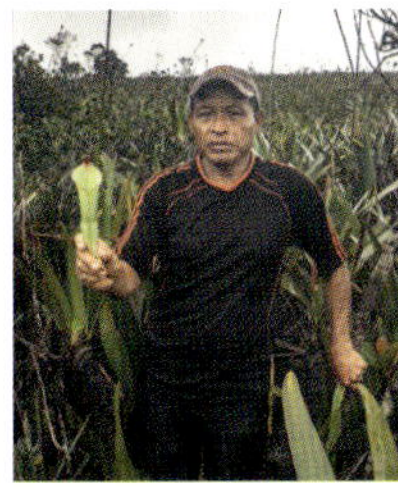

Utricularia quelchii on the summit of Roraima-tepui, near Lake Gladys, 2023.

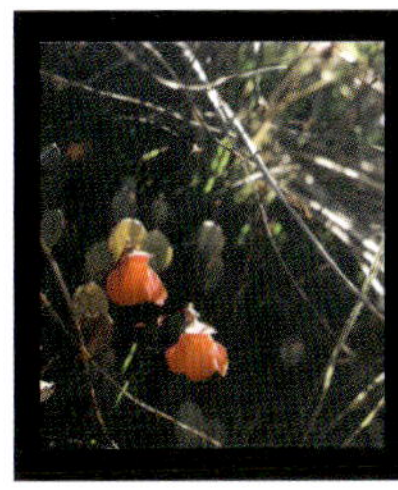

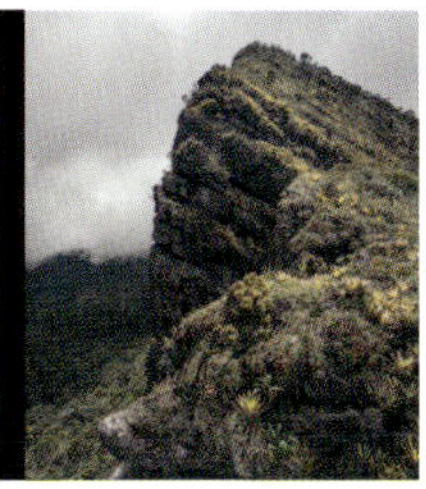

Sandstone ridges surrounding the upper plateau under Pico da Neblina. Pico da Neblina National Park, 2025.

Dead frond of *Pterozonium spectabile* from Auyán-tepui, covered in lichens. 2020.

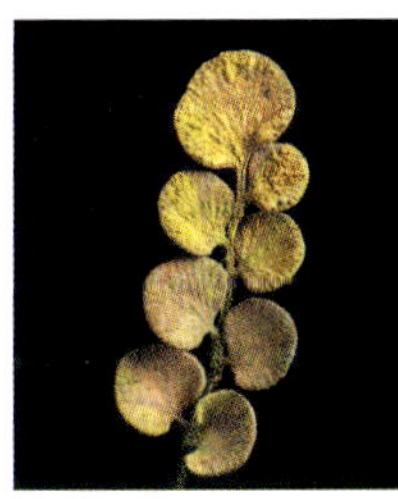

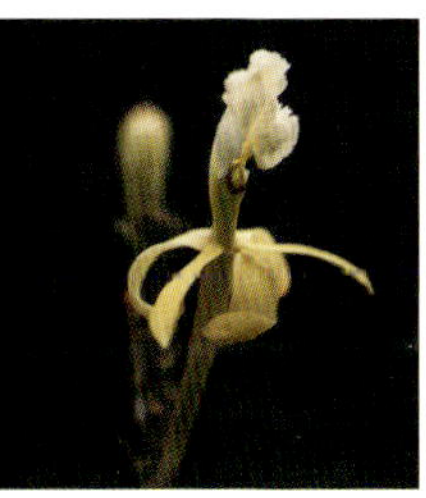

Epidendrum katarun-yariku in the upper montane cloud forest of Serra Imeri. Pico da Neblina National Park, 2025.

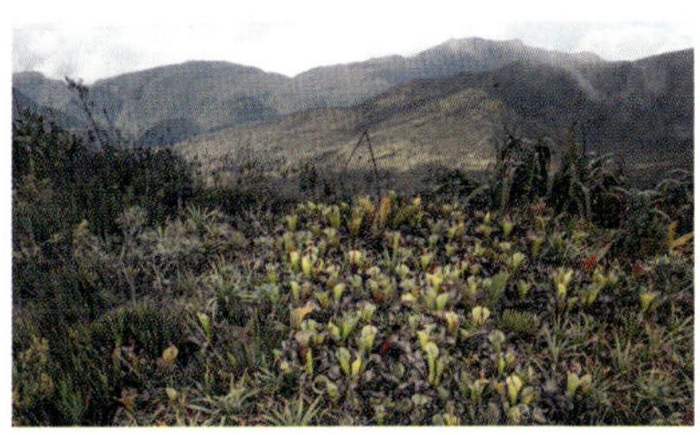

Population of *Heliamphora neblinae* on the ridges of Serra Imeri. Pico da Neblina National Park, 2025.

Utricularia humboldtii growing inside the tank of *Brocchinia tatei*. Upper slopes of Serra Imeri. Pico da Neblina National Park, 2025.

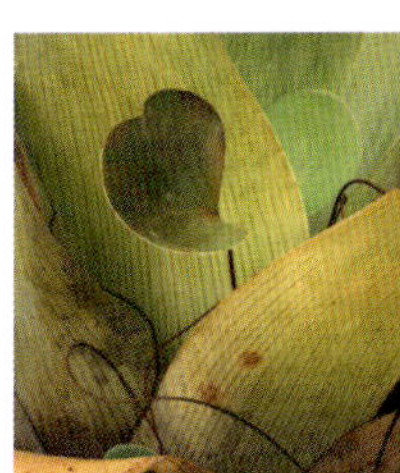

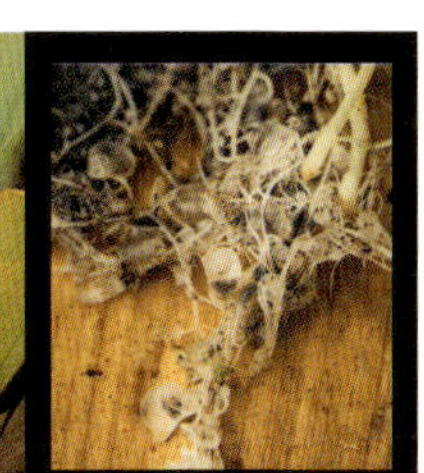

Traps ("bladders") of *Utricularia humboldtii*. Upper slopes of Serra Imeri, Pico da Neblina National Park, 2025.

Bejaria imthurnii on the summit of Roraima-tepui. Canaima National Park, 2023.

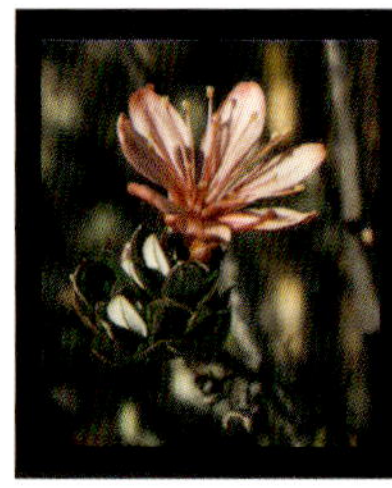

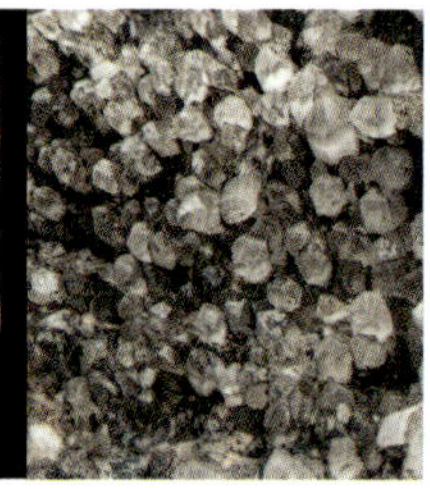

Cluster of quartz crystals in the so-called "Crystal Valley" (Valle de los Cristales) on the summit of Roraima-tepui. Canaima National Park, 2023.

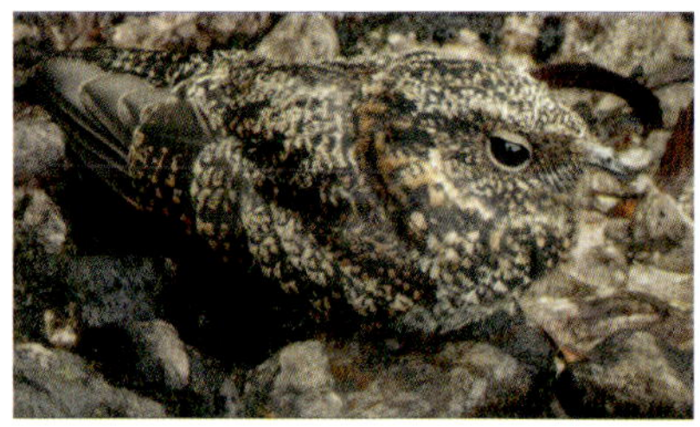

Nightjar, likely a Blackish nightjar - *Nyctipolus nigrescens*. Upper Pantepui zone (over 2,000 m above sea level) on the trail to Pico da Neblina (Yaripo). Pico da Neblina National Park, 2025.

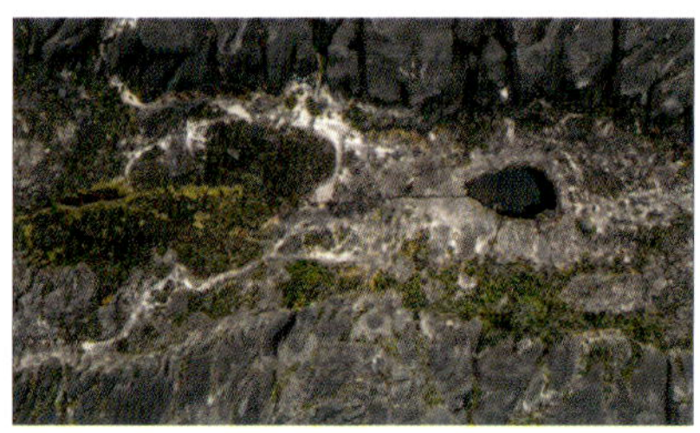

Sinkhole on the summit of Roraima-tepui, known as "El Foso". Canaima National Park, 2023.

Pico da Neblina (Yaripo) – summit with clouds rolling over. Pico da Neblina National Park, 2025.

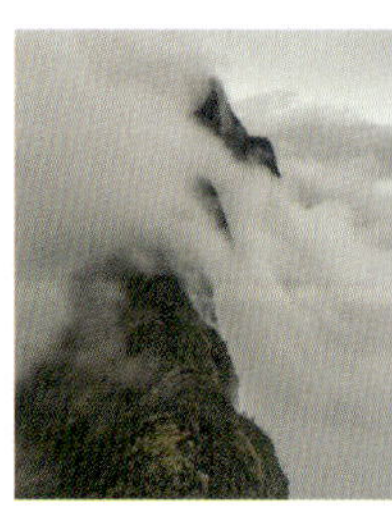

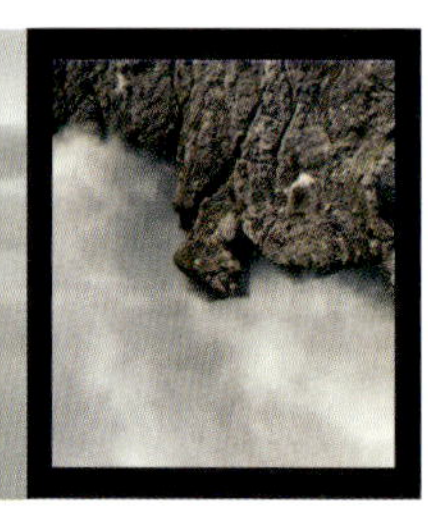

Edge of the summit plateau of Roraima-tepui. Canaima National Park, 2023.

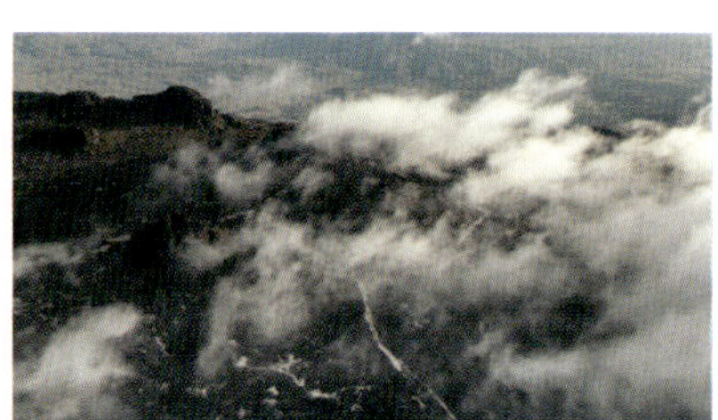

Aerial view of the summit of Roraima-tepui, with Gran Sabana visible far below in the background. Canaima National Park, 2023.

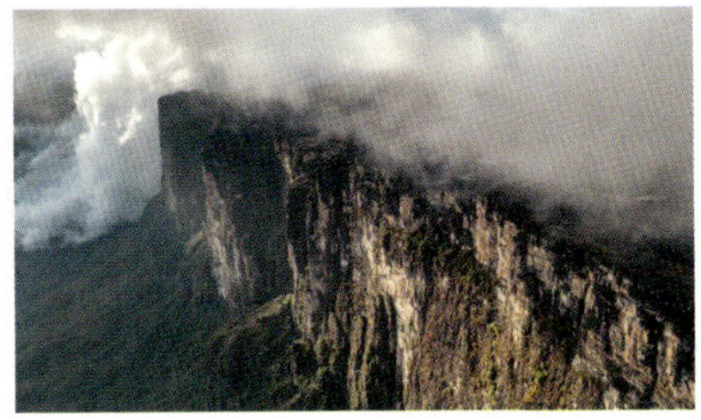

Aerial views of the cliffs of Roraima-tepui.
Canaima National Park, 2023.

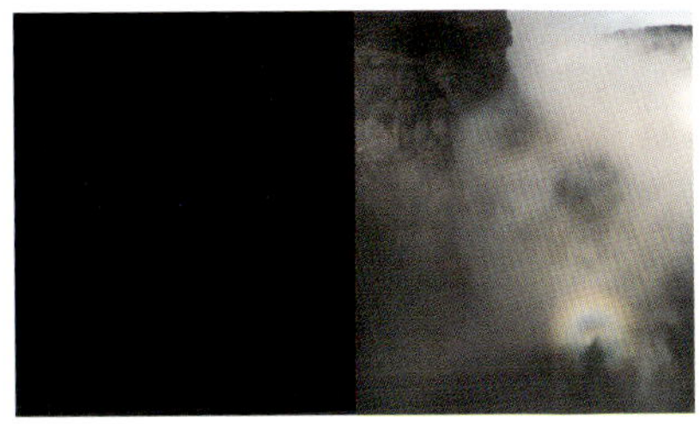

Brocken spectre. Self-portrait
on the summit of Roraima-tepui, 2023.

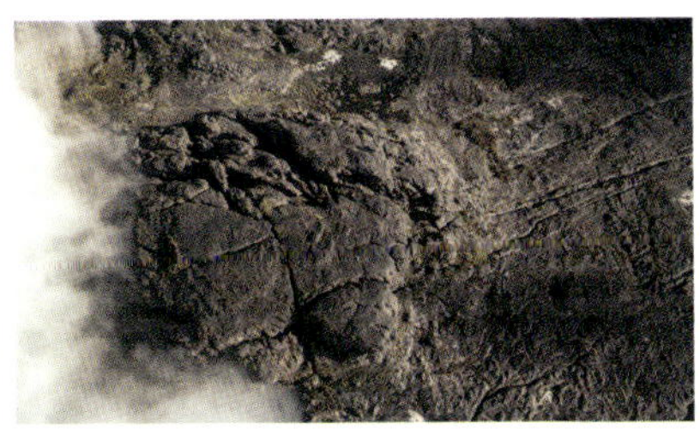

Cover photo: Aerial view of the summit
of Mount Roraima (Roraima-tepui).
Canaima National Park, 2023.

ACKNOWLEDGEMENTS

I would like to express my sincere gratitude to each and every person who made this project possible – especially my expedition companions, collaborators, scientific contributors, advisors, Indigenous guides and assistants, hosts and all the friends I made along the way during those journeys. This work wouldn't be possible without you.

Most special thanks to:

Darrell Carpenay
Orson Hinds
Stewart McPherson
Francesco Sauro
Calio Elliman
Freddy Vergara
Michal Golos
Tensing Rodriguez
Daniela Barbieri
Alessandro Beltrame
Alfredo Brunetti
Marco Mecchia
Andrea Pasqualini
Dillon Ross
Patrizio Rubcich
Leonardo Colavita
Sergio Guzmán
Andrés Aponte-Gutiérrez
Maciej Moskwa
Hondel Hunter
Ackley Phillip
Kelly Phillip
Byron Krammer
Frank Esteen
Casey Hastings
Mario Hastings
Romario Hastings
Charlie Elliman
Alex Smith
Lennox Percy
Lee Williams
Brad Wilson
Agenor Rodrigues Teixeira
Esmeraldino Campos da Silva
Alberto Rabelo
Andreas Wistuba
Doug Binns
André Witschi
Claudia Kuehni
Chetan Bhatt
Helen Fletcher
Michael Page
Antonio Hitcher
Javier Mesa
Catherine Fitzgibbon
Joelin Chani
Carlos Chani
Rosaura Chani
Humberto Chani
Juan Mora
Yonatan Pozas
Nestor Lezama
Ildemaro Lezama
Feliz Lezama
Wuilder Contreras
José Tovar
Judith Rosales
José Grande Allende
Lionel Hernández
Otto Huber
Fernando Rivadavia
Alastair Robinson
H. David Clarke
Philippe J.R. Kok
Terry W. Henkel
Bruce Holst
Karen Redden
Orlando Meléndez
Alan Reid Smith
Joep Moonen
Thomas Croat
Michel Boudrie
Bruce Hoffman

Also, with gratitude for their hospitality and support – thanks to the Indigenous communities of:

Arecuna
Taurepang
Kamarakoto
Akawaio
Patamona
Macushi
Wapishana
Yanomami

especially in the territories of:

Santa Teresita de Kavanayén
Yunék
Paraitepuy de Roraima
Wuarapata
Purpurken
Liwo Riwo
Paruima
Kako
Makuripai
Kumarakapay / San Francisco de Yuruaní
Murubik
Shiriri
Maturacá

EXPEDITIONS

The material presented in this book is a result of expeditions undertaken in the years 2017–2026:

Acopán-tepui & Cueva del Fantasma, Venezuela – 2017
Kaieteur Falls & South Rupununi, Guyana – 2018
Ptari-tepui & Gran Sabana, Venezuela – 2018
Vichada & Guaviare, Colombia – 2018
Waukauyengtipu & Uchii River Uplands, Guyana – 2019
The Prow of Mount Roraima, Guyana – 2019
Mount Roraima, Venezuela – 2023
Pico da Neblina (Yaripo), Brazil – 2025
Kumerau Falls & Kaieteur Falls, Guyana – 2026

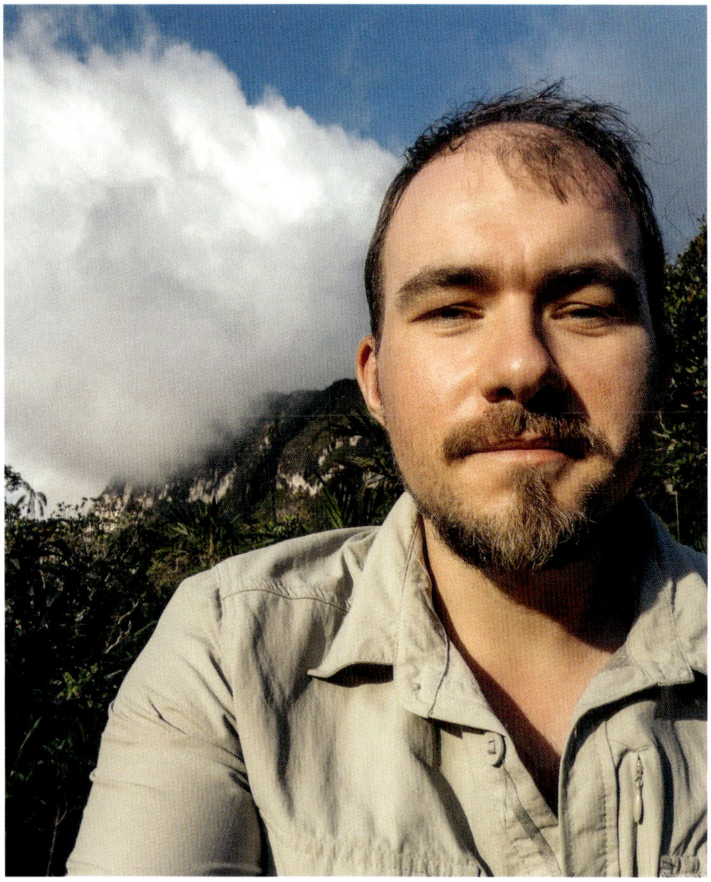

Mateusz Wrazidlo is a Silesian engineer, photographer, author and, above all, an avid naturalist. Born in 1993 in Rydułtowy in the south of Poland, he has co-organised and participated in numerous expeditions to Guyana, Venezuela, Colombia, Brazil and Svalbard, among many others. The Guiana Shield remains his primary field of focus for research and photography.

He combines Silesian engineering traditions with a deep passion for the natural world. Since his early childhood, he has nurtured a keen interest in botany, with a particular focus on the montane flora of the Guiana Highlands. He has expanded his knowledge of the plant world by combining practical experience growing demanding species in his conservatory with fieldwork in their natural environments. His contributions to botany and biogeography have been published in multiple scientific journals and magazines.

Mateusz is a Fellow of the Royal Geographical Society and the Explorers Club.

BIBLIOGRAPHY - QUOTATION SOURCES

CHAPTER 1: Gallegos, Rómulo. *Canaima*. 1935. Translated by Jaime Tello. Caracas: North American Association of Venezuela, 1984.

CHAPTER 2: Boddam-Whetham, John W. *Roraima and British Guiana, With a Glance at Bermuda, the West Indies, and the Spanish Main*. London: Hurst & Blackett, 1879.

CHAPTER 3: Schomburgk, Richard. *Botanical Reminiscences in British Guiana*. Adelaide: W.C. Cox, Government Printer, 1876.

CHAPTER 4: Swan, Michael. *The Marches of El Dorado*. London: Jonathan Cape, 1958.

CHAPTER 5: Im Thurn, Everard. "The Ascent of Mount Roraima." *Proceedings of the Royal Geographical Society and Monthly Record of Geography*, vol. 7, no. 8, August 1885. London: Edward Stanford, 1885.

Published in 2026 by Unicorn
an imprint of Unicorn Publishing Group
Charleston Studio
Meadow Business Centre
Lewes BN8 5RW
www.unicornpublishing.org

Text © Mateusz Wrazidlo
Images © Mateusz Wrazidlo
Captions © Mateusz Wrazidlo
Foreword © Jane Goodall

Graphic design by Barabasz Opalko
Photo selection and editorial by Karolina Jonderko
Pre-press by Zbigniew Kordys
Topographic contours by Muhammad Akmal
Proofreading by Michael Eckhardt
Printed in Serbia by Publikum

Mateusz Wrazidlo has asserted his moral right under the Copyright, Designs and Patents Act 1988 to be identified as the author of this work.

All rights reserved. No part of the contents of this book may be reproduced, stored in or introduced into a retrieval system, or transmitted, in any form or by any means (electronic, mechanical, photocopying, recording or otherwise), without the prior written permission of the copyright holder and the above publisher of this book.

Project completed without the use of generative AI technologies. Without limiting the author's and publisher's exclusive rights, any unauthorized use of the publication to train generative artificial intelligence (AI) technologies is expressly prohibited.

Every effort has been made to trace copyright holders and to obtain their permission for the use of copyrighted material. The publisher apologises for any errors or omissions and would be grateful to be notified of any corrections that should be incorporated in future reprints or editions of this book.

ISBN 978-1-917458-83-2

10 9 8 7 6 5 4 3 2 1